The Complete Poems of Henry Wadsworth Longfellow - Part I

Henry Wadsworth Longfellow

THE COMPLETE POETICAL WORKS OF HENRY WADSWORTH LONGFELLOW

(From the PUBLISHER'S NOTE: "The present Household Edition of Mr. Longfellow's Poetical Writings . . . contains all his original verse that he wished to preserve, and all his translations except the Divina Commedia. The poems are printed as nearly as possible in chronological order . . . Boston, Autumn, 1902." Houghton Mifflin Company.)

CONTENTS.

VOICES OF THE NIGHT

<Greek poem here—Euripides.>

PRELUDE.

Pleasant it was, when woods were green,
  And winds were soft and low,
To lie amid some sylvan scene.
Where, the long drooping boughs between,
Shadows dark and sunlight sheen
  Alternate come and go;

Or where the denser grove receives
  No sunlight from above,
But the dark foliage interweaves
In one unbroken roof of leaves,
Underneath whose sloping eaves
  The shadows hardly move.

Beneath some patriarchal tree
  I lay upon the ground;
His hoary arms uplifted he,
And all the broad leaves over me
Clapped their little hands in glee,
  With one continuous sound;—

A slumberous sound, a sound that brings
  The feelings of a dream,
As of innumerable wings,
As, when a bell no longer swings,
Faint the hollow murmur rings
  O'er meadow, lake, and stream.

And dreams of that which cannot die,
  Bright visions, came to me,
As lapped in thought I used to lie,
And gaze into the summer sky,
Where the sailing clouds went by,
  Like ships upon the sea;

Dreams that the soul of youth engage

Ere Fancy has been quelled;
Old legends of the monkish page,
Traditions of the saint and sage,
Tales that have the rime of age,
  And chronicles of Eld.

And, loving still these quaint old themes,
  Even in the city's throng
I feel the freshness of the streams,
That, crossed by shades and sunny gleams,
Water the green land of dreams,
  The holy land of song.

Therefore, at Pentecost, which brings
  The Spring, clothed like a bride,
When nestling buds unfold their wings,
And bishop's-caps have golden rings,
Musing upon many things,
  I sought the woodlands wide.

The green trees whispered low and mild;
  It was a sound of joy!
They were my playmates when a child,
And rocked me in their arms so wild!
Still they looked at me and smiled,
  As if I were a boy;

And ever whispered, mild and low,
  "Come, be a child once more!"
And waved their long arms to and fro,
And beckoned solemnly and slow;
O, I could not choose but go
  Into the woodlands hoar, —

Into the blithe and breathing air,
  Into the solemn wood,
Solemn and silent everywhere
Nature with folded hands seemed there
Kneeling at her evening prayer!
  Like one in prayer I stood.

Before me rose an avenue
  Of tall and sombrous pines;

Abroad their fan-like branches grew,
And, where the sunshine darted through,
Spread a vapor soft and blue,
  In long and sloping lines.

And, falling on my weary brain,
  Like a fast-falling shower,
The dreams of youth came back again,
Low lispings of the summer rain,
Dropping on the ripened grain,
  As once upon the flower.

Visions of childhood! Stay, O stay!
  Ye were so sweet and wild!
And distant voices seemed to say,
"It cannot be! They pass away!
Other themes demand thy lay;
  Thou art no more a child!

"The land of Song within thee lies,
  Watered by living springs;
The lids of Fancy's sleepless eyes
Are gates unto that Paradise,
Holy thoughts, like stars, arise,
  Its clouds are angels' wings.

"Learn, that henceforth thy song shall be,
  Not mountains capped with snow,
Nor forests sounding like the sea,
Nor rivers flowing ceaselessly,
Where the woodlands bend to see
  The bending heavens below.

"There is a forest where the din
  Of iron branches sounds!
A mighty river roars between,
And whosoever looks therein
Sees the heavens all black with sin,
  Sees not its depths, nor bounds.

"Athwart the swinging branches cast,
  Soft rays of sunshine pour;
Then comes the fearful wintry blast

Our hopes, like withered leaves, fail fast;
Pallid lips say, 'It is past!
  We can return no more!,

"Look, then, into thine heart, and write!
  Yes, into Life's deep stream!
All forms of sorrow and delight,
All solemn Voices of the Night,
That can soothe thee, or affright, —
  Be these henceforth thy theme."

HYMN TO THE NIGHT.

[Greek quotation]

I heard the trailing garments of the Night
    Sweep through her marble halls!
I saw her sable skirts all fringed with light
    From the celestial walls!

I felt her presence, by its spell of might,
    Stoop o'er me from above;
The calm, majestic presence of the Night,
    As of the one I love.

I heard the sounds of sorrow and delight,
    The manifold, soft chimes,
That fill the haunted chambers of the Night
    Like some old poet's rhymes.

From the cool cisterns of the midnight air
    My spirit drank repose;
The fountain of perpetual peace flows there, —
    From those deep cisterns flows.

O holy Night! from thee I learn to bear
    What man has borne before!
Thou layest thy finger on the lips of Care,
    And they complain no more.

Peace! Peace! Orestes-like I breathe this prayer!
    Descend with broad-winged flight,
The welcome, the thrice-prayed for, the most fair,
    The best-beloved Night!

A PSALM OF LIFE.

WHAT THE HEART OF THE YOUNG MAN SAID TO THE
PSALMIST.

Tell me not, in mournful numbers,
  Life is but an empty dream!
For the soul is dead that slumbers,
  And things are not what they seem.

Life is real! Life is earnest!
  And the grave is not its goal;
Dust thou art, to dust returnest,
  Was not spoken of the soul.

Not enjoyment, and not sorrow,
  Is our destined end or way;
But to act, that each to-morrow
  Find us farther than to-day.

Art is long, and Time is fleeting,
  And our hearts, though stout and brave,
Still, like muffled drums, are beating
  Funeral marches to the grave.

In the world's broad field of battle,
  In the bivouac of Life,
Be not like dumb, driven cattle!
  Be a hero in the strife!

Trust no Future, howe'er pleasant!
  Let the dead Past bury its dead!
Act,—act in the living Present!
  Heart within, and God o'erhead!

Lives of great men all remind us
  We can make our lives sublime,
And, departing, leave behind us
  Footprints on the sands of time;—

Footprints, that perhaps another,
  Sailing o'er life's solemn main,

A forlorn and shipwrecked brother,
  Seeing, shall take heart again.

Let us, then, be up and doing,
  With a heart for any fate;
Still achieving, still pursuing,
  Learn to labor and to wait.

THE REAPER AND THE FLOWERS.

There is a Reaper, whose name is Death,
  And, with his sickle keen,
He reaps the bearded grain at a breath,
  And the flowers that grow between.

"Shall I have naught that is fair?" saith he;
  "Have naught but the bearded grain?
Though the breath of these flowers is sweet to me,
  I will give them all back again."

He gazed at the flowers with tearful eyes,
  He kissed their drooping leaves;
It was for the Lord of Paradise
  He bound them in his sheaves.

"My Lord has need of these flowerets gay,"
  The Reaper said, and smiled;
"Dear tokens of the earth are they,
  Where he was once a child.

"They shall all bloom in fields of light,
  Transplanted by my care,
And saints, upon their garments white,
  These sacred blossoms wear."

And the mother gave, in tears and pain,
  The flowers she most did love;
She knew she should find them all again
  In the fields of light above.

O, not in cruelty, not in wrath,
  The Reaper came that day;
'T was an angel visited the green earth,
  And took the flowers away.

THE LIGHT OF STARS.

The night is come, but not too soon;
  And sinking silently,
All silently, the little moon
  Drops down behind the sky.

There is no light in earth or heaven
  But the cold light of stars;
And the first watch of night is given
  To the red planet Mars.

Is it the tender star of love?
  The star of love and dreams?
O no! from that blue tent above,
  A hero's armor gleams.

And earnest thoughts within me rise,
  When I behold afar,
Suspended in the evening skies,
  The shield of that red star.

O star of strength! I see thee stand
  And smile upon my pain;
Thou beckonest with thy mailed hand,
  And I am strong again.

Within my breast there is no light
  But the cold light of stars;
I give the first watch of the night
  To the red planet Mars.

The star of the unconquered will,
  He rises in my breast,
Serene, and resolute, and still,
  And calm, and self-possessed.

And thou, too, whosoe'er thou art,
  That readest this brief psalm,
As one by one thy hopes depart,
  Be resolute and calm.

O fear not in a world like this,
  And thou shalt know erelong,
Know how sublime a thing it is
  To suffer and be strong.

FOOTSTEPS OF ANGELS.

When the hours of Day are numbered,
  And the voices of the Night
Wake the better soul, that slumbered,
  To a holy, calm delight;

Ere the evening lamps are lighted,
  And, like phantoms grim and tall,
Shadows from the fitful firelight
  Dance upon the parlor wall;

Then the forms of the departed
  Enter at the open door;
The beloved, the true-hearted,
  Come to visit me once more;

He, the young and strong, who cherished
  Noble longings for the strife,
By the roadside fell and perished,
  Weary with the march of life!

They, the holy ones and weakly,
  Who the cross of suffering bore,
Folded their pale hands so meekly,
  Spake with us on earth no more!

And with them the Being Beauteous,
  Who unto my youth was given,
More than all things else to love me,
  And is now a saint in heaven.

With a slow and noiseless footstep
  Comes that messenger divine,
Takes the vacant chair beside me,
  Lays her gentle hand in mine.

And she sits and gazes at me
  With those deep and tender eyes,
Like the stars, so still and saint-like,
  Looking downward from the skies.

Uttered not, yet comprehended,
  Is the spirit's voiceless prayer,
Soft rebukes, in blessings ended,
  Breathing from her lips of air.

Oh, though oft depressed and lonely,
  All my fears are laid aside,
If I but remember only
  Such as these have lived and died!

FLOWERS.

Spake full well, in language quaint and olden,
  One who dwelleth by the castled Rhine,
When he called the flowers, so blue and golden,
  Stars, that in earth's firmament do shine.

Stars they are, wherein we read our history,
  As astrologers and seers of eld;
Yet not wrapped about with awful mystery,
  Like the burning stars, which they beheld.

Wondrous truths, and manifold as wondrous,
  God hath written in those stars above;
But not less in the bright flowerets under us
  Stands the revelation of his love.

Bright and glorious is that revelation,
  Written all over this great world of ours;
Making evident our own creation,
  In these stars of earth, these golden flowers.

And the Poet, faithful and far-seeing,
  Sees, alike in stars and flowers, a part
Of the self-same, universal being,
  Which is throbbing in his brain and heart.

Gorgeous flowerets in the sunlight shining,
  Blossoms flaunting in the eye of day,
Tremulous leaves, with soft and silver lining,
  Buds that open only to decay;

Brilliant hopes, all woven in gorgeous tissues,
  Flaunting gayly in the golden light;
Large desires, with most uncertain issues,
  Tender wishes, blossoming at night!

These in flowers and men are more than seeming;
  Workings are they of the self-same powers,
Which the Poet, in no idle dreaming,
  Seeth in himself and in the flowers.

Everywhere about us are they glowing,
  Some like stars, to tell us Spring is born;
Others, their blue eyes with tears o'er-flowing,
  Stand like Ruth amid the golden corn;

Not alone in Spring's armorial bearing,
  And in Summer's green-emblazoned field,
But in arms of brave old Autumn's wearing,
  In the centre of his brazen shield;

Not alone in meadows and green alleys,
  On the mountain-top, and by the brink
Of sequestered pools in woodland valleys,
  Where the slaves of nature stoop to drink;

Not alone in her vast dome of glory,
  Not on graves of bird and beast alone,
But in old cathedrals, high and hoary,
  On the tombs of heroes, carved in stone;

In the cottage of the rudest peasant,
  In ancestral homes, whose crumbling towers,
Speaking of the Past unto the Present,
  Tell us of the ancient Games of Flowers;

In all places, then, and in all seasons,
  Flowers expand their light and soul-like wings,
Teaching us, by most persuasive reasons,
  How akin they are to human things.

And with childlike, credulous affection
  We behold their tender buds expand;
Emblems of our own great resurrection,
  Emblems of the bright and better land.

THE BELEAGUERED CITY.

I have read, in some old, marvellous tale,
  Some legend strange and vague,
That a midnight host of spectres pale
  Beleaguered the walls of Prague.

Beside the Moldau's rushing stream,
  With the wan moon overhead,
There stood, as in an awful dream,
  The army of the dead.

White as a sea-fog, landward bound,
  The spectral camp was seen,
And, with a sorrowful, deep sound,
  The river flowed between.

No other voice nor sound was there,
  No drum, nor sentry's pace;
The mist-like banners clasped the air,
  As clouds with clouds embrace.

But when the old cathedral bell
  Proclaimed the morning prayer,
The white pavilions rose and fell
  On the alarmed air.

Down the broad valley fast and far
  The troubled army fled;
Up rose the glorious morning star,
  The ghastly host was dead.

I have read, in the marvellous heart of man,
  That strange and mystic scroll,
That an army of phantoms vast and wan
  Beleaguer the human soul.

Encamped beside Life's rushing stream,
  In Fancy's misty light,
Gigantic shapes and shadows gleam
  Portentous through the night.

Upon its midnight battle-ground
  The spectral camp is seen,
And, with a sorrowful, deep sound,
  Flows the River of Life between.

No other voice nor sound is there,
  In the army of the grave;
No other challenge breaks the air,
  But the rushing of Life's wave.

And when the solemn and deep churchbell
  Entreats the soul to pray,
The midnight phantoms feel the spell,
  The shadows sweep away.

Down the broad Vale of Tears afar
  The spectral camp is fled;
Faith shineth as a morning star,
  Our ghastly fears are dead.

MIDNIGHT MASS FOR THE DYING YEAR

Yes, the Year is growing old,
  And his eye is pale and bleared!
Death, with frosty hand and cold,
  Plucks the old man by the beard,
    Sorely, sorely!

The leaves are falling, falling,
  Solemnly and slow;
Caw! caw! the rooks are calling,
  It is a sound of woe,
    A sound of woe!

Through woods and mountain passes
  The winds, like anthems, roll;
They are chanting solemn masses,
  Singing, "Pray for this poor soul,
    Pray, pray!"

And the hooded clouds, like friars,
  Tell their beads in drops of rain,
And patter their doleful prayers;
  But their prayers are all in vain,
    All in vain!

There he stands in the foul weather,
  The foolish, fond Old Year,
Crowned with wild flowers and with heather,
  Like weak, despised Lear,
    A king, a king!

Then comes the summer-like day,
  Bids the old man rejoice!
His joy! his last! O, the man gray
  Loveth that ever-soft voice,
    Gentle and low.

To the crimson woods he saith,
  To the voice gentle and low
Of the soft air, like a daughter's breath,
  "Pray do not mock me so!

Do not laugh at me!"

And now the sweet day is dead;
  Cold in his arms it lies;
No stain from its breath is spread
  Over the glassy skies,
    No mist or stain!

Then, too, the Old Year dieth,
  And the forests utter a moan,
Like the voice of one who crieth
  In the wilderness alone,
    "Vex not his ghost!"

Then comes, with an awful roar,
  Gathering and sounding on,
The storm-wind from Labrador,
  The wind Euroclydon,
    The storm-wind!

Howl! howl! and from the forest
  Sweep the red leaves away!
Would, the sins that thou abhorrest,
  O Soul! could thus decay,
    And be swept away!
For there shall come a mightier blast,
  There shall be a darker day;

And the stars, from heaven down-cast
  Like red leaves be swept away!
    Kyrie, eleyson!
    Christe, eleyson!

            ****

18

EARLIER POEMS

AN APRIL DAY

When the warm sun, that brings
Seed-time and harvest, has returned again,
'T is sweet to visit the still wood, where springs
    The first flower of the plain.

I love the season well,
When forest glades are teeming with bright forms,
Nor dark and many-folded clouds foretell
    The coming-on of storms.

From the earth's loosened mould
The sapling draws its sustenance, and thrives;
Though stricken to the heart with winter's cold,
    The drooping tree revives.

The softly-warbled song
Comes from the pleasant woods, and colored wings
Glance quick in the bright sun, that moves along
    The forest openings.

When the bright sunset fills
The silver woods with light, the green slope throws
Its shadows in the hollows of the hills,
    And wide the upland glows.

And when the eve is born,
In the blue lake the sky, o'er-reaching far,
Is hollowed out and the moon dips her horn,
    And twinkles many a star.

Inverted in the tide
Stand the gray rocks, and trembling shadows throw,
And the fair trees look over, side by side,
    And see themselves below.

Sweet April! many a thought
Is wedded unto thee, as hearts are wed;
Nor shall they fail, till, to its autumn brought,
Life's golden fruit is shed.

AUTUMN

With what a glory comes and goes the year!
The buds of spring, those beautiful harbingers
Of sunny skies and cloudless times, enjoy
Life's newness, and earth's garniture spread out;
And when the silver habit of the clouds
Comes down upon the autumn sun, and with
A sober gladness the old year takes up
His bright inheritance of golden fruits,
A pomp and pageant fill the splendid scene.

  There is a beautiful spirit breathing now
Its mellow richness on the clustered trees,
And, from a beaker full of richest dyes,
Pouring new glory on the autumn woods,
And dipping in warm light the pillared clouds.
Morn on the mountain, like a summer bird,
Lifts up her purple wing, and in the vales
The gentle wind, a sweet and passionate wooer,
Kisses the blushing leaf, and stirs up life
Within the solemn woods of ash deep-crimsoned,
And silver beech, and maple yellow-leaved,
Where Autumn, like a faint old man, sits down
By the wayside a-weary. Through the trees
The golden robin moves. The purple finch,
That on wild cherry and red cedar feeds,
A winter bird, comes with its plaintive whistle,
And pecks by the witch-hazel, whilst aloud
From cottage roofs the warbling blue-bird sings,
And merrily, with oft-repeated stroke,
Sounds from the threshing-floor the busy flail.

  O what a glory doth this world put on
For him who, with a fervent heart, goes forth
Under the bright and glorious sky, and looks
On duties well performed, and days well spent!
For him the wind, ay, and the yellow leaves,
Shall have a voice, and give him eloquent teachings.
He shall so hear the solemn hymn that Death
Has lifted up for all, that he shall go
To his long resting-place without a tear.

WOODS IN WINTER.

When winter winds are piercing chill,
  And through the hawthorn blows the gale,
With solemn feet I tread the hill,
  That overbrows the lonely vale.

O'er the bare upland, and away
  Through the long reach of desert woods,
The embracing sunbeams chastely play,
  And gladden these deep solitudes.

Where, twisted round the barren oak,
  The summer vine in beauty clung,
And summer winds the stillness broke,
  The crystal icicle is hung.

Where, from their frozen urns, mute springs
  Pour out the river's gradual tide,
Shrilly the skater's iron rings,
  And voices fill the woodland side.

Alas! how changed from the fair scene,
  When birds sang out their mellow lay,
And winds were soft, and woods were green,
  And the song ceased not with the day!

But still wild music is abroad,
  Pale, desert woods! within your crowd;
And gathering winds, in hoarse accord,
  Amid the vocal reeds pipe loud.

Chill airs and wintry winds! my ear
  Has grown familiar with your song;
I hear it in the opening year,
  I listen, and it cheers me long.

HYMN OF THE MORAVIAN NUNS OF BETHLEHEM

AT THE CONSECRATION OF PULASKI'S BANNER.

When the dying flame of day
Through the chancel shot its ray,
Far the glimmering tapers shed
Faint light on the cowled head;
And the censer burning swung,
Where, before the altar, hung
The crimson banner, that with prayer
Had been consecrated there.
And the nuns' sweet hymn was heard the while,
Sung low, in the dim, mysterious aisle.

"Take thy banner! May it wave
Proudly o'er the good and brave;
When the battle's distant wail
Breaks the sabbath of our vale.
When the clarion's music thrills
To the hearts of these lone hills,
When the spear in conflict shakes,
And the strong lance shivering breaks.

"Take thy banner! and, beneath
The battle-cloud's encircling wreath,
Guard it, till our homes are free!
Guard it! God will prosper thee!
In the dark and trying hour,
In the breaking forth of power,
In the rush of steeds and men,
His right hand will shield thee then.

"Take thy banner! But when night
Closes round the ghastly fight,
If the vanquished warrior bow,
Spare him! By our holy vow,
By our prayers and many tears,
By the mercy that endears,
Spare him! he our love hath shared!
Spare him! as thou wouldst be spared!

"Take thy banner! and if e'er
Thou shouldst press the soldier's bier,
And the muffled drum should beat
To the tread of mournful feet,
Then this crimson flag shall be

Martial cloak and shroud for thee."

The warrior took that banner proud,
And it was his martial cloak and shroud!

SUNRISE ON THE HILLS

I stood upon the hills, when heaven's wide arch
Was glorious with the sun's returning march,
And woods were brightened, and soft gales
Went forth to kiss the sun-clad vales.
The clouds were far beneath me; bathed in light,
They gathered mid-way round the wooded height,
And, in their fading glory, shone
Like hosts in battle overthrown.
As many a pinnacle, with shifting glance.
Through the gray mist thrust up its shattered lance,
And rocking on the cliff was left
The dark pine blasted, bare, and cleft.
The veil of cloud was lifted, and below
Glowed the rich valley, and the river's flow
Was darkened by the forest's shade,
Or glistened in the white cascade;
Where upward, in the mellow blush of day,
The noisy bittern wheeled his spiral way.

I heard the distant waters dash,
I saw the current whirl and flash,
And richly, by the blue lake's silver beach,
The woods were bending with a silent reach.
Then o'er the vale, with gentle swell,
The music of the village bell
Came sweetly to the echo-giving hills;
And the wild horn, whose voice the woodland fills,
Was ringing to the merry shout,
That faint and far the glen sent out,
Where, answering to the sudden shot, thin smoke,
Through thick-leaved branches, from the dingle broke.

If thou art worn and hard beset
With sorrows, that thou wouldst forget,
If thou wouldst read a lesson, that will keep
Thy heart from fainting and thy soul from sleep,
Go to the woods and hills! No tears
Dim the sweet look that Nature wears.

THE SPIRIT OF POETRY

There is a quiet spirit in these woods,
That dwells where'er the gentle south-wind blows;
Where, underneath the white-thorn, in the glade,
The wild flowers bloom, or, kissing the soft air,
The leaves above their sunny palms outspread.
With what a tender and impassioned voice
It fills the nice and delicate ear of thought,
When the fast ushering star of morning comes
O'er-riding the gray hills with golden scarf;
Or when the cowled and dusky-sandaled Eve,
In mourning weeds, from out the western gate,
Departs with silent pace! That spirit moves
In the green valley, where the silver brook,
From its full laver, pours the white cascade;
And, babbling low amid the tangled woods,
Slips down through moss-grown stones with endless laughter.
And frequent, on the everlasting hills,
Its feet go forth, when it doth wrap itself
In all the dark embroidery of the storm,
And shouts the stern, strong wind. And here, amid
The silent majesty of these deep woods,
Its presence shall uplift thy thoughts from earth,
As to the sunshine and the pure, bright air
Their tops the green trees lift. Hence gifted bards
Have ever loved the calm and quiet shades.
For them there was an eloquent voice in all
The sylvan pomp of woods, the golden sun,
The flowers, the leaves, the river on its way,
Blue skies, and silver clouds, and gentle winds,
The swelling upland, where the sidelong sun
Aslant the wooded slope, at evening, goes,
Groves, through whose broken roof the sky looks in,
Mountain, and shattered cliff, and sunny vale,
The distant lake, fountains, and mighty trees,
In many a lazy syllable, repeating
Their old poetic legends to the wind.

   And this is the sweet spirit, that doth fill
The world; and, in these wayward days of youth,
My busy fancy oft embodies it,

As a bright image of the light and beauty
That dwell in nature; of the heavenly forms
We worship in our dreams, and the soft hues
That stain the wild bird's wing, and flush the clouds
When the sun sets. Within her tender eye
The heaven of April, with its changing light,
And when it wears the blue of May, is hung,
And on her lip the rich, red rose. Her hair
Is like the summer tresses of the trees,
When twilight makes them brown, and on her cheek
Blushes the richness of an autumn sky,
With ever-shifting beauty. Then her breath,
It is so like the gentle air of Spring,
As, front the morning's dewy flowers, it comes
Full of their fragrance, that it is a joy
To have it round us, and her silver voice
Is the rich music of a summer bird,
Heard in the still night, with its passionate cadence.

BURIAL OF THE MINNISINK

On sunny slope and beechen swell,
The shadowed light of evening fell;
And, where the maple's leaf was brown,
With soft and silent lapse came down,
The glory, that the wood receives,
At sunset, in its golden leaves.

Far upward in the mellow light
Rose the blue hills. One cloud of white,
Around a far uplifted cone,
In the warm blush of evening shone;
An image of the silver lakes,
By which the Indian's soul awakes.

But soon a funeral hymn was heard
Where the soft breath of evening stirred
The tall, gray forest; and a band
Of stern in heart, and strong in hand,
Came winding down beside the wave,
To lay the red chief in his grave.

They sang, that by his native bowers
He stood, in the last moon of flowers,
And thirty snows had not yet shed
Their glory on the warrior's head;
But, as the summer fruit decays,
So died he in those naked days.

A dark cloak of the roebuck's skin
Covered the warrior, and within
Its heavy folds the weapons, made
For the hard toils of war, were laid;
The cuirass, woven of plaited reeds,
And the broad belt of shells and beads.

Before, a dark-haired virgin train
Chanted the death dirge of the slain;
Behind, the long procession came
Of hoary men and chiefs of fame,
With heavy hearts, and eyes of grief,

Leading the war-horse of their chief.

Stripped of his proud and martial dress,
Uncurbed, unreined, and riderless,
With darting eye, and nostril spread,
And heavy and impatient tread,
He came; and oft that eye so proud
Asked for his rider in the crowd.

They buried the dark chief; they freed
Beside the grave his battle steed;
And swift an arrow cleaved its way
To his stern heart! One piercing neigh
Arose, and, on the dead man's plain,
The rider grasps his steed again.

L' ENVOI

Ye voices, that arose
After the Evening's close,
And whispered to my restless heart repose!

Go, breathe it in the ear
Of all who doubt and fear,
And say to them, "Be of good cheer!"

Ye sounds, so low and calm,
That in the groves of balm
Seemed to me like an angel's psalm!

Go, mingle yet once more
With the perpetual roar
Of the pine forest dark and hoar!

Tongues of the dead, not lost
But speaking from deaths frost,
Like fiery tongues at Pentecost!

Glimmer, as funeral lamps,
Amid the chills and damps
Of the vast plain where Death encamps!

BALLADS AND OTHER POEMS

THE SKELETON IN ARMOR

"Speak! speak I thou fearful guest
Who, with thy hollow breast
Still in rude armor drest,
    Comest to daunt me!
Wrapt not in Eastern balms,
Bat with thy fleshless palms
Stretched, as if asking alms,
    Why dost thou haunt me?"

Then, from those cavernous eyes
Pale flashes seemed to rise,
As when the Northern skies
    Gleam in December;
And, like the water's flow
Under December's snow,
Came a dull voice of woe
    From the heart's chamber.

"I was a Viking old!
My deeds, though manifold,
No Skald in song has told,
    No Saga taught thee!
Take heed, that in thy verse
Thou dost the tale rehearse,
Else dread a dead man's curse;
    For this I sought thee.

"Far in the Northern Land,
By the wild Baltic's strand,
I, with my childish hand,
    Tamed the gerfalcon;
And, with my skates fast-bound,
Skimmed the half-frozen Sound,
    That the poor whimpering hound
Trembled to walk on.

"Oft to his frozen lair
Tracked I the grisly bear,

While from my path the hare
  Fled like a shadow;
Oft through the forest dark
Followed the were-wolf's bark,
Until the soaring lark
  Sang from the meadow.

"But when I older grew,
Joining a corsair's crew,
O'er the dark sea I flew
  With the marauders.
Wild was the life we led;
Many the souls that sped,
Many the hearts that bled,
  By our stern orders.

"Many a wassail-bout
Wore the long Winter out;
Often our midnight shout
  Set the cocks crowing,
As we the Berserk's tale
Measured in cups of ale,
Draining the oaken pail,
  Filled to o'erflowing.

"Once as I told in glee
Tales of the stormy sea,
Soft eyes did gaze on me,
  Burning yet tender;
And as the white stars shine
On the dark Norway pine,
On that dark heart of mine
  Fell their soft splendor.

"I wooed the blue-eyed maid,
Yielding, yet half afraid,
And in the forest's shade
  Our vows were plighted.
Under its loosened vest
Fluttered her little breast
Like birds within their nest
  By the hawk frighted.

"Bright in her father's hall
Shields gleamed upon the wall,
Loud sang the minstrels all,
  Chanting his glory;
When of old Hildebrand
I asked his daughter's hand,
Mute did the minstrels stand
  To hear my story.

"While the brown ale he quaffed,
Loud then the champion laughed,
And as the wind-gusts waft
  The sea-foam brightly,
So the loud laugh of scorn,
Out of those lips unshorn,
From the deep drinking-horn
  Blew the foam lightly.

"She was a Prince's child,
I but a Viking wild,
And though she blushed and smiled,
  I was discarded!
Should not the dove so white
Follow the sea-mew's flight,
Why did they leave that night
  Her nest unguarded?

"Scarce had I put to sea,
Bearing the maid with me,
Fairest of all was she
  Among the Norsemen!
When on the white sea-strand,
Waving his armed hand,
Saw we old Hildebrand,
  With twenty horsemen.

"Then launched they to the blast,
Bent like a reed each mast,
Yet we were gaining fast,
  When the wind failed us;
And with a sudden flaw
Came round the gusty Skaw,
So that our foe we saw

Laugh as he hailed us.

"And as to catch the gale
Round veered the flapping sail,
Death I was the helmsman's hail,
  Death without quarter!
Mid-ships with iron keel
Struck we her ribs of steel
Down her black hulk did reel
  Through the black water!

"As with his wings aslant,
Sails the fierce cormorant,
Seeking some rocky haunt
  With his prey laden,
So toward the open main,
Beating to sea again,
Through the wild hurricane,
  Bore I the maiden.

"Three weeks we westward bore,
And when the storm was o'er,
Cloud-like we saw the shore
  Stretching to leeward;
There for my lady's bower
Built I the lofty tower,
Which, to this very hour,
  Stands looking seaward.

"There lived we many years;
Time dried the maiden's tears
She had forgot her fears,
  She was a mother.
Death closed her mild blue eyes,
Under that tower she lies;
Ne'er shall the sun arise
  On such another!

"Still grew my bosom then.
Still as a stagnant fen!
Hateful to me were men,
  The sunlight hateful!
In the vast forest here,

Clad in my warlike gear,
Fell I upon my spear,
  O, death was grateful!

"Thus, seamed with many scars,
Bursting these prison bars,
Up to its native stars
  My soul ascended!
There from the flowing bowl
Deep drinks the warrior's soul,
Skoal! to the Northland! skoal!"
  Thus the tale ended.

THE WRECK OF THE HESPERUS

It was the schooner Hesperus,
   That sailed the wintry sea;
And the skipper had taken his little daughter,
   To bear him company.

Blue were her eyes as the fairy-flax,
   Her cheeks like the dawn of day,
And her bosom white as the hawthorn buds,
   That ope in the month of May.

The skipper he stood beside the helm,
   His pipe was in his month,
And he watched how the veering flaw did blow
   The smoke now West, now South.

Then up and spake an old Sailor,
   Had sailed to the Spanish Main,
"I pray thee, put into yonder port,
   For I fear a hurricane.

"Last night, the moon had a golden ring,
   And to-night no moon we see!"
The skipper, he blew a whiff from his pipe,
   And a scornful laugh laughed he.

Colder and louder blew the wind,
   A gale from the Northeast.
The snow fell hissing in the brine,
   And the billows frothed like yeast.

Down came the storm, and smote amain
   The vessel in its strength;
She shuddered and paused, like a frighted steed,
   Then leaped her cable's length.

"Come hither! come hither! my little daughter,
   And do not tremble so;
For I can weather the roughest gale
   That ever wind did blow."

He wrapped her warm in his seaman's coat
  Against the stinging blast;
He cut a rope from a broken spar,
  And bound her to the mast.

"O father! I hear the church-bells ring,
  O say, what may it be?"
"'Tis a fog-bell on a rock-bound coast!" —
  And he steered for the open sea.

"O father! I hear the sound of guns,
  O say, what may it be?"
"Some ship in distress, that cannot live
  In such an angry sea!"

"O father! I see a gleaming light
  O say, what may it be?"
But the father answered never a word,
  A frozen corpse was he.

Lashed to the helm, all stiff and stark,
  With his face turned to the skies,
The lantern gleamed through the gleaming snow
  On his fixed and glassy eyes.

Then the maiden clasped her hands and prayed
  That saved she might be;
And she thought of Christ, who stilled the wave,
  On the Lake of Galilee.

And fast through the midnight dark and drear,
  Through the whistling sleet and snow,
Like a sheeted ghost, the vessel swept
  Tow'rds the reef of Norman's Woe.

And ever the fitful gusts between
  A sound came from the land;
It was the sound of the trampling surf
  On the rocks and the hard sea-sand.

The breakers were right beneath her bows,
  She drifted a dreary wreck,
And a whooping billow swept the crew

Like icicles from her deck.

She struck where the white and fleecy waves
  Looked soft as carded wool,
But the cruel rocks, they gored her side
  Like the horns of an angry bull.

Her rattling shrouds, all sheathed in ice,
  With the masts went by the board;
Like a vessel of glass, she stove and sank,
  Ho! ho! the breakers roared!

At daybreak, on the bleak sea-beach,
  A fisherman stood aghast,
To see the form of a maiden fair,
  Lashed close to a drifting mast.

The salt sea was frozen on her breast,
  The salt tears in her eyes;
And he saw her hair, like the brown sea-weed,
  On the billows fall and rise.

Such was the wreck of the Hesperus,
  In the midnight and the snow!
Christ save us all from a death like this,
  On the reef of Norman's Woe!

THE VILLAGE BLACKSMITH

Under a spreading chestnut-tree
  The village smithy stands;
The smith, a mighty man is he,
  With large and sinewy hands;
And the muscles of his brawny arms
  Are strong as iron bands.

His hair is crisp, and black, and long,
  His face is like the tan;
His brow is wet with honest sweat,
  He earns whate'er he can,
And looks the whole world in the face,
  For he owes not any man.

Week in, week out, from morn till night,
  You can hear his bellows blow;
You can hear him swing his heavy sledge,
  With measured beat and slow,
Like a sexton ringing the village bell,
  When the evening sun is low.

And children coming home from school
  Look in at the open door;
They love to see the flaming forge,
  And bear the bellows roar,
And catch the burning sparks that fly
  Like chaff from a threshing-floor.

He goes on Sunday to the church,
  And sits among his boys;
He hears the parson pray and preach,
  He hears his daughter's voice,
Singing in the village choir,
  And it makes his heart rejoice.

It sounds to him like her mother's voice,
  Singing in Paradise!
He needs must think of her once more,
  How in the grave she lies;
And with his hard, rough hand he wipes

A tear out of his eyes.

Toiling,—rejoicing,—sorrowing,
  Onward through life he goes;
Each morning sees some task begin,
  Each evening sees it close
Something attempted, something done,
  Has earned a night's repose.

Thanks, thanks to thee, my worthy friend,
For the lesson thou hast taught!
Thus at the flaming forge of life
  Our fortunes must be wrought;
Thus on its sounding anvil shaped
  Each burning deed and thought.

ENDYMION

The rising moon has hid the stars;
Her level rays, like golden bars,
  Lie on the landscape green,
  With shadows brown between.

And silver white the river gleams,
As if Diana, in her dreams,
  Had dropt her silver bow
  Upon the meadows low.

On such a tranquil night as this,
She woke Endymion with a kiss,
  When, sleeping in the grove,
  He dreamed not of her love.

Like Dian's kiss, unasked, unsought,
Love gives itself, but is not bought;
  Nor voice, nor sound betrays
  Its deep, impassioned gaze.

It comes, — the beautiful, the free,
The crown of all humanity, —
  In silence and alone
  To seek the elected one.

It lifts the boughs, whose shadows deep
Are Life's oblivion, the soul's sleep,
  And kisses the closed eyes
  Of him, who slumbering lies.

O weary hearts! O slumbering eyes!
O drooping souls, whose destinies
  Are fraught with fear and pain,
  Ye shall be loved again!

No one is so accursed by fate,
No one so utterly desolate,
  But some heart, though unknown,
  Responds unto his own.

Responds,—as if with unseen wings,
An angel touched its quivering strings;
  And whispers, in its song,
   "'Where hast thou stayed so long?"

IT IS NOT ALWAYS MAY

No hay pajaros en los nidos de antano.
      Spanish Proverb

The sun is bright,—the air is clear,
  The darting swallows soar and sing.
And from the stately elms I hear
  The bluebird prophesying Spring.

So blue you winding river flows,
  It seems an outlet from the sky,
Where waiting till the west-wind blows,
  The freighted clouds at anchor lie.

All things are new;—the buds, the leaves,
  That gild the elm-tree's nodding crest,
And even the nest beneath the eaves;—
  There are no birds in last year's nest!

All things rejoice in youth and love,
  The fulness of their first delight!
And learn from the soft heavens above
  The melting tenderness of night.

Maiden, that read'st this simple rhyme,
  Enjoy thy youth, it will not stay;
Enjoy the fragrance of thy prime,
  For oh, it is not always May!

Enjoy the Spring of Love and Youth,
  To some good angel leave the rest;
For Time will teach thee soon the truth,
  There are no birds in last year's nest!

THE RAINY DAY

The day is cold, and dark, and dreary
It rains, and the wind is never weary;
The vine still clings to the mouldering wall,
But at every gust the dead leaves fall,
   And the day is dark and dreary.

My life is cold, and dark, and dreary;
It rains, and the wind is never weary;
My thoughts still cling to the mouldering Past,
But the hopes of youth fall thick in the blast,
   And the days are dark and dreary.

Be still, sad heart! and cease repining;
Behind the clouds is the sun still shining;
Thy fate is the common fate of all,
Into each life some rain must fall,
   Some days must be dark and dreary.

GOD'S-ACRE.

I like that ancient Saxon phrase, which calls
  The burial-ground God's-Acre! It is just;
It consecrates each grave within its walls,
  And breathes a benison o'er the sleeping dust.

God's-Acre! Yes, that blessed name imparts
  Comfort to those, who in the grave have sown
The seed that they had garnered in their hearts,
  Their bread of life, alas! no more their own.

Into its furrows shall we all be cast,
  In the sure faith, that we shall rise again
At the great harvest, when the archangel's blast
  Shall winnow, like a fan, the chaff and grain.

Then shall the good stand in immortal bloom,
  In the fair gardens of that second birth;
And each bright blossom mingle its perfume
  With that of flowers, which never bloomed on earth.

With thy rude ploughshare, Death, turn up the sod,
  And spread the furrow for the seed we sow;
This is the field and Acre of our God,
  This is the place where human harvests grow!

TO THE RIVER CHARLES.

River! that in silence windest
 Through the meadows, bright and free,
Till at length thy rest thou findest
 In the bosom of the sea!

Four long years of mingled feeling,
 Half in rest, and half in strife,
I have seen thy waters stealing
 Onward, like the stream of life.

Thou hast taught me, Silent River!
 Many a lesson, deep and long;
Thou hast been a generous giver;
 I can give thee but a song.

Oft in sadness and in illness,
 I have watched thy current glide,
Till the beauty of its stillness
 Overflowed me, like a tide.

And in better hours and brighter,
 When I saw thy waters gleam,
I have felt my heart beat lighter,
 And leap onward with thy stream.

Not for this alone I love thee,
 Nor because thy waves of blue
From celestial seas above thee
 Take their own celestial hue.

Where yon shadowy woodlands hide thee,
 And thy waters disappear,
Friends I love have dwelt beside thee,
 And have made thy margin dear.

More than this;—thy name reminds me
 Of three friends, all true and tried;
And that name, like magic, binds me
 Closer, closer to thy side.

Friends my soul with joy remembers!
  How like quivering flames they start,
When I fan the living embers
  On the hearth-stone of my heart!

'T is for this, thou Silent River!
  That my spirit leans to thee;
Thou hast been a generous giver,
  Take this idle song from me.

BLIND BARTIMEUS

Blind Bartimeus at the gates
Of Jericho in darkness waits;
He hears the crowd;—he hears a breath
Say, "It is Christ of Nazareth!"
And calls, in tones of agony,
<Greek here>

The thronging multitudes increase;
Blind Bartimeus, hold thy peace!
But still, above the noisy crowd,
The beggar's cry is shrill and loud;
Until they say, "He calleth thee!"
<Greek here>

Then saith the Christ, as silent stands
The crowd, "What wilt thou at my hands?"
And he replies, "O give me light!
Rabbi, restore the blind man's sight.
And Jesus answers, '<Greek here>'
<Greek here>!

Ye that have eyes, yet cannot see,
In darkness and in misery,
Recall those mighty Voices Three,
<Greek here>!
<Greek here>!
<Greek here>!

THE GOBLET OF LIFE

Filled is Life's goblet to the brim;
And though my eyes with tears are dim,
I see its sparkling bubbles swim,
And chant a melancholy hymn
  With solemn voice and slow.

No purple flowers,—no garlands green,
Conceal the goblet's shade or sheen,
Nor maddening draughts of Hippocrene,
Like gleams of sunshine, flash between
  Thick leaves of mistletoe.

This goblet, wrought with curious art,
Is filled with waters, that upstart,
When the deep fountains of the heart,
By strong convulsions rent apart,
  Are running all to waste.

And as it mantling passes round,
With fennel is it wreathed and crowned,
Whose seed and foliage sun-imbrowned
Are in its waters steeped and drowned,
  And give a bitter taste.

Above the lowly plants it towers,
The fennel, with its yellow flowers,
And in an earlier age than ours
Was gifted with the wondrous powers,
  Lost vision to restore.

It gave new strength, and fearless mood;
And gladiators, fierce and rude,
Mingled it in their daily food;
And he who battled and subdued,
  A wreath of fennel wore.

Then in Life's goblet freely press,
The leaves that give it bitterness,
Nor prize the colored waters less,
For in thy darkness and distress

New light and strength they give!

And he who has not learned to know
How false its sparkling bubbles show,
How bitter are the drops of woe,
With which its brim may overflow,
   He has not learned to live.

The prayer of Ajax was for light;
Through all that dark and desperate fight
The blackness of that noonday night
He asked but the return of sight,
   To see his foeman's face.

Let our unceasing, earnest prayer
Be, too, for light,—for strength to bear
Our portion of the weight of care,
That crushes into dumb despair
   One half the human race.

O suffering, sad humanity!
O ye afflicted one; who lie
Steeped to the lips in misery,
Longing, and yet afraid to die,
   Patient, though sorely tried!

I pledge you in this cup of grief,
Where floats the fennel's bitter leaf!
The Battle of our Life is brief
The alarm,—the struggle,—the relief,
   Then sleep we side by side.

MAIDENHOOD

Maiden! with the meek, brown eyes,
In whose orbs a shadow lies
Like the dusk in evening skies!

Thou whose locks outshine the sun,
Golden tresses, wreathed in one,
As the braided streamlets run!

Standing, with reluctant feet,
Where the brook and river meet,
Womanhood and childhood fleet!

Gazing, with a timid glance,
On the brooklet's swift advance,
On the river's broad expanse!

Deep and still, that gliding stream
Beautiful to thee must seem,
As the river of a dream.

Then why pause with indecision,
When bright angels in thy vision
Beckon thee to fields Elysian?

Seest thou shadows sailing by,
As the dove, with startled eye,
Sees the falcon's shadow fly?

Hearest thou voices on the shore,
That our ears perceive no more,
Deafened by the cataract's roar?

O, thou child of many prayers!
Life hath quicksands, — Life hath snares
Care and age come unawares!

Like the swell of some sweet tune,
Morning rises into noon,
May glides onward into June.

Childhood is the bough, where slumbered
Birds and blossoms many-numbered;—
Age, that bough with snows encumbered.

Gather, then, each flower that grows,
When the young heart overflows,
To embalm that tent of snows.

Bear a lily in thy hand;
Gates of brass cannot withstand
One touch of that magic wand.

Bear through sorrow, wrong, and ruth,
In thy heart the dew of youth,
On thy lips the smile of truth!

O, that dew, like balm, shall steal
Into wounds that cannot heal,
Even as sleep our eyes doth seal;

And that smile, like sunshine, dart
Into many a sunless heart,
For a smile of God thou art.

EXCELSIOR

The shades of night were falling fast,
As through an Alpine village passed
A youth, who bore, 'mid snow and ice,
A banner with the strange device,
    Excelsior!

His brow was sad; his eye beneath,
Flashed like a falchion from its sheath,
And like a silver clarion rung
The accents of that unknown tongue,
    Excelsior!

In happy homes he saw the light
Of household fires gleam warm and bright;
Above, the spectral glaciers shone,
And from his lips escaped a groan,
    Excelsior!

"Try not the Pass!" the old man said:
"Dark lowers the tempest overhead,
The roaring torrent is deep and wide!
And loud that clarion voice replied,
    Excelsior!

"Oh stay," the maiden said, "and rest
Thy weary head upon this breast!"
A tear stood in his bright blue eye,
But still he answered, with a sigh,
    Excelsior!

"Beware the pine-tree's withered branch!
Beware the awful avalanche!"
This was the peasant's last Good-night,
A voice replied, far up the height,
    Excelsior!

At break of day, as heavenward
The pious monks of Saint Bernard
Uttered the oft-repeated prayer,
A voice cried through the startled air,

  Excelsior!

A traveller, by the faithful hound,
Half-buried in the snow was found,
Still grasping in his hand of ice
That banner with the strange device,
  Excelsior!

There in the twilight cold and gray,
Lifeless, but beautiful, he lay,
And from the sky, serene and far,
A voice fell, like a falling star,
  Excelsior!

POEMS ON SLAVERY.

[The following poems, with one exception, were written at sea, in the latter part of October, 1842. I had not then heard of Dr. Channing's death. Since that event, the poem addressed to him is no longer appropriate. I have decided, however, to let it remain as it was written, in testimony of my admiration for a great and good man.]

TO WILLIAM E. CHANNING

The pages of thy book I read,
  And as I closed each one,
My heart, responding, ever said,
  "Servant of God! well done!"

Well done! Thy words are great and bold;
  At times they seem to me,
Like Luther's, in the days of old,
  Half-battles for the free.

Go on, until this land revokes
  The old and chartered Lie,
The feudal curse, whose whips and yokes
  Insult humanity.

A voice is ever at thy side
  Speaking in tones of might,
Like the prophetic voice, that cried
  To John in Patmos, "Write!"

Write! and tell out this bloody tale;
  Record this dire eclipse,
This Day of Wrath, this Endless Wail,
  This dread Apocalypse!

THE SLAVE'S DREAM

Beside the ungathered rice he lay,
  His sickle in his hand;
His breast was bare, his matted hair
  Was buried in the sand.
Again, in the mist and shadow of sleep,
  He saw his Native Land.

Wide through the landscape of his dreams
  The lordly Niger flowed;
Beneath the palm-trees on the plain
  Once more a king he strode;
And heard the tinkling caravans
  Descend the mountain-road.

He saw once more his dark-eyed queen
  Among her children stand;
They clasped his neck, they kissed his cheeks,
  They held him by the hand! —
A tear burst from the sleeper's lids
  And fell into the sand.

And then at furious speed he rode
  Along the Niger's bank;
His bridle-reins were golden chains,
  And, with a martial clank,
At each leap he could feel his scabbard of steel
  Smiting his stallion's flank.

Before him, like a blood-red flag,
  The bright flamingoes flew;
From morn till night he followed their flight,
  O'er plains where the tamarind grew,
Till he saw the roofs of Caffre huts,
  And the ocean rose to view.

At night he heard the lion roar,
  And the hyena scream,
And the river-horse, as he crushed the reeds
  Beside some hidden stream;
And it passed, like a glorious roll of drums,

Through the triumph of his dream.

The forests, with their myriad tongues,
  Shouted of liberty;
And the Blast of the Desert cried aloud,
  With a voice so wild and free,
That he started in his sleep and smiled
  At their tempestuous glee.

He did not feel the driver's whip,
  Nor the burning heat of day;
For Death had illumined the Land of Sleep,
  And his lifeless body lay
A worn-out fetter, that the soul
  Had broken and thrown away!

THE GOOD PART

THAT SHALL NOT BE TAKEN AWAY

She dwells by Great Kenhawa's side,
  In valleys green and cool;
And all her hope and all her pride
  Are in the village school.

Her soul, like the transparent air
  That robes the hills above,
Though not of earth, encircles there
  All things with arms of love.

And thus she walks among her girls
  With praise and mild rebukes;
Subduing e'en rude village churls
  By her angelic looks.

She reads to them at eventide
  Of One who came to save;
To cast the captive's chains aside
  And liberate the slave.

And oft the blessed time foretells
  When all men shall be free;
And musical, as silver bells,
  Their falling chains shall be.

And following her beloved Lord,
  In decent poverty,
She makes her life one sweet record
  And deed of charity.

For she was rich, and gave up all
  To break the iron bands
Of those who waited in her hall,
  And labored in her lands.

Long since beyond the Southern Sea
  Their outbound sails have sped,
While she, in meek humility,

Now earns her daily bread.

It is their prayers, which never cease,
  That clothe her with such grace;
Their blessing is the light of peace
  That shines upon her face.

THE SLAVE IN THE DISMAL SWAMP

In dark fens of the Dismal Swamp
  The hunted Negro lay;
He saw the fire of the midnight camp,
And heard at times a horse's tramp
  And a bloodhound's distant bay.

Where will-o'-the-wisps and glow-worms shine,
  In bulrush and in brake;
Where waving mosses shroud the pine,
And the cedar grows, and the poisonous vine
  Is spotted like the snake;

Where hardly a human foot could pass,
  Or a human heart would dare,
On the quaking turf of the green morass
He crouched in the rank and tangled grass,
  Like a wild beast in his lair.

A poor old slave, infirm and lame;
  Great scars deformed his face;
On his forehead he bore the brand of shame,
And the rags, that hid his mangled frame,
  Were the livery of disgrace.

All things above were bright and fair,
  All things were glad and free;
Lithe squirrels darted here and there,
And wild birds filled the echoing air
  With songs of Liberty!

On him alone was the doom of pain,
  From the morning of his birth;
On him alone the curse of Cain
Fell, like a flail on the garnered grain,
  And struck him to the earth!

THE SLAVE SINGING AT MIDNIGHT

Loud he sang the psalm of David!
He, a Negro and enslaved,
Sang of Israel's victory,
Sang of Zion, bright and free.

In that hour, when night is calmest,
Sang he from the Hebrew Psalmist,
In a voice so sweet and clear
That I could not choose but hear,

Songs of triumph, and ascriptions,
Such as reached the swart Egyptians,
When upon the Red Sea coast
Perished Pharaoh and his host.

And the voice of his devotion
Filled my soul with strange emotion;
For its tones by turns were glad,
Sweetly solemn, wildly sad.

Paul and Silas, in their prison,
Sang of Christ, the Lord arisen,
And an earthquake's arm of might
Broke their dungeon-gates at night.

But, alas! what holy angel
Brings the Slave this glad evangel?
And what earthquake's arm of might
Breaks his dungeon-gates at night?

THE WITNESSES

In Ocean's wide domains,
  Half buried in the sands,
Lie skeletons in chains,
  With shackled feet and hands.

Beyond the fall of dews,
  Deeper than plummet lies,
Float ships, with all their crews,
  No more to sink nor rise.

There the black Slave-ship swims,
  Freighted with human forms,
Whose fettered, fleshless limbs
  Are not the sport of storms.

These are the bones of Slaves;
  They gleam from the abyss;
They cry, from yawning waves,
  "We are the Witnesses!"

Within Earth's wide domains
  Are markets for men's lives;
Their necks are galled with chains,
  Their wrists are cramped with gyves.

Dead bodies, that the kite
  In deserts makes its prey;
Murders, that with affright
  Scare school-boys from their play!

All evil thoughts and deeds;
  Anger, and lust, and pride;
The foulest, rankest weeds,
  That choke Life's groaning tide!

These are the woes of Slaves;
  They glare from the abyss;
They cry, from unknown graves,
  "We are the Witnesses!

THE QUADROON GIRL

The Slaver in the broad lagoon
  Lay moored with idle sail;
He waited for the rising moon,
  And for the evening gale.

Under the shore his boat was tied,
  And all her listless crew
Watched the gray alligator slide
  Into the still bayou.

Odors of orange-flowers, and spice,
  Reached them from time to time,
Like airs that breathe from Paradise
  Upon a world of crime.

The Planter, under his roof of thatch,
  Smoked thoughtfully and slow;
The Slaver's thumb was on the latch,
  He seemed in haste to go.

He said, "My ship at anchor rides
  In yonder broad lagoon;
I only wait the evening tides,
  And the rising of the moon.

Before them, with her face upraised,
  In timid attitude,
Like one half curious, half amazed,
  A Quadroon maiden stood.

Her eyes were large, and full of light,
  Her arms and neck were bare;
No garment she wore save a kirtle bright,
  And her own long, raven hair.

And on her lips there played a smile
  As holy, meek, and faint,
As lights in some cathedral aisle
  The features of a saint.

"The soil is barren,—the farm is old";
  The thoughtful planter said;
Then looked upon the Slaver's gold,
  And then upon the maid.

His heart within him was at strife
  With such accursed gains:
For he knew whose passions gave her life,
  Whose blood ran in her veins.

But the voice of nature was too weak;
  He took the glittering gold!
Then pale as death grew the maiden's cheek,
  Her hands as icy cold.

The Slaver led her from the door,
  He led her by the hand,
To be his slave and paramour
  In a strange and distant land!

THE WARNING

Beware! The Israelite of old, who tore
  The lion in his path, — when, poor and blind,
He saw the blessed light of heaven no more,
  Shorn of his noble strength and forced to grind
In prison, and at last led forth to be
A pander to Philistine revelry, —

Upon the pillars of the temple laid
  His desperate hands, and in its overthrow
Destroyed himself, and with him those who made
  A cruel mockery of his sightless woe;
The poor, blind Slave, the scoff and jest of all,
Expired, and thousands perished in the fall!

There is a poor, blind Samson in this land,
  Shorn of his strength and bound in bonds of steel,
Who may, in some grim revel, raise his hand,
  And shake the pillars of this Commonweal,
Till the vast Temple of our liberties.
A shapeless mass of wreck and rubbish lies.

THE SPANISH STUDENT

DRAMATIS PERSONAE

VICTORIAN

HYPOLITO	Students of Alcala.
THE COUNT OF LARA	
DON CARLOS	Gentlemen of Madrid.
THE ARCHBISHOP OF TOLEDO.	
A CARDINAL.	
BELTRAN CRUZADO	Count of the Gypsies.
BARTOLOME ROMAN	A young Gypsy.
THE PADRE CURA OF GUADARRAMA.	
PEDRO CRESPO	Alcalde.
PANCHO	Alguacil.
FRANCISCO	Lara's Servant.
CHISPA	Victorian's Servant.
BALTASAR	Innkeeper.
PRECIOSA	A Gypsy Girl.
ANGELICA	A poor Girl.
MARTINA	The Padre Cura's Niece.
DOLORES	Preciosa's Maid.
Gypsies, Musicians, etc.	

ACT I.

SCENE I.—The COUNT OF LARA'S chambers. Night. The COUNT
in his dressing-gown, smoking and conversing with DON CARLOS.

  Lara. You were not at the play tonight, Don Carlos;
How happened it?

  Don C. I had engagements elsewhere.
Pray who was there?

  Lara. Why all the town and court.
The house was crowded; and the busy fans
Among the gayly dressed and perfumed ladies
Fluttered like butterflies among the flowers.

There was the Countess of Medina Celi;
The Goblin Lady with her Phantom Lover,
Her Lindo Don Diego; Dona Sol,
And Dona Serafina, and her cousins.

  Don C. What was the play?

  Lara. It was a dull affair;
One of those comedies in which you see,
As Lope says, the history of the world
Brought down from Genesis to the Day of Judgment.
There were three duels fought in the first act,
Three gentlemen receiving deadly wounds,
Laying their hands upon their hearts, and saying,
"O, I am dead!" a lover in a closet,
An old hidalgo, and a gay Don Juan,
A Dona Inez with a black mantilla,
Followed at twilight by an unknown lover,
Who looks intently where he knows she is not!

  Don C. Of course, the Preciosa danced to-night?

  Lara. And never better. Every footstep fell
As lightly as a sunbeam on the water.
I think the girl extremely beautiful.

  Don C. Almost beyond the privilege of woman!
I saw her in the Prado yesterday.
Her step was royal,—queen-like,—and her face
As beautiful as a saint's in Paradise.

  Lara. May not a saint fall from her Paradise,
And be no more a saint?

  Don C.   Why do you ask?

  Lara. Because I have heard it said this angel fell,
And though she is a virgin outwardly,
Within she is a sinner; like those panels
Of doors and altar-pieces the old monks
Painted in convents, with the Virgin Mary
On the outside, and on the inside Venus!
  Don C. You do her wrong; indeed, you do her wrong!

She is as virtuous as she is fair.

   Lara. How credulous you are! Why look you, friend,
There's not a virtuous woman in Madrid,
In this whole city! And would you persuade me
That a mere dancing-girl, who shows herself,
Nightly, half naked, on the stage, for money,
And with voluptuous motions fires the blood
Of inconsiderate youth, is to be held
A model for her virtue?

   Don C.   You forget
She is a Gypsy girl.

   Lara.   And therefore won
The easier.

   Don C. Nay, not to be won at all!
The only virtue that a Gypsy prizes
Is chastity. That is her only virtue.
Dearer than life she holds it. I remember
A Gypsy woman, a vile, shameless bawd,
Whose craft was to betray the young and fair;
And yet this woman was above all bribes.
And when a noble lord, touched by her beauty,
The wild and wizard beauty of her race,
Offered her gold to be what she made others,
She turned upon him, with a look of scorn,
And smote him in the face!

   Lara.   And does that prove
That Preciosa is above suspicion?

   Don C. It proves a nobleman may be repulsed
When he thinks conquest easy. I believe
That woman, in her deepest degradation,
Holds something sacred, something undefiled,
Some pledge and keepsake of her higher nature,
And, like the diamond in the dark, retains
Some quenchless gleam of the celestial light!

   Lara. Yet Preciosa would have taken the gold.
   Don C. (rising). I do not think so.

Lara.   I am sure of it.
But why this haste? Stay yet a little longer,
And fight the battles of your Dulcinea.

  Don C. 'T is late. I must begone, for if I stay
You will not be persuaded.

  Lara.   Yes; persuade me.

  Don C. No one so deaf as he who will not hear!

 Lara. No one so blind as he who will not see!

  Don C. And so good night. I wish you pleasant dreams,
And greater faith in woman.   [Exit.

  Lara.   Greater faith!
I have the greatest faith; for I believe
Victorian is her lover. I believe
That I shall be to-morrow; and thereafter
Another, and another, and another,
Chasing each other through her zodiac,
As Taurus chases Aries.

(Enter FRANCISCO with a casket.)

      Well, Francisco,
What speed with Preciosa?

  Fran.   None, my lord.
She sends your jewels back, and bids me tell you
She is not to be purchased by your gold.

  Lara. Then I will try some other way to win her.
Pray, dost thou know Victorian?

  Fran.   Yes, my lord;
I saw him at the jeweller's to-day.

  Lara. What was he doing there?

  Fran.   I saw him buy
A golden ring, that had a ruby in it.

Lara. Was there another like it?

Fran.   One so like it
I could not choose between them.

Lara.   It is well.
To-morrow morning bring that ring to me.
Do not forget. Now light me to my bed.
                [Exeunt.

> SCENE II. — A street in Madrid. Enter CHISPA, followed by
> musicians, with a bagpipe, guitars, and other instruments.

Chispa. Abernuncio Satanas! and a plague on all lovers who
ramble about at night, drinking the elements, instead of
sleeping quietly in their beds. Every dead man to his cemetery,
say I; and every friar to his monastery. Now, here's my master,
Victorian, yesterday a cow-keeper, and to-day a gentleman;
yesterday a student, and to-day a lover; and I must be up later
than the nightingale, for as the abbot sings so must the
sacristan respond. God grant he may soon be married, for then
shall all this serenading cease. Ay, marry! marry! marry!
Mother, what does marry mean? It means to spin, to bear
children, and to weep, my daughter! And, of a truth, there is
something more in matrimony than the wedding-ring. (To the
musicians.) And now, gentlemen, Pax vobiscum! as the ass said to
the cabbages. Pray, walk this way; and don't hang down your
heads. It is no disgrace to have an old father and a ragged
shirt. Now, look you, you are gentlemen who lead the life of
crickets; you enjoy hunger by day and noise by night. Yet, I
beseech you, for this once be not loud, but pathetic; for it is a
serenade to a damsel in bed, and not to the Man in the Moon.
Your object is not to arouse and terrify, but to soothe and bring
lulling dreams. Therefore, each shall not play upon his
instrument as if it were the only one in the universe, but
gently, and with a certain modesty, according with the others.
Pray, how may I call thy name, friend?

First Mus. Geronimo Gil, at your service.

Chispa. Every tub smells of the wine that is in it. Pray,
Geronimo, is not Saturday an unpleasant day with thee?

First Mus. Why so?

Chispa. Because I have heard it said that Saturday is an
unpleasant day with those who have but one shirt. Moreover, I
have seen thee at the tavern, and if thou canst run as fast as
thou canst drink, I should like to hunt hares with thee. What
instrument is that?

First Mus. An Aragonese bagpipe.

Chispa. Pray, art thou related to the bagpiper of Bujalance,
who asked a maravedi for playing, and ten for leaving off?

First Mus. No, your honor.

Chispa. I am glad of it. What other instruments have we?

Second and Third Musicians. We play the bandurria.

Chispa. A pleasing instrument. And thou?

Fourth Mus. The fife.

Chispa. I like it; it has a cheerful, soul-stirring sound,
that soars up to my lady's window like the song of a swallow.
And you others?

Other Mus. We are the singers, please your honor.

Chispa. You are too many. Do you think we are going to sing
mass in the cathedral of Cordova? Four men can make but little
use of one shoe, and I see not how you can all sing in one song.
But follow me along the garden wall. That is the way my master
climbs to the lady's window, it is by the Vicar's skirts that the
Devil climbs into the belfry. Come, follow me, and make no
noise.
      [Exeunt.

SCENE III. — PRECIOSA'S chamber. She stands at the open window.

Prec. How slowly through the lilac-scented air
Descends the tranquil moon! Like thistle-down
The vapory clouds float in the peaceful sky;
And sweetly from yon hollow vaults of shade
The nightingales breathe out their souls in song.
And hark! what songs of love, what soul-like sounds,
Answer them from below!

SERENADE.

Stars of the summer night!
  Far in yon azure deeps,
Hide, hide your golden light!
  She sleeps!
My lady sleeps!
  Sleeps!

Moon of the summer night!
  Far down yon western steeps,
Sink, sink in silver light!
  She sleeps!
My lady sleeps!
  Sleeps!

Wind of the summer night!
  Where yonder woodbine creeps,
Fold, fold thy pinions light!
  She sleeps!
My lady sleeps!
  Sleeps!

Dreams of the summer night!
  Tell her, her lover keeps
Watch! while in slumbers light
  She sleeps
My lady sleeps
  Sleeps!

(Enter VICTORIAN by the balcony.)

Vict. Poor little dove! Thou tremblest like a leaf!

Prec. I am so frightened! 'T is for thee I tremble!
I hate to have thee climb that wall by night!
Did no one see thee?

Vict.   None, my love, but thou.

Prec. 'T is very dangerous; and when thou art gone
I chide myself for letting thee come here
Thus stealthily by night. Where hast thou been?
Since yesterday I have no news from thee.

Vict. Since yesterday I have been in Alcala.
Erelong the time will come, sweet Preciosa,
When that dull distance shall no more divide us;
And I no more shall scale thy wall by night
To steal a kiss from thee, as I do now.

Prec. An honest thief, to steal but what thou givest.

Vict. And we shall sit together unmolested,
And words of true love pass from tongue to tongue,
As singing birds from one bough to another.

Prec. That were a life to make time envious!
I knew that thou wouldst come to me to-night.
I saw thee at the play.

Vict.   Sweet child of air!
Never did I behold thee so attired
And garmented in beauty as to-night!
What hast thou done to make thee look so fair?

Prec. Am I not always fair?

Vict.   Ay, and so fair
That I am jealous of all eyes that see thee,
And wish that they were blind.

Prec.   I heed them not;
When thou art present, I see none but thee!

72

Vict. There's nothing fair nor beautiful, but takes
Something from thee, that makes it beautiful.

Prec. And yet thou leavest me for those dusty books.

Vict. Thou comest between me and those books too often!
I see thy face in everything I see!
The paintings in the chapel wear thy looks,
The canticles are changed to sarabands,
And with the leaned doctors of the schools
I see thee dance cachuchas.

Prec.   In good sooth,
I dance with learned doctors of the schools
To-morrow morning.

Vict. And with whom, I pray?

Prec. A grave and reverend Cardinal, and his Grace
The Archbishop of Toledo.

Vict.   What mad jest
Is this?

Prec. It is no jest; indeed it is not.

Vict.   Prithee, explain thyself.

Prec.   Why, simply thus.
Thou knowest the Pope has sent here into Spain
To put a stop to dances on the stage.

Vict. I have heard it whispered.

Prec.   Now the Cardinal,
Who for this purpose comes, would fain behold
With his own eyes these dances; and the Archbishop
Has sent for me—

Vict. That thou mayst dance before them!
Now viva la cachucha! It will breathe
The fire of youth into these gray old men!
'T will be thy proudest conquest!

Prec. Saving one.
And yet I fear these dances will be stopped,
And Preciosa be once more a beggar.

 Vict. The sweetest beggar that e'er asked for alms;
With such beseeching eyes, that when I saw thee
I gave my heart away!

 Prec. Dost thou remember
When first we met?

 Vict. It was at Cordova,
In the cathedral garden. Thou wast sitting
Under the orange-trees, beside a fountain.

 Prec. 'T was Easter-Sunday. The full-blossomed trees
Filled all the air with fragrance and with joy.
The priests were singing, and the organ sounded,
And then anon the great cathedral bell.
It was the elevation of the Host.
We both of us fell down upon our knees,
Under the orange boughs, and prayed together.
I never had been happy till that moment.

 Vict. Thou blessed angel!

 Prec. And when thou wast gone
I felt an acting here. I did not speak
To any one that day. But from that day
Bartolome grew hateful unto me.

 Vict. Remember him no more. Let not his shadow
Come between thee and me. Sweet Preciosa!
I loved thee even then, though I was silent!

 Prec. I thought I ne'er should see thy face again.
Thy farewell had a sound of sorrow in it.

 Vict. That was the first sound in the song of love!
Scarce more than silence is, and yet a sound.
Hands of invisible spirits touch the strings
Of that mysterious instrument, the soul,
And play the prelude of our fate. We hear

The voice prophetic, and are not alone.

  Prec. That is my faith. Dust thou believe these warnings?

  Vict. So far as this. Our feelings and our thoughts
Tend ever on, and rest not in the Present.
As drops of rain fall into some dark well,
And from below comes a scarce audible sound,
So fall our thoughts into the dark Hereafter,
And their mysterious echo reaches us.

  Prec. I have felt it so, but found no words to say it!
I cannot reason; I can only feel!
But thou hast language for all thoughts and feelings.
Thou art a scholar; and sometimes I think
We cannot walk together in this world!
The distance that divides us is too great!
Henceforth thy pathway lies among the stars;
I must not hold thee back.

  Vict.   Thou little sceptic!
Dost thou still doubt? What I most prize in woman
Is her affections, not her intellect!
The intellect is finite; but the affections
Are infinite, and cannot be exhausted.
Compare me with the great men of the earth;
What am I? Why, a pygmy among giants!
But if thou lovest,—mark me! I say lovest,
The greatest of thy sex excels thee not!
The world of the affections is thy world,
Not that of man's ambition. In that stillness
Which most becomes a woman, calm and holy,
Thou sittest by the fireside of the heart,
Feeding its flame. The element of fire
Is pure. It cannot change nor hide its nature,
But burns as brightly in a Gypsy camp
As in a palace hall. Art thou convinced?

  Prec. Yes, that I love thee, as the good love heaven;
But not that I am worthy of that heaven.
How shall I more deserve it?

  Vict.   Loving more.

Prec. I cannot love thee more; my heart is full.

Vict. Then let it overflow, and I will drink it,
As in the summer-time the thirsty sands
Drink the swift waters of the Manzanares,
And still do thirst for more.

A Watchman (in the street). Ave Maria
Purissima! 'T is midnight and serene!

Vict. Hear'st thou that cry?

Prec.   It is a hateful sound,
To scare thee from me!

Vict.   As the hunter's horn
Doth scare the timid stag, or bark of hounds
The moor-fowl from his mate.

Prec.   Pray, do not go!

Vict. I must away to Alcala to-night.
Think of me when I am away.

Prec.   Fear not!
I have no thoughts that do not think of thee.

Vict. (giving her a ring).
And to remind thee of my love, take this;
A serpent, emblem of Eternity;
A ruby,—say, a drop of my heart's blood.

Prec. It is an ancient saying, that the ruby
Brings gladness to the wearer, and preserves
The heart pure, and, if laid beneath the pillow,
Drives away evil dreams. But then, alas!
It was a serpent tempted Eve to sin.

Vict. What convent of barefooted Carmelites
Taught thee so much theology?

Prec. (laying her hand upon his mouth). Hush! hush!
Good night! and may all holy angels guard thee!

Vict. Good night! good night! Thou art my guardian angel!
I have no other saint than thou to pray to!

(He descends by the balcony.)

 Prec. Take care, and do not hurt thee. Art thou safe?

 Vict. (from the garden).
Safe as my love for thee! But art thou safe?
Others can climb a balcony by moonlight
As well as I. Pray shut thy window close;
I am jealous of the perfumed air of night
That from this garden climbs to kiss thy lips.

 Prec. (throwing down her handkerchief).
Thou silly child! Take this to blind thine eyes.
It is my benison!

 Vict.   And brings to me
Sweet fragrance from thy lips, as the soft wind
Wafts to the out-bound mariner the breath
Of the beloved land he leaves behind.

 Prec. Make not thy voyage long.

 Vict.   To-morrow night
Shall see me safe returned. Thou art the star
To guide me to an anchorage. Good night!
My beauteous star! My star of love, good night!

 Prec. Good night!

 Watchman (at a distance). Ave Maria Purissima!

             Scene IV. — An inn on the road to Alcala.
          BALTASAR asleep on a bench. Enter CHISPA.

 Chispa. And here we are, halfway to Alcala, between cocks and
midnight. Body o' me! what an inn this is! The lights out, and
the landlord asleep. Hola! ancient Baltasar!

 Bal. (waking). Here I am.

Chispa. Yes, there you are, like a one-eyed Alcalde in a town without inhabitants. Bring a light, and let me have supper.

Bal. Where is your master?

Chispo. Do not trouble yourself about him. We have stopped a moment to breathe our horses; and, if he chooses to walk up and down in the open air, looking into the sky as one who hears it rain, that does not satisfy my hunger, you know. But be quick, for I am in a hurry, and every man stretches his legs according to the length of his coverlet. What have we here?

Bal. (setting a light on the table). Stewed rabbit.

Chispa (eating).   Conscience of Portalegre! Stewed kitten, you mean!

Bal. And a pitcher of Pedro Ximenes, with a roasted pear in it.

Chispa (drinking). Ancient Baltasar, amigo! You know how to cry wine and sell vinegar. I tell you this is nothing but Vino Tinto of La Mancha, with a tang of the swine-skin.

Bal. I swear to you by Saint Simon and Judas, it is all as I say.

Chispa. And I swear to you by Saint Peter and Saint Paul, that it is no such thing. Moreover, your supper is like the hidalgo's dinner, very little meat and a great deal of tablecloth.

Bal. Ha! ha! ha!

Chispa. And more noise than nuts.

Bal. Ha! ha! ha! You must have your joke, Master Chispa. But shall I not ask Don Victorian in, to take a draught of the PedroXimenes?

Chispa. No; you might as well say, "Don't-you-want-some?" to a dead man.

Bal. Why does he go so often to Madrid?

Chispa. For the same reason that he eats no supper. He is in love. Were you ever in love, Baltasar?

Bal. I was never out of it, good Chispa. It has been the torment of my life.

Chispa. What! are you on fire, too, old hay-stack? Why, we shall never be able to put you out.

Vict. (without). Chispa!

Chispa. Go to bed, Pero Grullo, for the cocks are crowing.

Vict. Ea! Chispa! Chispa!

Chispa. Ea! Senor. Come with me, ancient Baltasar, and bring water for the horses. I will pay for the supper tomorrow.
        [Exeunt.

SCENE V. — VICTORIAN'S chambers at Alcala. HYPOLITO asleep
            inan arm-chair. He awakes slowly.

Hyp. I must have been asleep! ay, sound asleep!
And it was all a dream. O sleep, sweet sleep
Whatever form thou takest, thou art fair,
Holding unto our lips thy goblet filled
Out of Oblivion's well, a healing draught!
The candles have burned low; it must be late.
Where can Victorian be? Like Fray Carrillo,
The only place in which one cannot find him
Is his own cell. Here's his guitar, that seldom
Feels the caresses of its master's hand.
Open thy silent lips, sweet instrument!
And make dull midnight merry with a song.

(He plays and sings.)

Padre Francisco!
Padre Francisco!
What do you want of Padre Francisco?
Here is a pretty young maiden
Who wants to confess her sins!

Open the door and let her come in,
I will shrive her from every sin.

(Enter VICTORIAN.)

Vict. Padre Hypolito! Padre Hypolito!

Hyp. What do you want of Padre Hypolito?

Vict. Come, shrive me straight; for, if love be a sin,
I am the greatest sinner that doth live.
I will confess the sweetest of all crimes,
A maiden wooed and won.

Hyp.   The same old tale
Of the old woman in the chimney-corner,
Who, while the pot boils, says, "Come here, my child;
I'll tell thee a story of my wedding-day."

Vict. Nay, listen, for my heart is full; so full
That I must speak.

Hyp.   Alas! that heart of thine
Is like a scene in the old play; the curtain
Rises to solemn music, and lo! enter
The eleven thousand virgins of Cologne!

Vict. Nay, like the Sibyl's volumes, thou shouldst say;
Those that remained, after the six were burned,
Being held more precious than the nine together.
But listen to my tale. Dost thou remember
The Gypsy girl we saw at Cordova
Dance the Romalis in the market-place?

Hyp. Thou meanest Preciosa.

Vict.   Ay, the same.
Thou knowest how her image haunted me
Long after we returned to Alcala.
She's in Madrid.

Hyp.   I know it.

Vict.   And I'm in love.

Hyp. And therefore in Madrid when thou shouldst be
In Alcala.

  Vict. O pardon me, my friend,
If I so long have kept this secret from thee;
But silence is the charm that guards such treasures,
And, if a word be spoken ere the time,
They sink again, they were not meant for us.

  Hyp. Alas! alas! I see thou art in love.
Love keeps the cold out better than a cloak.
It serves for food and raiment. Give a Spaniard
His mass, his olla, and his Dona Luisa —
Thou knowest the proverb. But pray tell me, lover,
How speeds thy wooing? Is the maiden coy?
Write her a song, beginning with an Ave;
Sing as the monk sang to the Virgin Mary,

        Ave! cujus calcem clare
        Nec centenni commendare
          Sciret Seraph studio!

  Vict. Pray, do not jest! This is no time for it!
I am in earnest!

  Hyp.   Seriously enamored?
What, ho! The Primus of great Alcala
Enamored of a Gypsy? Tell me frankly,
How meanest thou?

  Vict.   I mean it honestly.

Hyp. Surely thou wilt not marry her!

Vict.   Why not?

  Hyp. She was betrothed to one Bartolome,
If I remember rightly, a young Gypsy
Who danced with her at Cordova.

  Vict.   They quarrelled,

And so the matter ended.

  Hyp.   But in truth
Thou wilt not marry her.

  Vict.   In truth I will.
The angels sang in heaven when she was born!
She is a precious jewel I have found
Among the filth and rubbish of the world.
I'll stoop for it; but when I wear it here,
Set on my forehead like the morning star,
The world may wonder, but it will not laugh.

  Hyp. If thou wear'st nothing else upon thy forehead,
'T will be indeed a wonder.

  Vict. ˙   Out upon thee
With thy unseasonable jests! Pray tell me,
Is there no virtue in the world?

  Hyp.   Not much.
What, think'st thou, is she doing at this moment;
Now, while we speak of her?

  Vict.   She lies asleep,
And from her parted lips her gentle breath
Comes like the fragrance from the lips of flowers.
Her tender limbs are still, and on her breast
The cross she prayed to, ere she fell asleep,
Rises and falls with the soft tide of dreams,
Like a light barge safe moored.

  Hyp.   Which means, in prose,
She's sleeping with her mouth a little open!

  Vict. O, would I had the old magician's glass
To see her as she lies in childlike sleep!

  Hyp. And wouldst thou venture?

  Vict.   Ay, indeed I would!

  Hyp. Thou art courageous. Hast thou e'er reflected

How much lies hidden in that one word, NOW?

   Vict. Yes; all the awful mystery of Life!
I oft have thought, my dear Hypolito,
That could we, by some spell of magic, change
The world and its inhabitants to stone,
In the same attitudes they now are in,
What fearful glances downward might we cast
Into the hollow chasms of human life!
What groups should we behold about the death-bed,
Putting to shame the group of Niobe!
What joyful welcomes, and what sad farewells!
What stony tears in those congealed eyes!
What visible joy or anguish in those cheeks!
What bridal pomps, and what funereal shows!
What foes, like gladiators, fierce and struggling!
What lovers with their marble lips together!

   Hyp. Ay, there it is! and, if I were in love,
That is the very point I most should dread.
This magic glass, these magic spells of thine,
Might tell a tale were better left untold.
For instance, they might show us thy fair cousin,
The Lady Violante, bathed in tears
Of love and anger, like the maid of Colchis,
Whom thou, another faithless Argonaut,
Having won that golden fleece, a woman's love,
Desertest for this Glauce.

   Vict.   Hold thy peace!
She cares not for me. She may wed another,
Or go into a convent, and, thus dying,
Marry Achilles in the Elysian Fields.

   Hyp. (rising). And so, good night! Good morning, I should say.

(Clock strikes three.)

Hark! how the loud and ponderous mace of Time
Knocks at the golden portals of the day!
And so, once more, good night! We'll speak more largely
Of Preciosa when we meet again.
Get thee to bed, and the magician, Sleep,

Shall show her to thee, in his magic glass,
In all her loveliness. Good night!
                         [Exit.

  Vict.   Good night!
But not to bed; for I must read awhile.

(Throws himself into the arm-chair which HYPOLITO has left, and
lays a large book open upon his knees.)

Must read, or sit in revery and watch
The changing color of the waves that break
Upon the idle sea-shore of the mind!
Visions of Fame! that once did visit me,
Making night glorious with your smile, where are ye?
O, who shall give me, now that ye are gone,
Juices of those immortal plants that bloom
Upon Olympus, making us immortal?
Or teach me where that wondrous mandrake grows
Whose magic root, torn from the earth with groans,
At midnight hour, can scare the fiends away,
And make the mind prolific in its fancies!
I have the wish, but want the will, to act!
Souls of great men departed! Ye whose words
Have come to light from the swift river of Time,
Like Roman swords found in the Tagus' bed,
Where is the strength to wield the arms ye bore?
From the barred visor of Antiquity
Reflected shines the eternal light of Truth,
As from a mirror! All the means of action—
The shapeless masses, the materials—
Lie everywhere about us. What we need
Is the celestial fire to change the flint
Into transparent crystal, bright and clear.
That fire is genius! The rude peasant sits
At evening in his smoky cot, and draws
With charcoal uncouth figures on the wall.
The son of genius comes, foot-sore with travel,
And begs a shelter from the inclement night.
He takes the charcoal from the peasant's hand,
And, by the magic of his touch at once
Transfigured, all its hidden virtues shine,
And, in the eyes of the astonished clown,

It gleams a diamond! Even thus transformed,
Rude popular traditions and old tales
Shine as immortal poems, at the touch
Of some poor, houseless, homeless, wandering bard,
Who had but a night's lodging for his pains.
But there are brighter dreams than those of Fame,
Which are the dreams of Love! Out of the heart
Rises the bright ideal of these dreams,
As from some woodland fount a spirit rises
And sinks again into its silent deeps,
Ere the enamored knight can touch her robe!
'T is this ideal that the soul of man,
Like the enamored knight beside the fountain,
Waits for upon the margin of Life's stream;
Waits to behold her rise from the dark waters,
Clad in a mortal shape! Alas! how many
Must wait in vain! The stream flows evermore,
But from its silent deeps no spirit rises!
Yet I, born under a propitious star,
Have found the bright ideal of my dreams.
Yes! she is ever with me. I can feel,
Here, as I sit at midnight and alone,
Her gentle breathing! on my breast can feel
The pressure of her head! God's benison
Rest ever on it! Close those beauteous eyes,
Sweet Sleep! and all the flowers that bloom at night
With balmy lips breathe in her ears my name!

(Gradually sinks asleep.)

ACT II.

SCENE I. — PRECIOSA'S chamber. Morning. PRECIOSA and
ANGELICA.

Prec. Why will you go so soon? Stay yet awhile.
The poor too often turn away unheard
From hearts that shut against them with a sound
That will be heard in heaven. Pray, tell me more
Of your adversities. Keep nothing from me.
What is your landlord's name?

Ang.   The Count of Lara.

Prec. The Count of Lara? O, beware that man!
Mistrust his pity,—hold no parley with him!
And rather die an outcast in the streets
Than touch his gold.

Ang.   You know him, then!

Prec.   As much
As any woman may, and yet be pure.
As you would keep your name without a blemish,
Beware of him!

Ang.   Alas! what can I do?
I cannot choose my friends. Each word of kindness,
Come whence it may, is welcome to the poor.

Prec. Make me your friend. A girl so young and fair
Should have no friends but those of her own sex.
What is your name?

Ang.   Angelica.

Prec.   That name
Was given you, that you might be an angel
To her who bore you! When your infant smile
Made her home Paradise, you were her angel.
O, be an angel still! She needs that smile.
So long as you are innocent, fear nothing.

No one can harm you! I am a poor girl,
Whom chance has taken from the public streets.
I have no other shield than mine own virtue.
That is the charm which has protected me!
Amid a thousand perils, I have worn it
Here on my heart! It is my guardian angel.

   Ang. (rising). I thank you for this counsel, dearest lady.

   Prec. Thank me by following it.

   Ang.   Indeed I will.

   Prec. Pray, do not go. I have much more to say.

   Ang. My mother is alone. I dare not leave her.

   Prec. Some other time, then, when we meet again.
You must not go away with words alone.

(Gives her a purse.)

Take this. Would it were more.

   Ang.   I thank you, lady.

   Prec. No thanks. To-morrow come to me again.
I dance to-night, — perhaps for the last time.
But what I gain, I promise shall be yours,
If that can save you from the Count of Lara.

   Ang. O, my dear lady! how shall I be grateful
For so much kindness?

   Prec.   I deserve no thanks,
Thank Heaven, not me.

   Ang.   Both Heaven and you.

   Prec.   Farewell.
Remember that you come again tomorrow.

   Ang. I will. And may the Blessed Virgin guard you,

And all good angels.   [Exit.

  Prec.   May they guard thee too,
And all the poor; for they have need of angels.
Now bring me, dear Dolores, my basquina,
My richest maja dress, — my dancing dress,
And my most precious jewels! Make me look
Fairer than night e'er saw me! I've a prize
To win this day, worthy of Preciosa!

(Enter BELTRAN CRUZADO.)

  Cruz. Ave Maria!

  Prec.   O God! my evil genius!
What seekest thou here to-day?

  Cruz.   Thyself, — my child.

  Prec. What is thy will with me?

  Cruz.   Gold! gold!

  Prec. I gave thee yesterday; I have no more.

  Cruz. The gold of the Busne, — give me his gold!

  Prec. I gave the last in charity to-day.

  Cruz. That is a foolish lie.

  Prec.   It is the truth.

  Cruz. Curses upon thee! Thou art not my child!
Hast thou given gold away, and not to me?
Not to thy father? To whom, then?

  Prec.   To one
Who needs it more.

  Cruz. No one can need it more.

  Prec. Thou art not poor.

Cruz. What, I, who lurk about
In dismal suburbs and unwholesome lanes
I, who am housed worse than the galley slave;
I, who am fed worse than the kennelled hound;
I, who am clothed in rags, —Beltran Cruzado, —
Not poor!

Prec. Thou hast a stout heart and strong hands.
Thou canst supply thy wants; what wouldst thou more?

Cruz. The gold of the Busne! give me his gold!

Prec. Beltran Cruzado! hear me once for all.
I speak the truth. So long as I had gold,
I gave it to thee freely, at all times,
Never denied thee; never had a wish
But to fulfil thine own. Now go in peace!
Be merciful, be patient, and ere long
Thou shalt have more.

Cruz.   And if I have it not,
Thou shalt no longer dwell here in rich chambers,
Wear silken dresses, feed on dainty food,
And live in idleness; but go with me,
Dance the Romalis in the public streets,
And wander wild again o'er field and fell;
For here we stay not long.

Prec.   What! march again?

Cruz. Ay, with all speed. I hate the crowded town!
I cannot breathe shut up within its gates
Air, —I want air, and sunshine, and blue sky,
The feeling of the breeze upon my face,
The feeling of the turf beneath my feet,
And no walls but the far-off mountain-tops.
Then I am free and strong, —once more myself,
Beltran Cruzado, Count of the Cales!

Prec.   God speed thee on thy march! —I cannot go.

Cruz. Remember who I am, and who thou art
Be silent and obey! Yet one thing more.

Bartolome Roman—

  Prec. (with emotion). O, I beseech thee
If my obedience and blameless life,
If my humility and meek submission
In all things hitherto, can move in thee
One feeling of compassion; if thou art
Indeed my father, and canst trace in me
One look of her who bore me, or one tone
That doth remind thee of her, let it plead
In my behalf, who am a feeble girl,
Too feeble to resist, and do not force me
To wed that man! I am afraid of him!
I do not love him! On my knees I beg thee
To use no violence, nor do in haste
What cannot be undone!

  Cruz.   O child, child, child!
Thou hast betrayed thy secret, as a bird
Betrays her nest, by striving to conceal it.
I will not leave thee here in the great city
To be a grandee's mistress. Make thee ready
To go with us; and until then remember
A watchful eye is on thee.   [Exit.

  Prec.   Woe is me!
I have a strange misgiving in my heart!
But that one deed of charity I'll do,
Befall what may; they cannot take that from me.

      SCENE II — A room in the ARCHBISHOP'S Palace. The
        ARCHBISHOP and a CARDINAL seated.

  Arch. Knowing how near it touched the public morals,
And that our age is grown corrupt and rotten
By such excesses, we have sent to Rome,
Beseeching that his Holiness would aid
In curing the gross surfeit of the time,
By seasonable stop put here in Spain
To bull-fights and lewd dances on the stage.
All this you know.

Card.   Know and approve.

 Arch.   And further,
That, by a mandate from his Holiness,
The first have been suppressed.

 Card.   I trust forever.
It was a cruel sport.

 Arch.   A barbarous pastime,
Disgraceful to the land that calls itself
Most Catholic and Christian.

 Card.   Yet the people
Murmur at this; and, if the public dances
Should be condemned upon too slight occasion,
Worse ills might follow than the ills we cure.
As Panem et Circenses was the cry
Among the Roman populace of old,
So Pan y Toros is the cry in Spain.
Hence I would act advisedly herein;
And therefore have induced your Grace to see
These national dances, ere we interdict them.

(Enter a Servant)

 Serv. The dancing-girl, and with her the musicians
Your Grace was pleased to order, wait without.

 Arch. Bid them come in. Now shall your eyes behold
In what angelic, yet voluptuous shape
The Devil came to tempt Saint Anthony.

(Enter PRECIOSA, with a mantle thrown over her head. She
advances slowly, in modest, half-timid attitude.)

 Card. (aside). O, what a fair and ministering angel
Was lost to heaven when this sweet woman fell!

 Prec. (kneeling before the ARCHBISHOP).
I have obeyed the order of your Grace.
If I intrude upon your better hours,
I proffer this excuse, and here beseech

Your holy benediction.

   Arch.   May God bless thee,
And lead thee to a better life. Arise.

   Card. (aside). Her acts are modest, and her words discreet!
I did not look for this! Come hither, child.
Is thy name Preciosa?

   Prec.   Thus I am called.

   Card. That is a Gypsy name. Who is thy father?

   Prec. Beltran Cruzado, Count of the Cales.

   Arch. I have a dim remembrance of that man:
He was a bold and reckless character,
A sun-burnt Ishmael!

   Card.   Dost thou remember
Thy earlier days?

   Prec. Yes; by the Darro's side
My childhood passed. I can remember still
The river, and the mountains capped with snow
The village, where, yet a little child,
I told the traveller's fortune in the street;
The smuggler's horse, the brigand and the shepherd;
The march across the moor; the halt at noon;
The red fire of the evening camp, that lighted
The forest where we slept; and, further back,
As in a dream or in some former life,
Gardens and palace walls.

   Arch.   'T is the Alhambra,
Under whose towers the Gypsy camp was pitched.
But the time wears; and we would see thee dance.

   Prec. Your Grace shall be obeyed.

(She lays aside her mantilla. The music of the cachucha is
played, and the dance begins.   The ARCHBISHOP and the
CARDINAL

look on with gravity and an occasional frown; then make signs to
each other; and, as the dance continues, become more and more
pleased and excited; and at length rise from their seats, throw
their caps in the air, and applaud vehemently as the scene
closes.)

SCENE III. — The Prado. A long avenue of trees leading to the gate
of Atocha. On the right the dome and spires of a convent. A
fountain. Evening, DON CARLOS and HYPOLITO meeting.

Don C. Hola! good evening, Don Hypolito.

Hyp. And a good evening to my friend, Don Carlos.
Some lucky star has led my steps this way.
I was in search of you.

Don. C.   Command me always.

Hyp. Do you remember, in Quevedo's Dreams,
The miser, who, upon the Day of Judgment,
Asks if his money-bags would rise?

Don C.   I do;
But what of that?

Hyp. I am that wretched man.

Don C. You mean to tell me yours have risen empty?

Hyp. And amen! said my Cid the Campeador.

Don C. Pray, how much need you?

Hyp.   Some half-dozen ounces,
Which, with due interest—

Don C. (giving his purse). What, am I a Jew
To put my moneys out at usury?
Here is my purse.

Hyp. Thank you. A pretty purse.
Made by the hand of some fair Madrilena;
Perhaps a keepsake.

Don C. No, 't is at your service.

Hyp. Thank you again. Lie there, good Chrysostom,
And with thy golden mouth remind me often,
I am the debtor of my friend.

Don C.   But tell me,
Come you to-day from Alcala?

Hyp.   This moment.

Don C. And pray, how fares the brave Victorian?

Hyp. Indifferent well; that is to say, not well.
A damsel has ensnared him with the glances
Of her dark, roving eyes, as herdsmen catch
A steer of Andalusia with a lazo.
He is in love.

Don C. And is it faring ill
To be in love?

Hyp.   In his case very ill.

Don C. Why so?

Hyp. For many reasons. First and foremost,
Because he is in love with an ideal;
A creature of his own imagination;
A child of air; an echo of his heart;
And, like a lily on a river floating,
She floats upon the river of his thoughts!

Don C. A common thing with poets. But who is
This floating lily? For, in fine, some woman,
Some living woman,—not a mere ideal,—
Must wear the outward semblance of his thought.
Who is it? Tell me.

Hyp.   Well, it is a woman!
But, look you, from the coffer of his heart
He brings forth precious jewels to adorn her,
As pious priests adorn some favorite saint

With gems and gold, until at length she gleams
One blaze of glory. Without these, you know,
And the priest's benediction, 't is a doll.

  Don C. Well, well! who is this doll?

  Hyp.   Why, who do you think?

  Don C. His cousin Violante.

  Hyp.   Guess again.
To ease his laboring heart, in the last storm
He threw her overboard, with all her ingots.

  Don C. I cannot guess; so tell me who it is.

  Hyp. Not I.

  Don. C. Why not?

  Hyp. (mysteriously). Why? Because Mari Franca
Was married four leagues out of Salamanca!

  Don C. Jesting aside, who is it?

  Hyp.   Preciosa.

  Don C. Impossible! The Count of Lara tells me
She is not virtuous.

  Hyp.   Did I say she was?
The Roman Emperor Claudius had a wife
Whose name was Messalina, as I think;
Valeria Messalina was her name.
But hist! I see him yonder through the trees,
Walking as in a dream.

  Don C.   He comes this way.

  Hyp. It has been truly said by some wise man,
That money, grief, and love cannot be hidden.

(Enter VICTORIAN in front.)

 Vict. Where'er thy step has passed is holy ground!
These groves are sacred! I behold thee walking
Under these shadowy trees, where we have walked
At evening, and I feel thy presence now;
Feel that the place has taken a charm from thee,
And is forever hallowed.

 Hyp.   Mark him well!
See how he strides away with lordly air,
Like that odd guest of stone, that grim Commander
Who comes to sup with Juan in the play.

 Don C. What ho! Victorian!

 Hyp.   Wilt thou sup with us?

 Vict. Hola! amigos! Faith, I did not see you.
How fares Don Carlos?

 Don C.   At your service ever.

 Vict. How is that young and green-eyed Gaditana
That you both wot of?

 Don C. Ay, soft, emerald eyes!
She has gone back to Cadiz.

 Hyp.   Ay de mi!

 Vict. You are much to blame for letting her go back.
A pretty girl; and in her tender eyes
Just that soft shade of green we sometimes see
In evening skies.

 Hyp. But, speaking of green eyes,
Are thine green?

 Vict.   Not a whit. Why so?

 Hyp.   I think
The slightest shade of green would be becoming,

For thou art jealous.

Vid.   No, I am not jealous.

Hyp. Thou shouldst be.

Vict.   Why?

Hyp.   Because thou art in love.
And they who are in love are always jealous.
Therefore thou shouldst be.

Vict.   Marry, is that all?
Farewell; I am in haste. Farewell, Don Carlos.
Thou sayest I should be jealous?

Hyp.   Ay, in truth
I fear there is reason. Be upon thy guard.
I hear it whispered that the Count of Lara
Lays siege to the same citadel.

Vict.   Indeed!
Then he will have his labor for his pains.

Hyp. He does not think so, and Don Carlos tells me
He boasts of his success.

Vict. How's this, Don Carlos?

Don. C. Some hints of it I heard from his own lips.
He spoke but lightly of the lady's virtue,
As a gay man might speak.

Vict.   Death and damnation!
I'll cut his lying tongue out of his mouth,
And throw it to my dog! But no, no, no!
This cannot be. You jest, indeed you jest.
Trifle with me no more. For otherwise
We are no longer friends. And so, fare well!
                    [Exit.

Hyp. Now what a coil is here! The Avenging Child
Hunting the traitor Quadros to his death,
And the Moor Calaynos, when he rode
To Paris for the ears of Oliver,
Were nothing to him! O hot-headed youth!
But come; we will not follow. Let us join
The crowd that pours into the Prado. There
We shall find merrier company; I see
The Marialonzos and the Almavivas,
And fifty fans, that beckon me already.
                    [Exeunt.

SCENE IV. — PRECIOSA'S chamber. She is sitting, with a book in
her hand, near a table, on which are flowers. A bird singing in its
    cage. The COUNT OF LARA enters behind unperceived.

Prec. (reads).
    All are sleeping, weary heart!
    Thou, thou only sleepless art!

Heigho! I wish Victorian were here.
I know not what it is makes me so restless!

(The bird sings.)

Thou little prisoner with thy motley coat,
That from thy vaulted, wiry dungeon singest,
Like thee I am a captive, and, like thee,
I have a gentle jailer. Lack-a-day!

    All are sleeping, weary heart!
    Thou, thou only sleepless art!
    All this throbbing, all this aching,
    Evermore shall keep thee waking,
    For a heart in sorrow breaking
    Thinketh ever of its smart!

Thou speakest truly, poet! and methinks
More hearts are breaking in this world of ours
Than one would say. In distant villages
And solitudes remote, where winds have wafted
The barbed seeds of love, or birds of passage

98

Scattered them in their flight, do they take root,
And grow in silence, and in silence perish.
Who hears the falling of the forest leaf?
Or who takes note of every flower that dies?
Heigho! I wish Victorian would come.
Dolores!

(Turns to lay down her boot and perceives the COUNT.)

    Ha!

Lara.   Senora, pardon me.

Prec. How's this? Dolores!

Lara.   Pardon me—

Prec.   Dolores!

Lara. Be not alarmed; I found no one in waiting.
If I have been too bold—

Prec. (turning her back upon him). You are too bold!
Retire! retire, and leave me!

Lara.   My dear lady,
First hear me! I beseech you, let me speak!
'T is for your good I come.

Prec. (turning toward him with indignation). Begone! begone!
You are the Count of Lara, but your deeds
Would make the statues of your ancestors
Blush on their tombs! Is it Castilian honor,
Is it Castilian pride, to steal in here
Upon a friendless girl, to do her wrong?
O shame! shame! shame! that you, a nobleman,
Should be so little noble in your thoughts
As to send jewels here to win my love,
And think to buy my honor with your gold!
I have no words to tell you how I scorn you!
Begone! The sight of you is hateful to me!
Begone, I say!

Lara. Be calm; I will not harm you.

Prec. Because you dare not.

Lara.   I dare anything!
Therefore beware! You are deceived in me.
In this false world, we do not always know
Who are our friends and who our enemies.
We all have enemies, and all need friends.
Even you, fair Preciosa, here at court
Have foes, who seek to wrong you.

Prec.   If to this
I owe the honor of the present visit,
You might have spared the coming. Raving spoken,
Once more I beg you, leave me to myself.

Lara. I thought it but a friendly part to tell you
What strange reports are current here in town.
For my own self, I do not credit them;
But there are many who, not knowing you,
Will lend a readier ear.

Prec.   There was no need
That you should take upon yourself the duty
Of telling me these tales.

Lara.   Malicious tongues
Are ever busy with your name.

Prec.   Alas!
I've no protectors. I am a poor girl,
Exposed to insults and unfeeling jests.
They wound me, yet I cannot shield myself.
I give no cause for these reports. I live
Retired; am visited by none.

Lara.   By none?
O, then, indeed, you are much wronged!

Prec.   How mean you?

Lara. Nay, nay; I will not wound your gentle soul

By the report of idle tales.

   Prec.   Speak out!
What are these idle tales? You need not spare me.

   Lara. I will deal frankly with you. Pardon me
This window, as I think, looks toward the street,
And this into the Prado, does it not?
In yon high house, beyond the garden wall, —
You see the roof there just above the trees, —
There lives a friend, who told me yesterday,
That on a certain night, —be not offended
If I too plainly speak, —he saw a man
Climb to your chamber window. You are silent!
I would not blame you, being young and fair —

(He tries to embrace her. She starts back, and draws a dagger
from her bosom.)

   Prec. Beware! beware! I am a Gypsy girl!
Lay not your hand upon me. One step nearer
And I will strike!

   Lara. Pray you, put up that dagger.
Fear not.

   Prec. I do not fear. I have a heart
In whose strength I can trust.

   Lara.   Listen to me
I come here as your friend, —I am your friend, —
And by a single word can put a stop
To all those idle tales, and make your name
Spotless as lilies are. Here on my knees,
Fair Preciosa! on my knees I swear,
I love you even to madness, and that love
Has driven me to break the rules of custom,
And force myself unasked into your presence.

(VICTORIAN enters behind.)

   Prec. Rise, Count of Lara! That is not the place
For such as you are. It becomes you not

To kneel before me. I am strangely moved
To see one of your rank thus low and humbled;
For your sake I will put aside all anger,
All unkind feeling, all dislike, and speak
In gentleness, as most becomes a woman,
And as my heart now prompts me. I no more
Will hate you, for all hate is painful to me.
But if, without offending modesty
And that reserve which is a woman's glory,
I may speak freely, I will teach my heart
To love you.

   Lara. O sweet angel!

   Prec.   Ay, in truth,
Far better than you love yourself or me.

   Lara. Give me some sign of this,—the slightest token.
Let me but kiss your hand!

   Prec.   Nay, come no nearer.
The words I utter are its sign and token.
Misunderstand me not! Be not deceived!
The love wherewith I love you is not such
As you would offer me. For you come here
To take from me the only thing I have,
My honor. You are wealthy, you have friends
And kindred, and a thousand pleasant hopes
That fill your heart with happiness; but I
Am poor, and friendless, having but one treasure,
And you would take that from me, and for what?
To flatter your own vanity, and make me
What you would most despise. O sir, such love,
That seeks to harm me, cannot be true love.
Indeed it cannot. But my love for you
Is of a different kind. It seeks your good.
It is a holier feeling. It rebukes
Your earthly passion, your unchaste desires,
And bids you look into your heart, and see
How you do wrong that better nature in you,
And grieve your soul with sin.

   Lara.   I swear to you,

I would not harm you; I would only love you.
I would not take your honor, but restore it,
And in return I ask but some slight mark
Of your affection. If indeed you love me,
As you confess you do, O let me thus
With this embrace—

  Vict. (rushing forward). Hold! hold! This is too much.
What means this outrage?

  Lara. First, what right have you
To question thus a nobleman of Spain?

  Vict. I too am noble, and you are no more!
Out of my sight!

  Lara.   Are you the master here?

  Vict. Ay, here and elsewhere, when the wrong of others
Gives me the right!

  Prec. (to LARA). Go! I beseech you, go!

  Vict. I shall have business with you, Count, anon!

  Lara. You cannot come too soon!
        [Exit.

  Prec.   Victorian!
O, we have been betrayed!

  Vict.   Ha! ha! betrayed!
'T is I have been betrayed, not we!—not we!

  Prec. Dost thou imagine—

  Vict.   I imagine nothing;
I see how 't is thou whilest the time away
When I am gone!

  Prec. O speak not in that tone!
It wounds me deeply.

Vict. 'T was not meant to flatter.

Prec. Too well thou knowest the presence of that man
Is hateful to me!

Vict.   Yet I saw thee stand
And listen to him, when he told his love.

Prec. I did not heed his words.

Vict.   Indeed thou didst,
And answeredst them with love.

Prec.   Hadst thou heard all—

Vict. I heard enough.

Prec.   Be not so angry with me.

Vict. I am not angry; I am very calm.

Prec. If thou wilt let me speak—

Vict.   Nay, say no more.
I know too much already. Thou art false!
I do not like these Gypsy marriages!
Where is the ring I gave thee?

Prec.   In my casket.

Vict. There let it rest! I would not have thee wear it:
I thought thee spotless, and thou art polluted!

Prec. I call the Heavens to witness—

Vict.   Nay, nay, nay!
Take not the name of Heaven upon thy lips!
They are forsworn!

Prec. Victorian! dear Victorian!

Vict. I gave up all for thee; myself, my fame,
My hopes of fortune, ay, my very soul!

And thou hast been my ruin! Now, go on!
Laugh at my folly with thy paramour,
And, sitting on the Count of Lara's knee,
Say what a poor, fond fool Victorian was!

(He casts her from him and rushes out.)

  Prec. And this from thee!

(Scene closes.)

  SCENE V. — The COUNT OF LARA'S rooms. Enter the COUNT.

  Lara. There's nothing in this world so sweet as love,
And next to love the sweetest thing is hate!
I've learned to hate, and therefore am revenged.
A silly girl to play the prude with me!
The fire that I have kindled —

(Enter FRANCISCO.)

          Well, Francisco,
What tidings from Don Juan?

  Fran.   Good, my lord;
He will be present.

  Lara.   And the Duke of Lermos?

  Fran. Was not at home.

  Lara.   How with the rest?

  Fran.   I've found
The men you wanted. They will all be there,
And at the given signal raise a whirlwind
Of such discordant noises, that the dance
Must cease for lack of music.

  Lara.   Bravely done.
Ah! little dost thou dream, sweet Preciosa,
What lies in wait for thee. Sleep shall not close

Thine eyes this night! Give me my cloak and sword. [Exeunt.

SCENE VI. — A retired spot beyond the city gates. Enter
VICTORIAN and HYPOLITO.

Vict. O shame! O shame! Why do I walk abroad
By daylight, when the very sunshine mocks me,
And voices, and familiar sights and sounds
Cry, "Hide thyself!" O what a thin partition
Doth shut out from the curious world the knowledge
Of evil deeds that have been done in darkness!
Disgrace has many tongues. My fears are windows,
Through which all eyes seem gazing. Every face
Expresses some suspicion of my shame,
And in derision seems to smile at me!

Hyp. Did I not caution thee? Did I not tell thee
I was but half persuaded of her virtue?

Vict. And yet, Hypolito, we may be wrong,
We may be over-hasty in condemning!
The Count of Lara is a cursed villain.

Hyp. And therefore is she cursed, loving him.

Vid. She does not love him! 'T is for gold! for gold!

Hyp. Ay, but remember, in the public streets
He shows a golden ring the Gypsy gave him,
A serpent with a ruby in its mouth.

Vict. She had that ring from me! God! she is false!
But I will be revenged! The hour is passed.
Where stays the coward?

Hyp.   Nay, he is no coward;
A villain, if thou wilt, but not a coward.
I've seen him play with swords; it is his pastime.
And therefore be not over-confident,
He'll task thy skill anon. Look, here he comes.

(Enter LARA followed by FRNANCISCO)

106

Lara. Good evening, gentlemen.

Hyp.   Good evening, Count.

Lara. I trust I have not kept you long in waiting.

Vict. Not long, and yet too long. Are you prepared?

Lara. I am.

Hyp.   It grieves me much to see this quarrel
Between you, gentlemen. Is there no way
Left open to accord this difference,
But you must make one with your swords?

Vict.   No! none!
I do entreat thee, dear Hypolito,
Stand not between me an my foe. Too long
Our tongues have spoken. Let these tongues of steel
End our debate. Upon your guard, Sir Count.

(They fight. VICTORIAN disarms the COUNT.)

Your life is mine; and what shall now withhold me
From sending your vile soul to its account?

Lara. Strike! strike!

Vict.   You are disarmed. I will not kill you.
I will not murder you. Take up your sword.

(FRANCISCO hands the COUNT his sword, and HYPOLITO
interposes.)

Hyp. Enough! Let it end here! The Count of Lara
Has shown himself a brave man, and Victorian
A generous one, as ever. Now be friends.
Put up your swords; for, to speak frankly to you,
Your cause of quarrel is too slight a thing
To move you to extremes.

Lara.   I am content,
I sought no quarrel. A few hasty words,

Spoken in the heat of blood, have led to this.

    Vict. Nay, something more than that.

    Lara.   I understand you.
Therein I did not mean to cross your path.
To me the door stood open, as to others.
But, had I known the girl belonged to you,
Never would I have sought to win her from you.
The truth stands now revealed; she has been false
To both of us.

    Vict.   Ay, false as hell itself!

    Lara. In truth, I did not seek her; she sought me;
And told me how to win her, telling me
The hours when she was oftenest left alone.

    Vict. Say, can you prove this to me? O, pluck out
These awful doubts, that goad me into madness!
Let me know all! all! all!

    Lara.   You shall know all.
Here is my page, who was the messenger
Between us. Question him. Was it not so,
Francisco?

    Fran. Ay, my lord.

    Lara.   If further proof
Is needful, I have here a ring she gave me.

    Vict. Pray let me see that ring! It is the same!

(Throws it upon the ground, and tramples upon it.)

Thus may she perish who once wore that ring!
Thus do I spurn her from me; do thus trample
Her memory in the dust! O Count of Lara,
We both have been abused, been much abused!
I thank you for your courtesy and frankness.
Though, like the surgeon's hand, yours gave me pain,
Yet it has cured my blindness, and I thank you.

I now can see the folly I have done,
Though 't is, alas! too late. So fare you well!
To-night I leave this hateful town forever.
Regard me as your friend. Once more farewell!

  Hyp. Farewell, Sir Count.

  [Exeunt VICTORIAN and HYPOLITO.

  Lara. Farewell! farewell! farewell!
Thus have I cleared the field of my worst foe!
I have none else to fear; the fight is done,
The citadel is stormed, the victory won!

[Exit with FRANCISCO.

SCENE VII. — A lane in the suburbs. Night. Enter CRUZADO and
BARTOLOME.

  Cruz. And so, Bartolome, the expedition failed. But where
wast thou for the most part?

  Bart. In the Guadarrama mountains, near San Ildefonso.

  Cruz. And thou bringest nothing back with thee? Didst thou
rob no one?

  Bart. There was no one to rob, save a party of students from
Segovia, who looked as if they would rob us; and a jolly little
friar, who had nothing in his pockets but a missal and a loaf of
bread.

  Cruz. Pray, then, what brings thee back to Madrid?

  Bart. First tell me what keeps thee here?

  Cruz. Preciosa.

  Bart. And she brings me back. Hast thou forgotten thy
promise?

  Cruz. The two years are not passed yet. Wait patiently. The
girl shall be thine.

Bart. I hear she has a Busne lover.

Cruz. That is nothing.

Bart. I do not like it. I hate him,—the son of a Busne
harlot. He goes in and out, and speaks with her alone, and I
must stand aside, and wait his pleasure.

Cruz. Be patient, I say. Thou shalt have thy revenge. When
the time comes, thou shalt waylay him.

Bart. Meanwhile, show me her house.

Cruz. Come this way. But thou wilt not find her. She dances
at the play to-night.

Bart. No matter. Show me the house.
　　　　　[Exeunt.

SCENE VIII. — The Theatre. The orchestra plays the cachucha.
Sound of castanets behind the scenes. The curtain rises, and
discovers PRECIOSA in the attitude of commencing the dance. The
cachucha. Tumult; hisses; cries of "Brava!" and "Afuera!" She
falters and pauses. The music stops. General confusion. PRECIOSA
faints.

SCENE IX. — The COUNT OF LARA'S chambers. LARA and his
friends at supper.

Lara. So, Caballeros, once more many thanks!
You have stood by me bravely in this matter.
Pray fill your glasses.

Don J. Did you mark, Don Luis,
How pale she looked, when first the noise began,
And then stood still, with her large eyes dilated!
Her nostrils spread! her lips apart! Her bosom
Tumultuous as the sea!

Don L.　　　I pitied her.

110

Lara. Her pride is humbled; and this very night
I mean to visit her.

Don J.   Will you serenade her?

Lara. No music! no more music!

Don L.   Why not music?
It softens many hearts.

Lara.   Not in the humor
She now is in. Music would madden her.

Don J. Try golden cymbals.

Don L.   Yes, try Don Dinero;
A mighty wooer is your Don Dinero.

Lara. To tell the truth, then, I have bribed her maid.
But, Caballeros, you dislike this wine.
A bumper and away; for the night wears.
A health to Preciosa.

(They rise and drink.)

All.   Preciosa.

Lara. (holding up his glass).
Thou bright and flaming minister of Love!
Thou wonderful magician! who hast stolen
My secret from me, and mid sighs of passion
Caught from my lips, with red and fiery tongue,
Her precious name! O nevermore henceforth
Shall mortal lips press thine; and nevermore
A mortal name be whispered in thine ear.
Go! keep my secret!

(Drinks and dashes the goblet down.)

Don J.   Ite! missa est!

(Scene closes.)

SCENE X. — Street and garden wall. Night. Enter CRUZADO and
BARTOLOME.

Cruz. This is the garden wall, and above it, yonder, is her
house. The window in which thou seest the light is her window.
But we will not go in now.

Bart. Why not?

Cruz. Because she is not at home.

Bart. No matter; we can wait. But how is this? The gate is
bolted. (Sound of guitars and voices in a neighboring street.)
Hark! There comes her lover with his infernal serenade! Hark!

SONG.

Good night! Good night, beloved!
  I come to watch o'er thee!
To be near thee, — to be near thee,
  Alone is peace for me.

Thine eyes are stars of morning,
  Thy lips are crimson flowers!
Good night! Good night beloved,
  While I count the weary hours.

Cruz. They are not coming this way.

Bart. Wait, they begin again.

SONG (coming nearer).

Ah! thou moon that shinest
  Argent-clear above!
All night long enlighten
  My sweet lady-love!
  Moon that shinest,
All night long enlighten!

Bart. Woe be to him, if he comes this way!

Cruz. Be quiet, they are passing down the street.

SONG (dying away).

The nuns in the cloister
  Sang to each other;
For so many sisters
  Is there not one brother!
Ay, for the partridge, mother!
The cat has run away with the partridge!
  Puss! puss! puss!

  Bart. Follow that! follow that!
Come with me. Puss! puss!

(Exeunt. On the opposite side enter the COUNT OF LARA and
gentlemen, with FRANCISCO.)

  Lara. The gate is fast. Over the wall, Francisco,
And draw the bolt. There, so, and so, and over.
Now, gentlemen, come in, and help me scale
Yon balcony. How now? Her light still burns.
Move warily. Make fast the gate, Francisco.

(Exeunt. Re-enter CRUZADO and BARTOLOME.)

  Bart. They went in at the gate. Hark! I hear them in the
garden. (Tries the gate.) Bolted again! Vive Cristo! Follow me
over the wall.

(They climb the wall.)

SCENE XI. — PRECIOSA'S bedchamber. Midnight. She is sleeping
     in an armchair, in an undress. DOLORES watching her.

  Dol. She sleeps at last!

(Opens the window, and listens.)

     All silent in the street,
And in the garden. Hark!

Prec. (in her sleep). I must go hence!
Give me my cloak!

Dol. He comes! I hear his footsteps.

Prec. Go tell them that I cannot dance to-night;
I am too ill! Look at me! See the fever
That burns upon my cheek! I must go hence.
I am too weak to dance.

(Signal from the garden.)

Dol. (from the window). Who's there?

Voice (from below).   A friend.

Dol. I will undo the door. Wait till I come.

Prec. I must go hence. I pray you do not harm me!
Shame! shame! to treat a feeble woman thus!
Be you but kind, I will do all things for you.
I'm ready now,—give me my castanets.
Where is Victorian? Oh, those hateful lamps!
They glare upon me like an evil eye.
I cannot stay. Hark! how they mock at me!
They hiss at me like serpents! Save me! save me!

(She wakes.)

How late is it, Dolores?

Dol.   It is midnight.

Prec. We must be patient. Smooth this pillow for me.

(She sleeps again. Noise from the garden, and voices.)

Voice. Muera!

Another Voice. O villains! villains!

Lara.   So! have at you!

Voice. Take that!

Lara.   O, I am wounded!

Dol. (shutting the window). Jesu Maria!

ACT III.

SCENE I. — A cross-road through a wood. In the background a distant village spire. VICTORIAN and HYPOLITO, as traveling students, with guitars, sitting under the trees. HYPOLITO plays and sings.

SONG.

   Ah, Love!
Perjured, false, treacherous Love!
   Enemy
Of all that mankind may not rue!
   Most untrue
To him who keeps most faith with thee.
   Woe is me!
The falcon has the eyes of the dove.
   Ah, Love!
Perjured, false, treacherous Love!

   Vict. Yes, Love is ever busy with his shuttle,
Is ever weaving into life's dull warp
Bright, gorgeous flowers and scenes Arcadian;
Hanging our gloomy prison-house about
With tapestries, that make its walls dilate
In never-ending vistas of delight.

   Hyp. Thinking to walk in those Arcadian pastures,
Thou hast run thy noble head against the wall.

SONG (continued).

   Thy deceits
Give us clearly to comprehend,
   Whither tend
All thy pleasures, all thy sweets!
   They are cheats,
Thorns below and flowers above.
   Ah, Love!
Perjured, false, treacherous Love!

   Vict. A very pretty song. I thank thee for it.

Hyp. It suits thy case.

Vict.   Indeed, I think it does.
What wise man wrote it?

Hyp.   Lopez Maldonado.

Vict. In truth, a pretty song.

Hyp.   With much truth in it.
I hope thou wilt profit by it; and in earnest
Try to forget this lady of thy love.

Vict. I will forget her! All dear recollections
Pressed in my heart, like flowers within a book,
Shall be torn out, and scattered to the winds!
I will forget her! But perhaps hereafter,
When she shall learn how heartless is the world,
A voice within her will repeat my name,
And she will say, "He was indeed my friend!"
O, would I were a soldier, not a scholar,
That the loud march, the deafening beat of drums,
The shattering blast of the brass-throated trumpet,
The din of arms, the onslaught and the storm,
And a swift death, might make me deaf forever
To the upbraidings of this foolish heart!

Hyp. Then let that foolish heart upbraid no more!
To conquer love, one need but will to conquer.

Vict. Yet, good Hypolito, it is in vain
I throw into Oblivion's sea the sword
That pierces me; for, like Excalibar,
With gemmed and flashing hilt, it will not sink.
There rises from below a hand that grasp it,
And waves it in the air; and wailing voices
Are heard along the shore.

Hyp.   And yet at last
Down sank Excalibar to rise no more.
This is not well. In truth, it vexes me.
Instead of whistling to the steeds of Time,
To make them jog on merrily with life's burden,

Like a dead weight thou hangest on the wheels.
Thou art too young, too full of lusty health
To talk of dying.

  Vict.   Yet I fain would die!
To go through life, unloving and unloved;
To feel that thirst and hunger of the soul
We cannot still; that longing, that wild impulse,
And struggle after something we have not
And cannot have; the effort to be strong
And, like the Spartan boy, to smile, and smile,
While secret wounds do bleed beneath our cloaks
All this the dead feel not, — the dead alone!
Would I were with them!

  Hyp.   We shall all be soon.

  Vict. It cannot be too soon; for I am weary
Of the bewildering masquerade of Life,
Where strangers walk as friends, and friends as strangers;
Where whispers overheard betray false hearts;
And through the mazes of the crowd we chase
Some form of loveliness, that smiles, and beckons,
And cheats us with fair words, only to leave us
A mockery and a jest; maddened, — confused, —
Not knowing friend from foe.

  Hyp.   Why seek to know?
Enjoy the merry shrove-tide of thy youth!
Take each fair mask for what it gives itself,
Nor strive to look beneath it.

  Vict.   I confess,
That were the wiser part. But Hope no longer
Comforts my soul. I am a wretched man,
Much like a poor and shipwrecked mariner,
Who, struggling to climb up into the boat,
Has both his bruised and bleeding hands cut off,
And sinks again into the weltering sea,
Helpless and hopeless!

  Hyp.   Yet thou shalt not perish.
The strength of thine own arm is thy salvation.

Above thy head, through rifted clouds, there shines
A glorious star. Be patient. Trust thy star!

(Sound of a village belt in the distance.)

  Vict. Ave Maria! I hear the sacristan
Ringing the chimes from yonder village belfry!
A solemn sound, that echoes far and wide
Over the red roofs of the cottages,
And bids the laboring hind a-field, the shepherd,
Guarding his flock, the lonely muleteer,
And all the crowd in village streets, stand still,
And breathe a prayer unto the blessed Virgin!

  Hyp. Amen! amen! Not half a league from hence
The village lies.

  Vict.   This path will lead us to it,
Over the wheat-fields, where the shadows sail
Across the running sea, now green, now blue,
And, like an idle mariner on the main,
Whistles the quail. Come, let us hasten on.
                    [Exeunt.

SCENE II. — Public square in the village of Guadarrama. The Ave Maria still tolling. A crowd of villagers, with their hats in their hands, as if in prayer. In front, a group of Gypsies. The bell rings a merrier peal. A Gypsy dance. Enter PANCHO, followed by PEDRO CRESPO.

  Pancho. Make room, ye vagabonds and Gypsy thieves!
Make room for the Alcalde and for me!

  Pedro C. Keep silence all! I have an edict here
From our most gracious lord, the King of Spain,
Jerusalem, and the Canary Islands,
Which I shall publish in the market-place.
Open your ears and listen!

(Enter the PADRE CURA at the door of his cottage.)

          Padre Cura,
Good day! and, pray you, hear this edict read.

  Padre C. Good day, and God be with you! Pray, what is it?

  Pedro C. An act of banishment against the Gypsies!

(Agitation and murmurs in the crowd.)

  Pancho. Silence!

  Pedro C. (reads). "I hereby order and command,
That the Egyptian an Chaldean strangers,
Known by the name of Gypsies, shall henceforth
Be banished from the realm, as vagabonds
And beggars; and if, after seventy days,
Any be found within our kingdom's bounds,
They shall receive a hundred lashes each;
The second time, shall have their ears cut off;
The third, be slaves for life to him who takes them,
Or burnt as heretics. Signed, I, the King."
Vile miscreants and creatures unbaptized!
You hear the law! Obey and disappear!

  Pancho. And if in seventy days you are not gone,
Dead or alive I make you all my slaves.

(The Gypsies go out in confusion, showing signs of fear and
discontent. PANCHO follows.)

  Padre C. A righteous law! A very righteous law!
Pray you, sit down.

Pedro C.   I thank you heartily.

(They seat themselves on a bench at the PADRE CURAS door.
Sound of guitars heard at a distance, approaching during the
dialogue which follows.)

A very righteous judgment, as you say.
Now tell me, Padre Cura, — you know all things,
How came these Gypsies into Spain?

Padre C.   Why, look you;
They came with Hercules from Palestine,
And hence are thieves and vagrants, Sir Alcalde,
As the Simoniacs from Simon Magus,
And, look you, as Fray Jayme Bleda says,
There are a hundred marks to prove a Moor
Is not a Christian, so 't is with the Gypsies.
They never marry, never go to mass,
Never baptize their children, nor keep Lent,
Nor see the inside of a church, — nor — nor —

Pedro C. Good reasons, good, substantial reasons all!
No matter for the other ninety-five.
They should be burnt, I see it plain enough,
They should be bunt.

(Enter VICTORIAN and HYPOLITO playing.)

Padre C. And pray, whom have we here?

Pedro C. More vagrants! By Saint Lazarus, more vagrants!

Hyp. Good evening, gentlemen! Is this Guadarrama?

Padre C. Yes, Guadarrama, and good evening to you.

Hyp. We seek the Padre Cura of the village;
And, judging from your dress and reverend mien,
You must be he.

Padre C.   I am. Pray, what's your pleasure?

Hyp. We are poor students, traveling in vacation.
You know this mark?

(Touching the wooden spoon in his hat-band.

Padre C. (joyfully). Ay, know it, and have worn it.

Pedro C. (aside). Soup-eaters! by the mass! The worst of vagrants!
And there's no law against them. Sir, your servant.
                [Exit.

Padre C. Your servant, Pedro Crespo.

Hyp.   Padre Cura,
Front the first moment I beheld your face,
I said within myself, "This is the man!"
There is a certain something in your looks,
A certain scholar-like and studious something, —
You understand, — which cannot be mistaken;
Which marks you as a very learned man,
In fine, as one of us.

Vict. (aside).   What impudence!

Hyp. As we approached, I said to my companion,
"That is the Padre Cura; mark my words!"
Meaning your Grace. "The other man," said I,
Who sits so awkwardly upon the bench,
Must be the sacristan."

Padre C.   Ah! said you so?
Why, that was Pedro Crespo, the alcalde!

Hyp. Indeed! you much astonish me! His air
Was not so full of dignity and grace
As an alcalde's should be.

Padre C.   That is true.
He's out of humor with some vagrant Gypsies,
Who have their camp here in the neighborhood.
There's nothing so undignified as anger.

Hyp. The Padre Cura will excuse our boldness,
If, from his well-known hospitality,
We crave a lodging for the night.

Padre C.   I pray you!
You do me honor! I am but too happy
To have such guests beneath my humble roof.
It is not often that I have occasion
To speak with scholars; and Emollit mores,
Nec sinit esse feros, Cicero says.

Hyp. 'T is Ovid, is it not?

Padre C.　　　　　No, Cicero.

Hyp. Your Grace is right. You are the better scholar.
Now what a dunce was I to think it Ovid!
But hang me if it is not! (Aside.)

Padre C.　　　　Pass this way.
He was a very great man, was Cicero!
Pray you, go in, go in! no ceremony.
　　　　　　　　　[Exeunt.

SCENE III. — A room in the PADRE CURA'S house. Enter the
PADRE and HYPOLITO.

Padre C. So then, Senor, you come from Alcala.
I am glad to hear it. It was there I studied.

Hyp. And left behind an honored name, no doubt.
How may I call your Grace?

Padre C.　　　　　Geronimo
De Santillana, at your Honor's service.

Hyp. Descended from the Marquis Santillana?
From the distinguished poet?

Padre C.　　　From the Marquis,
Not from the poet.

Hyp.　　Why, they were the same.
Let me embrace you! O some lucky star
Has brought me hither! Yet once more!—once more!
Your name is ever green in Alcala,
And our professor, when we are unruly,
Will shake his hoary head, and say, "Alas!
It was not so in Santillana's time!"

Padre C. I did not think my name remembered there.

Hyp. More than remembered; it is idolized.

Padre C. Of what professor speak you?

Hyp. Timoneda.

Padre C. I don't remember any Timoneda.

Hyp. A grave and sombre man, whose beetling brow
O'erhangs the rushing current of his speech
As rocks o'er rivers hang. Have you forgotten?

Padre C. Indeed, I have. O, those were pleasant days,
Those college days! I ne'er shall see the like!
I had not buried then so many hopes!
I had not buried then so many friends!
I've turned my back on what was then before me;
And the bright faces of my young companions
Are wrinkled like my own, or are no more.
Do you remember Cueva?

Hyp.   Cueva? Cueva?

Padre C. Fool that I am! He was before your time.
You're a mere boy, and I am an old man.

Hyp. I should not like to try my strength with you.

Padre C. Well, well. But I forget; you must be hungry.
Martina! ho! Martina! 'T is my niece.

(Enter MARTINA.)

Hyp. You may be proud of such a niece as that.
I wish I had a niece. Emollit mores.
   (Aside.)
He was a very great man, was Cicero!
Your servant, fair Martina.

Mart.   Servant, sir.

Padre C. This gentleman is hungry. See thou to it.
Let us have supper.

Mart.   'T will be ready soon.

Padre C. And bring a bottle of my Val-de-Penas

Out of the cellar. Stay; I'll go myself.
Pray you. Senor, excuse me.   [Exit.

Hyp.   Hist! Martina!
One word with you. Bless me I what handsome eyes!
To-day there have been Gypsies in the village.
Is it not so?

Mart. There have been Gypsies here.

Hyp. Yes, and have told your fortune.

Mart. (embarrassed). Told my fortune?

Hyp. Yes, yes; I know they did. Give me your hand.
I'll tell you what they said. They said,—they said,
The shepherd boy that loved you was a clown,
And him you should not marry. Was it not?

Mart. (surprised). How know you that?

Hyp.   O, I know more than that,
What a soft, little hand! And then they said,
A cavalier from court, handsome, and tall
And rich, should come one day to marry you,
And you should be a lady. Was it not!
He has arrived, the handsome cavalier.

(Tries to kiss her. She runs off. Enter VICTORIAN, with a
letter.)

Vict. The muleteer has come.

Hyp.   So soon?

Vict.   I found him
Sitting at supper by the tavern door,
And, from a pitcher that he held aloft
His whole arm's length, drinking the blood-red wine.

Hyp. What news from Court?

Vict. He brought this letter only.

(Reads.)

O cursed perfidy! Why did I let
That lying tongue deceive me! Preciosa,
Sweet Preciosa! how art thou avenged!

  Hyp. What news is this, that makes thy cheek turn pale,
And thy hand tremble?

  Vict.   O, most infamous!
The Count of Lara is a worthless villain!

  Hyp. That is no news, forsooth.

  Vict.   He strove in vain
To steal from me the jewel of my soul,
The love of Preciosa. Not succeeding,
He swore to be revenged; and set on foot
A plot to ruin her, which has succeeded.
She has been hissed and hooted from the stage,
Her reputation stained by slanderous lies
Too foul to speak of; and, once more a beggar,
She roams a wanderer over God's green earth
Housing with Gypsies!

  Hyp.   To renew again
The Age of Gold, and make the shepherd swains
Desperate with love, like Gasper Gil's Diana.
Redit et Virgo!

  Vict.   Dear Hypolito,
How have I wronged that meek, confiding heart!
I will go seek for her; and with my tears
Wash out the wrong I've done her!

  Hyp.   O beware!
Act not that folly o'er again.

  Vict.   Ay, folly,
Delusion, madness, call it what thou wilt,
I will confess my weakness, —I still love her!
Still fondly love her!

(Enter the PADRE CURA.)

Hyp.   Tell us, Padre Cura,
Who are these Gypsies in the neighborhood?

Padre C. Beltran Cruzado and his crew.

Vict.   Kind Heaven,
I thank thee! She is found! is found again!

Hyp. And have they with them a pale, beautiful girl,
Called Preciosa?

Padre C.   Ay, a pretty girl.
The gentleman seems moved.

Hyp.   Yes, moved with hunger,
He is half famished with this long day's journey.

Padre C. Then, pray you, come this way. The supper waits.
                [Exeunt.

SCENE IV. — A post-house on the road to Segovia, not far from the village of Guadarrama. Enter CHISPA, cracking a whip, and singing the cachucha.

Chispa. Halloo! Don Fulano! Let us have horses, and quickly. Alas, poor Chispa! what a dog's life dost thou lead! I thought, when I left my old master Victorian, the student, to serve my new master Don Carlos, the gentleman, that I, too, should lead the life of a gentleman; should go to bed early, and get up late. For when the abbot plays cards, what can you expect of the friars? But, in running away from the thunder, I have run into the lightning. Here I am in hot chase after my master and his Gypsy girl. And a good beginning of the week it is, as he said who was hanged on Monday morning.

(Enter DON CARLOS)

Don C. Are not the horses ready yet?

Chispa. I should think not, for the hostler seems to be

127

asleep. Ho! within there! Horses! horses! horses! (He knocks at the gate with his whip, and enter MOSQUITO, putting on his jacket.)

Mosq. Pray, have a little patience. I'm not a musket.

Chispa. Health and pistareens! I'm glad to see you come on dancing, padre! Pray, what's the news?

Mosq. You cannot have fresh horses; because there are none.

Chispa. Cachiporra! Throw that bone to another dog. Do I look like your aunt?

Mosq. No; she has a beard.

Chispa. Go to! go to!

Mosq. Are you from Madrid?

Chispa. Yes; and going to Estramadura. Get us horses.

Mosq. What's the news at Court?

Chispa. Why, the latest news is, that I am going to set up a coach, and I have already bought the whip.

(Strikes him round the legs.)

Mosq. Oh! oh! You hurt me!

Don C. Enough of this folly. Let us have horses. (Gives money to MOSQUITO.) It is almost dark; and we are in haste. But tell me, has a band of Gypsies passed this way of late?

Mosq. Yes; and they are still in the neighborhood.

Don C. And where?

Mosq. Across the fields yonder, in the woods near Guadarrama.
                    [Exit.

Don C. Now this is lucky. We will visit the Gypsy camp.

Chispa. Are you not afraid of the evil eye? Have you a stag's horn with you?

Don C. Fear not. We will pass the night at the village.

Chispa. And sleep like the Squires of Hernan Daza, nine under one blanket.

Don C. I hope we may find the Preciosa among them.

Chispa. Among the Squires?

Don C. No; among the Gypsies, blockhead!

Chispa. I hope we may; for we are giving ourselves trouble enough on her account. Don't you think so? However, there is no catching trout without wetting one's trousers. Yonder come the horses.
                    [Exeunt.

SCENE V. — The Gypsy camp in the forest. Night. Gypsies working at a forge. Others playing cards by the firelight. Gypsies (at the forge sing).

On the top of a mountain I stand,
With a crown of red gold in my hand,
Wild Moors come trooping over the lea
O how from their fury shall I flee, flee, flee?
O how from their fury shall I flee?

First Gypsy (playing). Down with your John-Dorados, my pigeon. Down with your John-Dorados, and let us make an end.

Gypsies (at the forge sing).

  Loud sang the Spanish cavalier,
  And thus his ditty ran;
  God send the Gypsy lassie here,
  And not the Gypsy man.

First Gypsy (playing). There you are in your morocco!

Second Gypsy. One more game. The Alcalde's doves against the Padre Cura's new moon.

First Gypsy. Have at you, Chirelin.

Gypsies (at the forge sing).

At midnight, when the moon began
  To show her silver flame,
There came to him no Gypsy man,
  The Gypsy lassie came.

(Enter BELTRAN CRUZADO.)

Cruz. Come hither, Murcigalleros and Rastilleros; leave work, leave play; listen to your orders for the night. (Speaking to the right.) You will get you to the village, mark you, by the stone cross.

Gypsies. Ay!

Cruz. (to the left). And you, by the pole with the hermit's head upon it.

Gypsies. Ay!

Cruz. As soon as you see the planets are out, in with you, and be busy with the ten commandments, under the sly, and Saint Martin asleep. D'ye hear?

Gypsies. Ay!

Cruz. Keep your lanterns open, and, if you see a goblin or a papagayo, take to your trampers. Vineyards and Dancing John is the word. Am I comprehended?

Gypsies. Ay! ay!

Cruz. Away, then!

(Exeunt severally. CRUZADO walks up the stage, and disappears among the trees. Enter PRECIOSA.)

Prec. How strangely gleams through the gigantic trees

The red light of the forge! Wild, beckoning shadows
Stalk through the forest, ever and anon
Rising and bending with the flickering flame,
Then flitting into darkness! So within me
Strange hopes and fears do beckon to each other,
My brightest hopes giving dark fears a being
As the light does the shadow. Woe is me
How still it is about me, and how lonely!

(BARTOLOME rushes in.)

Bart. Ho! Preciosa!

Prec.   O Bartolome!
Thou here?

Bart.   Lo! I am here.

Prec.   Whence comest thou?

Bart. From the rough ridges of the wild Sierra,
From caverns in the rocks, from hunger, thirst,
And fever! Like a wild wolf to the sheepfold.
Come I for thee, my lamb.

Prec.   O touch me not!
The Count of Lara's blood is on thy hands!
The Count of Lara's curse is on thy soul!
Do not come near me! Pray, begone from here
Thou art in danger! They have set a price
Upon thy head!

Bart.   Ay, and I've wandered long
Among the mountains; and for many days
Have seen no human face, save the rough swineherd's.
The wind and rain have been my sole companions.
I shouted to them from the rocks thy name,
And the loud echo sent it back to me,
Till I grew mad. I could not stay from thee,
And I am here! Betray me, if thou wilt.

Prec. Betray thee? I betray thee?

131

Bart.   Preciosa!
I come for thee! for thee I thus brave death!
Fly with me o'er the borders of this realm!
Fly with me!

 Prec. Speak of that no more. I cannot.
I'm thine no longer.

 Bart.   O, recall the time
When we were children! how we played together,
How we grew up together; how we plighted
Our hearts unto each other, even in childhood!
Fulfil thy promise, for the hour has come.
I'm hunted from the kingdom, like a wolf!
Fulfil thy promise.

 Prec. 'T was my father's promise.
Not mine. I never gave my heart to thee,
Nor promised thee my hand!

 Bart. False tongue of woman!
And heart more false!

 Prec. Nay, listen unto me.
I will speak frankly. I have never loved thee;
I cannot love thee. This is not my fault,
It is my destiny. Thou art a man
Restless and violent. What wouldst thou with me,
A feeble girl, who have not long to live,
Whose heart is broken? Seek another wife,
Better than I, and fairer; and let not
Thy rash and headlong moods estrange her from thee.
Thou art unhappy in this hopeless passion,
I never sought thy love; never did aught
To make thee love me. Yet I pity thee,
And most of all I pity thy wild heart,
That hurries thee to crimes and deeds of blood,
Beware, beware of that.

 Bart. For thy dear sake
I will be gentle. Thou shalt teach me patience.

 Prec. Then take this farewell, and depart in peace.

Thou must not linger here.

Bart.   Come, come with me.

Prec. Hark! I hear footsteps.

Bart.   I entreat thee, come!

Prec. Away! It is in vain.

Bart.   Wilt thou not come?

Prec. Never!

Bart.   Then woe, eternal woe, upon thee!
Thou shalt not be another's. Thou shalt die.
            [Exit.

Prec. All holy angels keep me in this hour!
Spirit of her who bore me, look upon me!
Mother of God, the glorified, protect me!
Christ and the saints, be merciful unto me!
Yet why should I fear death? What is it to die?
To leave all disappointment, care, and sorrow,
To leave all falsehood, treachery, and unkindness,
All ignominy, suffering, and despair,
And be at rest forever! O dull heart,
Be of good cheer! When thou shalt cease to beat,
Then shalt thou cease to suffer and complain!

(Enter VICTORIAN and HYPOLITO behind.)

Vict. 'T is she! Behold, how beautiful she stands
Under the tent-like trees!

Hyp.   A woodland nymph!

Vict. I pray thee, stand aside. Leave me.

Hyp.   Be wary.
Do not betray thyself too soon.

Vict. (disguising his voice). Hist! Gypsy!

Prec. (aside, with emotion).
That voice! that voice from heaven! O speak again!
Who is it calls?

Vict.   A friend.

Prec. (aside). 'T is he! 'T is he!
I thank thee, Heaven, that thou hast heard my prayer,
And sent me this protector! Now be strong,
Be strong, my heart! I must dissemble here.
False friend or true?

Vict. A true friend to the true;
Fear not; come hither. So; can you tell fortunes?

Prec. Not in the dark. Come nearer to the fire.
Give me your hand. It is not crossed, I see.

Vict. (putting a piece of gold into her hand). There is the
cross.

Prec.   Is 't silver?

Vict.   No, 't is gold.

Prec. There's a fair lady at the Court, who loves you,
And for yourself alone.

Vict.   Fie! the old story!
Tell me a better fortune for my money;
Not this old woman's tale!

Prec.   You are passionate;
And this same passionate humor in your blood
Has marred your fortune. Yes; I see it now;
The line of life is crossed by many marks.
Shame! shame! O you have wronged the maid who loved you!
How could you do it?

Vict.   I never loved a maid;
For she I loved was then a maid no more.

Prec. How know you that?

Vict. A little bird in the air
Whispered the secret.

  Prec. There, take back your gold!
Your hand is cold, like a deceiver's hand!
There is no blessing in its charity!
Make her your wife, for you have been abused;
And you shall mend your fortunes, mending hers.

  Vict. (aside). How like an angel's speaks the tongue of woman,
When pleading in another's cause her own!
That is a pretty ring upon your finger.
Pray give it me. (Tries to take the ring.)

  Prec. No; never from my hand
Shall that be taken!

  Vict. Why, 't is but a ring.
I'll give it back to you; or, if I keep it,
Will give you gold to buy you twenty such.

  Prec. Why would you have this ring?

  Vict. A traveller's fancy,
A whim, and nothing more. I would fain keep it
As a memento of the Gypsy camp
In Guadarrama, and the fortune-teller
Who sent me back to wed a widowed maid.
Pray, let me have the ring.

  Prec. No, never! never!
I will not part with it, even when I die;
But bid my nurse fold my pale fingers thus,
That it may not fall from them. 'T is a token
Of a beloved friend, who is no more.

  Vict. How? dead?

  Prec. Yes; dead to me; and worse than dead.
He is estranged! And yet I keep this ring.
I will rise with it from my grave hereafter,
To prove to him that I was never false.

Vict. (aside). Be still, my swelling heart! one moment, still!
Why, 't is the folly of a love-sick girl.
Come, give it me, or I will say 't is mine,
And that you stole it.

Prec.   O, you will not dare
To utter such a falsehood!

Vict.   I not dare?
Look in my face, and say if there is aught
I have not dared, I would not dare for thee!

(She rushes into his arms.)

Prec. 'T is thou! 't is thou! Yes; yes; my heart's elected!
My dearest-dear Victorian! my soul's heaven!
Where hast thou been so long? Why didst thou leave me?

Vict. Ask me not now, my dearest Preciosa.
Let me forget we ever have been parted!

Prec. Hadst thou not come —

Vict. I pray thee, do not chide me!

Prec. I should have perished here among these Gypsies.

Vict. Forgive me, sweet! for what I made thee suffer.
Think'st thou this heart could feel a moment's joy,
Thou being absent? O, believe it not!
Indeed, since that sad hour I have not slept,
For thinking of the wrong I did to thee
Dost thou forgive me? Say, wilt thou forgive me?

Prec. I have forgiven thee. Ere those words of anger
Were in the book of Heaven writ down against thee,
I had forgiven thee.

Vict.   I'm the veriest fool
That walks the earth, to have believed thee false.
It was the Count of Lara —

Prec.   That bad man

Has worked me harm enough. Hast thou not heard—

   Vict. I have heard all. And yet speak on, speak on!
Let me but hear thy voice, and I am happy;
For every tone, like some sweet incantation,
Calls up the buried past to plead for me.
Speak, my beloved, speak into my heart,
Whatever fills and agitates thine own.

(They walk aside.)

   Hyp. All gentle quarrels in the pastoral poets,
All passionate love scenes in the best romances,
All chaste embraces on the public stage,
All soft adventures, which the liberal stars
Have winked at, as the natural course of things,
Have been surpassed here by my friend, the student,
And this sweet Gypsy lass, fair Preciosa!

   Prec. Senor Hypolito! I kiss your hand.
Pray, shall I tell your fortune?

   Hyp.   Not to-night;
For, should you treat me as you did Victorian,
And send me back to marry maids forlorn,
My wedding day would last from now till Christmas.

   Chispa (within). What ho! the Gypsies, ho! Beltran Cruzado!
Halloo! halloo! halloo! halloo!

(Enters booted, with a whip and lantern.

   Vict.   What now
Why such a fearful din? Hast thou been robbed?

   Chispa. Ay, robbed and murdered; and good evening to you,
My worthy masters.

   Vict. Speak; what brings thee here?

   CHISPA (to PRECIOSA).
Good news from Court; good news! Beltran Cruzado,
The Count of the Cales, is not your father,

But your true father has returned to Spain
Laden with wealth. You are no more a Gypsy.

  Vict. Strange as a Moorish tale!

  Chispa.   And we have all
Been drinking at the tavern to your health,
As wells drink in November, when it rains.

  Vict. Where is the gentlemen?

  Chispa.   As the old song says,
      His body is in Segovia,
        His soul is in Madrid,

  Prec. Is this a dream? O, if it be a dream,
Let me sleep on, and do not wake me yet!
Repeat thy story! Say I'm not deceived!
Say that I do not dream! I am awake;
This is the Gypsy camp; this is Victorian,
And this his friend, Hypolito! Speak! speak!
Let me not wake and find it all a dream!

  Vict. It is a dream, sweet child! a waking dream,
A blissful certainty, a vision bright
Of that rare happiness, which even on earth
Heaven gives to those it loves. Now art thou rich,
As thou wast ever beautiful and good;
And I am now the beggar.

  Prec. (giving him her hand). I have still
A hand to give.

  Chispa (aside). And I have two to take.
I've heard my grandmother say, that Heaven gives almonds
To those who have no teeth. That's nuts to crack,
I've teeth to spare, but where shall I find almonds?

  Vict. What more of this strange story?

  Chispa.   Nothing more.
Your friend, Don Carlos, is now at the village
Showing to Pedro Crespo, the Alcalde,

138

The proofs of what I tell you. The old hag,
Who stole you in your childhood, has confessed;
And probably they'll hang her for the crime,
To make the celebration more complete.

  Vict. No; let it be a day of general joy;
Fortune comes well to all, that comes not late.
Now let us join Don Carlos.

  Hyp.   So farewell,
The student's wandering life! Sweet serenades,
Sung under ladies' windows in the night,
And all that makes vacation beautiful!
To you, ye cloistered shades of Alcala,
To you, ye radiant visions of romance,
Written in books, but here surpassed by truth,
The Bachelor Hypolito returns,
And leaves the Gypsy with the Spanish Student.

SCENE VI. — A pass in the Guadarrama mountains. Early morning.
    A muleteer crosses the stage, sitting sideways on his mule and
          lighting a paper cigar with flint and steel.

SONG.

If thou art sleeping, maiden,
  Awake and open thy door,
'T is the break of day, and we must away,
  O'er meadow, and mount, and moor.

Wait not to find thy slippers,
  But come with thy naked feet;
We shall have to pass through the dewy grass,
  And waters wide and fleet.

(Disappears down the pass. Enter a Monk. A shepherd appears on
the rocks above.)

  Monk. Ave Maria, gratia plena. Ola! good man!

  Shep. Ola!

Monk. Is this the road to Segovia?

Shep. It is, your reverence.

Monk. How far is it?

Shep. I do not know.

Monk. What is that yonder in the valley?

Shep. San Ildefonso.

Monk. A long way to breakfast.

Shep. Ay, marry.

Monk. Are there robbers in these mountains?

Shep. Yes, and worse than that.

Monk. What?

Shep. Wolves.

Monk. Santa Maria! Come with me to San Ildefonso, and thou shalt be well rewarded.

Shep. What wilt thou give me?

Monk. An Agnus Dei and my benediction.

(They disappear. A mounted Contrabandista passes, wrapped in his cloak, and a gun at his saddle-bow. He goes down the pass singing.)

SONG.

Worn with speed is my good steed,
And I march me hurried, worried;
Onward, caballito mio,
With the white star in thy forehead!
Onward, for here comes the Ronda,
And I hear their rifles crack!
Ay, jaleo! Ay, ay, jaleo!

Ay, jaleo! They cross our track.

(Song dies away. Enter PRECIOSA, on horseback, attended by
VICTORIAN, HYPOLITO, DON CARLOS, and CHISPA, on foot,
and armed.)

  Vict. This is the highest point. Here let us rest.
See, Preciosa, see how all about us
Kneeling, like hooded friars, the misty mountains
Receive the benediction of the sun!
O glorious sight!

  Prec.   Most beautiful indeed!

  Hyp. Most wonderful!

  Vict.   And in the vale below,
Where yonder steeples flash like lifted halberds,
San Ildefonso, from its noisy belfries,
Sends up a salutation to the morn,
As if an army smote their brazen shields,
And shouted victory!

  Prec.   And which way lies Segovia?

  Vict. At a great distance yonder.
Dost thou not see it?

  Prec.   No. I do not see it.

  Vict. The merest flaw that dents the horizon's edge.
There, yonder!

  Hyp.   'T is a notable old town,
Boasting an ancient Roman aqueduct,
And an Alcazar, builded by the Moors,
Wherein, you may remember, poor Gil Blas
Was fed on Pan del Rey. O, many a time
Out of its grated windows have I looked
Hundreds of feet plumb down to the Eresma,
That, like a serpent through the valley creeping,
Glides at its foot.

Prec.   O yes! I see it now,
Yet rather with my heart than with mine eyes,
So faint it is. And all my thoughts sail thither,
Freighted with prayers and hopes, and forward urged
Against all stress of accident, as in
The Eastern Tale, against the wind and tide
Great ships were drawn to the Magnetic Mountains,
And there were wrecked, and perished in the sea!
(She weeps.)

 Vict. O gentle spirit! Thou didst bear unmoved
Blasts of adversity and frosts of fate!
But the first ray of sunshine that falls on thee
Melts thee to tears! O, let thy weary heart
Lean upon mine! and it shall faint no more,
Nor thirst, nor hunger; but be comforted
And filled with my affection.

 Prec.   Stay no longer!
My father waits. Methinks I see him there,
Now looking from the window, and now watching
Each sound of wheels or footfall in the street,
And saying, "Hark! she comes!" O father! father!

(They descend the pass. CHISPA remains behind.)

 Chispa. I have a father, too, but he is a dead one. Alas and alack-a-day. Poor was I born, and poor do I remain. I neither win nor lose. Thus I was, through the world, half the time on foot, and the other half walking; and always as merry as a thunder-storm in the night. And so we plough along, as the fly said to the ox. Who knows what may happen? Patience, and shuffle the cards! I am not yet so bald that you can see my brains; and perhaps, after all, I shall some day go to Rome, and come back Saint Peter. Benedicite!
[Exit.

(A pause. Then enter BARTOLOME wildly, as if in pursuit, with a carbine in his hand.)

 Bart. They passed this way! I hear their horses' hoofs!
Yonder I see them! Come, sweet caramillo,
This serenade shall be the Gypsy's last!

(Fires down the pass.)

Ha! ha! Well whistled, my sweet caramillo!
Well whistled!—I have missed her!—O my God!

(The shot is returned. BARTOLOME falls).

THE BELFRY OF BRUGES AND OTHER POEMS

THE BELFRY OF BRUGES
CARILLON

In the ancient town of Bruges,
In the quaint old Flemish city,
As the evening shades descended,
Low and loud and sweetly blended,
Low at times and loud at times,
And changing like a poet's rhymes,
Rang the beautiful wild chimes
From the Belfry in the market
Of the ancient town of Bruges.

Then, with deep sonorous clangor
Calmly answering their sweet anger,
When the wrangling bells had ended,
Slowly struck the clock eleven,
And, from out the silent heaven,
Silence on the town descended.
Silence, silence everywhere,
On the earth and in the air,
Save that footsteps here and there
Of some burgher home returning,
By the street lamps faintly burning,
For a moment woke the echoes
Of the ancient town of Bruges.

But amid my broken slumbers
Still I heard those magic numbers,
As they loud proclaimed the flight
And stolen marches of the night;
Till their chimes in sweet collision
Mingled with each wandering vision,
Mingled with the fortune-telling
Gypsy-bands of dreams and fancies,
Which amid the waste expanses
Of the silent land of trances
Have their solitary dwelling;
All else seemed asleep in Bruges,
In the quaint old Flemish city.

And I thought how like these chimes
Are the poet's airy rhymes,
All his rhymes and roundelays,
His conceits, and songs, and ditties,
From the belfry of his brain,
Scattered downward, though in vain,
On the roofs and stones of cities!
For by night the drowsy ear
Under its curtains cannot hear,
And by day men go their ways,
Hearing the music as they pass,
But deeming it no more, alas!
Than the hollow sound of brass.

Yet perchance a sleepless wight,
Lodging at some humble inn
In the narrow lanes of life,
When the dusk and hush of night
Shut out the incessant din
Of daylight and its toil and strife,
May listen with a calm delight
To the poet's melodies,
Till he hears, or dreams he hears,
Intermingled with the song,
Thoughts that he has cherished long;
Hears amid the chime and singing
The bells of his own village ringing,
And wakes, and finds his slumberous eyes
Wet with most delicious tears.

Thus dreamed I, as by night I lay
In Bruges, at the Fleur-de-Ble,
Listening with a wild delight
To the chimes that, through the night
Bang their changes from the Belfry
Of that quaint old Flemish city.

THE BELFRY OF BRUGES

In the market-place of Bruges stands the belfry old and brown;
Thrice consumed and thrice rebuilded, still it watches o'er the
town.

As the summer morn was breaking, on that lofty tower I stood,
And the world threw off the darkness, like the weeds of widowhood.

Thick with towns and hamlets studded, and with streams and
vapors gray,
Like a shield embossed with silver, round and vast the landscape
lay.

At my feet the city slumbered. From its chimneys, here and there,
Wreaths of snow-white smoke, ascending, vanished, ghost-like, into
air.

Not a sound rose from the city at that early morning hour,
But I heard a heart of iron beating in the ancient tower.

From their nests beneath the rafters sang the swallows wild and
high;
And the world, beneath me sleeping, seemed more distant than the
sky.

Then most musical and solemn, bringing back the olden times,
With their strange, unearthly changes rang the melancholy chimes,

Like the psalms from some old cloister, when the nuns sing in the
choir;
And the great bell tolled among them, like the chanting of a friar.

Visions of the days departed, shadowy phantoms filled my brain;
They who live in history only seemed to walk the earth again;

All the Foresters of Flanders, — mighty Baldwin Bras de Fer,
Lyderick du Bucq and Cressy Philip, Guy de Dampierre.

I beheld the pageants splendid that adorned those days of old;
Stately dames, like queens attended, knights who bore the Fleece of
Gold

Lombard and Venetian merchants with deep-laden argosies;
Ministers from twenty nations; more than royal pomp and ease.

I beheld proud Maximilian, kneeling humbly on the ground;
I beheld the gentle Mary, hunting with her hawk and hound;

And her lighted bridal-chamber, where a duke slept with the queen,
And the armed guard around them, and the sword unsheathed
        between.

I beheld the Flemish weavers, with Namur and Juliers bold,
Marching homeward from the bloody battle of the Spurs of Gold;

Saw the light at Minnewater, saw the White Hoods moving west,
Saw great Artevelde victorious scale the Golden Dragon's nest.

And again the whiskered Spaniard all the land with terror smote;
And again the wild alarum sounded from the tocsin's throat;

Till the bell of Ghent responded o'er lagoon and dike of sand,
"I am Roland! I am Roland! there is victory in the land!"

Then the sound of drums aroused me. The awakened city's roar
Chased the phantoms I had summoned back into their graves once
        more.

Hours had passed away like minutes; and, before I was aware,
Lo! the shadow of the belfry crossed the sun-illumined square.

A GLEAM OF SUNSHINE

This is the place. Stand still, my steed,
  Let me review the scene,
And summon from the shadowy Past
  The forms that once have been.

The Past and Present here unite
  Beneath Time's flowing tide,
Like footprints hidden by a brook,
  But seen on either side.

Here runs the highway to the town;
  There the green lane descends,
Through which I walked to church with thee,
  O gentlest of my friends!

The shadow of the linden-trees
  Lay moving on the grass;
Between them and the moving boughs,
  A shadow, thou didst pass.

Thy dress was like the lilies,
  And thy heart as pure as they:
One of God's holy messengers
  Did walk with me that day.

I saw the branches of the trees
  Bend down thy touch to meet,
The clover-blossoms in the grass
  Rise up to kiss thy feet,

"Sleep, sleep to-day, tormenting cares,
  Of earth and folly born!"
Solemnly sang the village choir
  On that sweet Sabbath morn.

Through the closed blinds the golden sun
  Poured in a dusty beam,
Like the celestial ladder seen
  By Jacob in his dream.

And ever and anon, the wind,
  Sweet-scented with the hay,
Turned o'er the hymn-book's fluttering leaves
  That on the window lay.

Long was the good man's sermon,
  Yet it seemed not so to me;
For he spake of Ruth the beautiful,
  And still I thought of thee.

Long was the prayer he uttered,
  Yet it seemed not so to me;
For in my heart I prayed with him,
  And still I thought of thee.

But now, alas! the place seems changed;
  Thou art no longer here:
Part of the sunshine of the scene
  With thee did disappear.

Though thoughts, deep-rooted in my heart,
  Like pine-trees dark and high,
Subdue the light of noon, and breathe
  A low and ceaseless sigh;

This memory brightens o'er the past,
  As when the sun, concealed
Behind some cloud that near us hangs
  Shines on a distant field.

THE ARSENAL AT SPRINGFIELD

This is the Arsenal. From floor to ceiling,
  Like a huge organ, rise the burnished arms;
But front their silent pipes no anthem pealing
  Startles the villages with strange alarms.

Ah! what a sound will rise, how wild and dreary,
  When the death-angel touches those swift keys
What loud lament and dismal Miserere
  Will mingle with their awful symphonies

I hear even now the infinite fierce chorus,
  The cries of agony, the endless groan,
Which, through the ages that have gone before us,
  In long reverberations reach our own.

On helm and harness rings the Saxon hammer,
  Through Cimbric forest roars the Norseman's song,
And loud, amid the universal clamor,
O'er distant deserts sounds the Tartar gong.

I hear the Florentine, who from his palace
  Wheels out his battle-bell with dreadful din,
And Aztec priests upon their teocallis
  Beat the wild war-drums made of serpent's skin;

The tumult of each sacked and burning village;
  The shout that every prayer for mercy drowns;
The soldiers' revels in the midst of pillage;
  The wail of famine in beleaguered towns;

The bursting shell, the gateway wrenched asunder,
  The rattling musketry, the clashing blade;
And ever and anon, in tones of thunder,
  The diapason of the cannonade.

Is it, O man, with such discordant noises,
  With such accursed instruments as these,
Thou drownest Nature's sweet and kindly voices,
  And jarrest the celestial harmonies?

Were half the power, that fills the world with terror,
  Were half the wealth, bestowed on camps and courts,
Given to redeem the human mind from error,
  There were no need of arsenals or forts:

The warrior's name would be a name abhorred!
  And every nation, that should lift again
Its hand against a brother, on its forehead
  Would wear forevermore the curse of Cain!

Down the dark future, through long generations,
  The echoing sounds grow fainter and then cease;
And like a bell, with solemn, sweet vibrations,
  I hear once more the voice of Christ say, "Peace!"

Peace! and no longer from its brazen portals
  The blast of War's great organ shakes the skies!
But beautiful as songs of the immortals,
  The holy melodies of love arise.

NUREMBERG

In the valley of the Pegnitz, where across broad meadow-lands
Rise the blue Franconian mountains, Nuremberg, the ancient, stands.

Quaint old town of toil and traffic, quaint old town of art and song,
Memories haunt thy pointed gables, like the rooks that round them
       throng:

Memories of the Middle Ages, when the emperors, rough and bold,
Had their dwelling in thy castle, time-defying, centuries old;

And thy brave and thrifty burghers boasted, in their uncouth rhyme,
That their great imperial city stretched its hand through every clime.

In the court-yard of the castle, bound with many an iron hand,
Stands the mighty linden planted by Queen Cunigunde's hand;

On the square the oriel window, where in old heroic days
Sat the poet Melchior singing Kaiser Maximilian's praise.

Everywhere I see around me rise the wondrous world of Art:
Fountains wrought with richest sculpture standing in the common
       mart;

And above cathedral doorways saints and bishops carved in stone,
By a former age commissioned as apostles to our own.

In the church of sainted Sebald sleeps enshrined his holy dust,
And in bronze the Twelve Apostles guard from age to age their trust;

In the church of sainted Lawrence stands a pix of sculpture rare,
Like the foamy sheaf of fountains, rising through the painted air.

Here, when Art was still religion, with a simple, reverent heart,
Lived and labored Albrecht Durer, the Evangelist of Art;

Hence in silence and in sorrow, toiling still with busy hand,
Like an emigrant he wandered, seeking for the Better Land.

Emigravit is the inscription on the tombstone where he lies;
Dead he is not, but departed, — for the artist never dies.

Fairer seems the ancient city, and the sunshine seems more fair,
That he once has trod its pavement, that he once has breathed its air!

Through these streets so broad and stately, these obscure and dismal
       lanes,
Walked of yore the Mastersingers, chanting rude poetic strains.

From remote and sunless suburbs came they to the friendly guild,
Building nests in Fame's great temple, as in spouts the swallows
       build.

As the weaver plied the shuttle, wove he too the mystic rhyme,
And the smith his iron measures hammered to the anvil's chime;

Thanking God, whose boundless wisdom makes the flowers of
       poesy bloom
In the forge's dust and cinders, in the tissues of the loom.

Here Hans Sachs, the cobbler-poet, laureate of the gentle craft,
Wisest of the Twelve Wise Masters, in huge folios sang and laughed.

But his house is now an ale-house, with a nicely sanded floor,
And a garland in the window, and his face above the door;

Painted by some humble artist, as in Adam Puschman's song,
As the old man gray and dove-like, with his great beard white and
       long.

And at night the swart mechanic comes to drown his cark and care,
Quaffing ale from pewter tankard; in the master's antique chair.

Vanished is the ancient splendor, and before my dreamy eye
Wave these mingled shapes and figures, like a faded tapestry.

Not thy Councils, not thy Kaisers, win for thee the world's regard;
But thy painter, Albrecht Durer, and Hans Sachs thy cobbler-bard.

Thus, O Nuremberg, a wanderer from a region far away,
As he paced thy streets and court-yards, sang in thought his careless
       lay:

Gathering from the pavement's crevice, as a floweret of the soil,
The nobility of labor,—the long pedigree of toil.

THE NORMAN BARON

Dans les moments de la vie ou la reflexion devient plus calme et plus profonde, ou l'interet et l'avarice parlent moins haut que la raison, dans les instants de chagrin domestique, de maladie, et de peril de mort, les nobles se repentirent de posseder des serfs, comme d'une chose peu agreable a Dieu, qui avait cree tous les hommes a son image.—THIERRY, Conquete de l'Angleterre.

In his chamber, weak and dying,
Was the Norman baron lying;
Loud, without, the tempest thundered
    And the castle-turret shook,

In this fight was Death the gainer,
Spite of vassal and retainer,
And the lands his sires had plundered,
    Written in the Doomsday Book.

By his bed a monk was seated,
Who in humble voice repeated
Many a prayer and pater-noster,
    From the missal on his knee;

And, amid the tempest pealing,
Sounds of bells came faintly stealing,
Bells, that from the neighboring kloster
    Rang for the Nativity.

In the hall, the serf and vassal
Held, that night their Christmas wassail;
Many a carol, old and saintly,
    Sang the minstrels and the waits;

And so loud these Saxon gleemen
Sang to slaves the songs of freemen,
That the storm was heard but faintly,
    Knocking at the castle-gates.

Till at length the lays they chanted
Reached the chamber terror-haunted,
Where the monk, with accents holy,

Whispered at the baron's ear.

Tears upon his eyelids glistened,
As he paused awhile and listened,
And the dying baron slowly
    Turned his weary head to hear.

"Wassail for the kingly stranger
Born and cradled in a manger!
King, like David, priest, like Aaron,
    Christ is born to set us free!"

And the lightning showed the sainted
Figures on the casement painted,
And exclaimed the shuddering baron,
    "Miserere, Domine!"

In that hour of deep contrition
He beheld, with clearer vision,
Through all outward show and fashion,
    Justice, the Avenger, rise.

All the pomp of earth had vanished,
Falsehood and deceit were banished,
Reason spake more loud than passion,
    And the truth wore no disguise.

Every vassal of his banner,
Every serf born to his manor,
All those wronged and wretched creatures,
    By his hand were freed again.

And, as on the sacred missal
He recorded their dismissal,
Death relaxed his iron features,
    And the monk replied, "Amen!"

Many centuries have been numbered
Since in death the baron slumbered
By the convent's sculptured portal,
    Mingling with the common dust:

But the good deed, through the ages
Living in historic pages,
Brighter grows and gleams immortal,
    Unconsumed by moth or rust

RAIN IN SUMMER

How beautiful is the rain!
After the dust and heat,
In the broad and fiery street,
In the narrow lane,
How beautiful is the rain!

How it clatters along the roofs,
Like the tramp of hoofs
How it gushes and struggles out
From the throat of the overflowing spout!

Across the window-pane
It pours and pours;
And swift and wide,
With a muddy tide,
Like a river down the gutter roars
The rain, the welcome rain!

The sick man from his chamber looks
At the twisted brooks;
He can feel the cool
Breath of each little pool;
His fevered brain
Grows calm again,
And he breathes a blessing on the rain.

From the neighboring school
Come the boys,
With more than their wonted noise
And commotion;
And down the wet streets
Sail their mimic fleets,
Till the treacherous pool
Ingulfs them in its whirling
And turbulent ocean.

In the country, on every side,
Where far and wide,
Like a leopard's tawny and spotted hide,
Stretches the plain,

To the dry grass and the drier grain
How welcome is the rain!

In the furrowed land
The toilsome and patient oxen stand;
Lifting the yoke encumbered head,
With their dilated nostrils spread,
They silently inhale
The clover-scented gale,
And the vapors that arise
From the well-watered and smoking soil.
For this rest in the furrow after toil
Their large and lustrous eyes
Seem to thank the Lord,
More than man's spoken word.

Near at hand,
From under the sheltering trees,
The farmer sees
His pastures, and his fields of grain,
As they bend their tops
To the numberless beating drops
Of the incessant rain.
He counts it as no sin
That he sees therein
Only his own thrift and gain.

These, and far more than these,
The Poet sees!
He can behold
Aquarius old
Walking the fenceless fields of air;
And from each ample fold
Of the clouds about him rolled
Scattering everywhere
The showery rain,
As the farmer scatters his grain.

He can behold
Things manifold
That have not yet been wholly told, —
Have not been wholly sung nor said.
For his thought, that never stops,

Follows the water-drops
Down to the graves of the dead,
Down through chasms and gulfs profound,
To the dreary fountain-head
Of lakes and rivers under ground;
And sees them, when the rain is done,
On the bridge of colors seven
Climbing up once more to heaven,
Opposite the setting sun.

Thus the Seer,
With vision clear,
Sees forms appear and disappear,
In the perpetual round of strange,
Mysterious change
From birth to death, from death to birth,
From earth to heaven, from heaven to earth;
Till glimpses more sublime
Of things, unseen before,
Unto his wondering eyes reveal
The Universe, as an immeasurable wheel
Turning forevermore
In the rapid and rushing river of Time.

TO A CHILD

Dear child! how radiant on thy mother's knee,
With merry-making eyes and jocund smiles,
Thou gazest at the painted tiles,
Whose figures grace,
With many a grotesque form and face.
The ancient chimney of thy nursery!
The lady with the gay macaw,
The dancing girl, the grave bashaw
With bearded lip and chin;
And, leaning idly o'er his gate,
Beneath the imperial fan of state,
The Chinese mandarin.

With what a look of proud command
Thou shakest in thy little hand
The coral rattle with its silver bells,
Making a merry tune!
Thousands of years in Indian seas
That coral grew, by slow degrees,
Until some deadly and wild monsoon
Dashed it on Coromandel's sand!
Those silver bells
Reposed of yore,
As shapeless ore,
Far down in the deep-sunken wells
Of darksome mines,
In some obscure and sunless place,
Beneath huge Chimborazo's base,
Or Potosi's o'erhanging pines
And thus for thee, O little child,
Through many a danger and escape,
The tall ships passed the stormy cape;
For thee in foreign lands remote,
Beneath a burning, tropic clime,
The Indian peasant, chasing the wild goat,
Himself as swift and wild,
In falling, clutched the frail arbute,
The fibres of whose shallow root,
Uplifted from the soil, betrayed
The silver veins beneath it laid,

The buried treasures of the miser, Time.

But, lo! thy door is left ajar!
Thou hearest footsteps from afar!
And, at the sound,
Thou turnest round
With quick and questioning eyes,
Like one, who, in a foreign land,
Beholds on every hand
Some source of wonder and surprise!
And, restlessly, impatiently,
Thou strivest, strugglest, to be free,
The four walls of thy nursery
Are now like prison walls to thee.
No more thy mother's smiles,
No more the painted tiles,
Delight thee, nor the playthings on the floor,
That won thy little, beating heart before;
Thou strugglest for the open door.

Through these once solitary halls
Thy pattering footstep falls.
The sound of thy merry voice
Makes the old walls
Jubilant, and they rejoice
With the joy of thy young heart,
O'er the light of whose gladness
No shadows of sadness
From the sombre background of memory start.

Once, ah, once, within these walls,
One whom memory oft recalls,
The Father of his Country, dwelt.
And yonder meadows broad and damp
The fires of the besieging camp
Encircled with a burning belt.
Up and down these echoing stairs,
Heavy with the weight of cares,
Sounded his majestic tread;
Yes, within this very room
Sat he in those hours of gloom,
Weary both in heart and head.

But what are these grave thoughts to thee?
Out, out! into the open air!
Thy only dream is liberty,
Thou carest little how or where.
I see thee eager at thy play,
Now shouting to the apples on the tree,
With cheeks as round and red as they;
And now among the yellow stalks,
Among the flowering shrubs and plants,
As restless as the bee.
Along the garden walks,
The tracks of thy small carriage-wheels I trace;
And see at every turn how they efface
Whole villages of sand-roofed tents,
That rise like golden domes
Above the cavernous and secret homes
Of wandering and nomadic tribes of ants.
Ah, cruel little Tamerlane,
Who, with thy dreadful reign,
Dost persecute and overwhelm
These hapless Troglodytes of thy realm!
What! tired already! with those suppliant looks,
And voice more beautiful than a poet's books,
Or murmuring sound of water as it flows.
Thou comest back to parley with repose;
This rustic seat in the old apple-tree,
With its o'erhanging golden canopy
Of leaves illuminate with autumnal hues,
And shining with the argent light of dews,
Shall for a season be our place of rest.
Beneath us, like an oriole's pendent nest,
From which the laughing birds have taken wing,
By thee abandoned, hangs thy vacant swing.
Dream-like the waters of the river gleam;
A sailless vessel drops adown the stream,
And like it, to a sea as wide and deep,
Thou driftest gently down the tides of sleep.

O child! O new-born denizen
Of life's great city! on thy head
The glory of the morn is shed,
Like a celestial benison!
Here at the portal thou dost stand,

And with thy little hand
Thou openest the mysterious gate
Into the future's undiscovered land.
I see its valves expand,
As at the touch of Fate!
Into those realms of love and hate,
Into that darkness blank and drear,
By some prophetic feeling taught,
I launch the bold, adventurous thought,
Freighted with hope and fear;
As upon subterranean streams,
In caverns unexplored and dark,
Men sometimes launch a fragile bark,
Laden with flickering fire,
And watch its swift-receding beams,
Until at length they disappear,
And in the distant dark expire.

By what astrology of fear or hope
Dare I to cast thy horoscope!
Like the new moon thy life appears;
A little strip of silver light,
And widening outward into night
The shadowy disk of future years;
And yet upon its outer rim,
A luminous circle, faint and dim,
And scarcely visible to us here,
Rounds and completes the perfect sphere;
A prophecy and intimation,
A pale and feeble adumbration,
Of the great world of light, that lies
Behind all human destinies.

Ah! if thy fate, with anguish fraught,
Should be to wet the dusty soil
With the hot tears and sweat of toil, —
To struggle with imperious thought,
Until the overburdened brain,
Weary with labor, faint with pain,
Like a jarred pendulum, retain
Only its motion, not its power, —
Remember, in that perilous hour,
When most afflicted and oppressed,

From labor there shall come forth rest.

And if a more auspicious fate
On thy advancing steps await
Still let it ever be thy pride
To linger by the laborer's side;
With words of sympathy or song
To cheer the dreary march along
Of the great army of the poor,
O'er desert sand, o'er dangerous moor.
Nor to thyself the task shall be
Without reward; for thou shalt learn
The wisdom early to discern
True beauty in utility;
As great Pythagoras of yore,
Standing beside the blacksmith's door,
And hearing the hammers, as they smote
The anvils with a different note,
Stole from the varying tones, that hung
Vibrant on every iron tongue,
The secret of the sounding wire.
And formed the seven-chorded lyre.

Enough! I will not play the Seer;
I will no longer strive to ope
The mystic volume, where appear
The herald Hope, forerunning Fear,
And Fear, the pursuivant of Hope.
Thy destiny remains untold;
For, like Acestes' shaft of old,
The swift thought kindles as it flies,
And burns to ashes in the skies.

THE OCCULTATION OF ORION

I saw, as in a dream sublime,
The balance in the hand of Time.
O'er East and West its beam impended;
And day, with all its hours of light,
Was slowly sinking out of sight,
While, opposite, the scale of night
Silently with the stars ascended.

Like the astrologers of eld,
In that bright vision I beheld
Greater and deeper mysteries.
I saw, with its celestial keys,
Its chords of air, its frets of fire,
The Samian's great Aeolian lyre,
Rising through all its sevenfold bars,
From earth unto the fixed stars.
And through the dewy atmosphere,
Not only could I see, but hear,
Its wondrous and harmonious strings,
In sweet vibration, sphere by sphere,
From Dian's circle light and near,
Onward to vaster and wider rings.
Where, chanting through his beard of snows,
Majestic, mournful, Saturn goes,
And down the sunless realms of space
Reverberates the thunder of his bass.

Beneath the sky's triumphal arch
This music sounded like a march,
And with its chorus seemed to be
Preluding some great tragedy.
Sirius was rising in the east;
And, slow ascending one by one,
The kindling constellations shone.
Begirt with many a blazing star,
Stood the great giant Algebar,
Orion, hunter of the beast!
His sword hung gleaming by his side,
And, on his arm, the lion's hide
Scattered across the midnight air

The golden radiance of its hair.

The moon was pallid, but not faint;
And beautiful as some fair saint,
Serenely moving on her way
In hours of trial and dismay.
As if she heard the voice of God,
Unharmed with naked feet she trod
Upon the hot and burning stars,
As on the glowing coals and bars,
That were to prove her strength, and try
Her holiness and her purity.

Thus moving on, with silent pace,
And triumph in her sweet, pale face,
She reached the station of Orion.
Aghast he stood in strange alarm!
And suddenly from his outstretched arm
Down fell the red skin of the lion
Into the river at his feet.
His mighty club no longer beat
The forehead of the bull; but he
Reeled as of yore beside the sea,
When, blinded by Oenopion,
He sought the blacksmith at his forge,
And, climbing up the mountain gorge,
Fixed his blank eyes upon the sun.

Then, through the silence overhead,
An angel with a trumpet said,
"Forevermore, forevermore,
The reign of violence is o'er!"
And, like an instrument that flings
Its music on another's strings,
The trumpet of the angel cast
Upon the heavenly lyre its blast,
And on from sphere to sphere the words
Re-echoed down the burning chords, —
"Forevermore, forevermore,
The reign of violence is o'er!"

THE BRIDGE

I stood on the bridge at midnight,
  As the clocks were striking the hour,
And the moon rose o'er the city,
  Behind the dark church-tower.

I saw her bright reflection
  In the waters under me,
Like a golden goblet falling
  And sinking into the sea.

And far in the hazy distance
  Of that lovely night in June,
The blaze of the flaming furnace
  Gleamed redder than the moon.

Among the long, black rafters
  The wavering shadows lay,
And the current that came from the ocean
  Seemed to lift and bear them away;

As, sweeping and eddying through them,
Rose the belated tide,
And, streaming into the moonlight,
  The seaweed floated wide.

And like those waters rushing
  Among the wooden piers,
A flood of thoughts came o'er me
  That filled my eyes with tears.

How often, oh, how often,
  In the days that had gone by,
I had stood on that bridge at midnight
  And gazed on that wave and sky!

How often, oh, how often,
  I had wished that the ebbing tide
Would bear me away on its bosom
  O'er the ocean wild and wide!

For my heart was hot and restless,
  And my life was full of care,
And the burden laid upon me
  Seemed greater than I could bear.

But now it has fallen from me,
  It is buried in the sea;
And only the sorrow of others
  Throws its shadow over me.

Yet whenever I cross the river
  On its bridge with wooden piers,
Like the odor of brine from the ocean
  Comes the thought of other years.

And I think how many thousands
  Of care-encumbered men,
Each bearing his burden of sorrow,
  Have crossed the bridge since then.

I see the long procession
  Still passing to and fro,
The young heart hot and restless,
  And the old subdued and slow!

And forever and forever,
  As long as the river flows,
As long as the heart has passions,
  As long as life has woes;

The moon and its broken reflection
  And its shadows shall appear,
As the symbol of love in heaven,
  And its wavering image here.

TO THE DRIVING CLOUD

Gloomy and dark art thou, O chief of the mighty Omahas;
Gloomy and dark as the driving cloud, whose name thou hast taken!
Wrapt in thy scarlet blanket, I see thee stalk through the city's
Narrow and populous streets, as once by the margin of rivers
Stalked those birds unknown, that have left us only their footprints.
What, in a few short years, will remain of thy race but the footprints?

How canst thou walk these streets, who hast trod the green turf of
        the prairies!
How canst thou breathe this air, who hast breathed the sweet air of
        the mountains!
Ah! 't is in vain that with lordly looks of disdain thou dost challenge
Looks of disdain in return, and question these walls and these
        pavements,
Claiming the soil for thy hunting-grounds, while down-trodden
        millions
Starve in the garrets of Europe, and cry from its caverns that they,
        too,
Have been created heirs of the earth, and claim its division!

Back, then, back to thy woods in the regions west of the Wabash!
There as a monarch thou reignest. In autumn the leaves of the maple
Pave the floors of thy palace-halls with gold, and in summer
Pine-trees waft through its chambers the odorous breath of their
        branches.
There thou art strong and great, a hero, a tamer of horses!
There thou chasest the stately stag on the banks of the Elkhorn,
Or by the roar of the Running-Water, or where the Omaha
Calls thee, and leaps through the wild ravine like a brave of the
Blackfeet!

Hark! what murmurs arise from the heart of those mountainous
        deserts?
Is it the cry of the Foxes and Crows, or the mighty Behemoth,
Who, unharmed, on his tusks once caught the bolts of the thunder,
And now lurks in his lair to destroy the race of the red man?
Far more fatal to thee and thy race than the Crows and the Foxes,
Far more fatal to thee and thy race than the tread of Behemoth,
Lo! the big thunder-canoe, that steadily breasts the Missouri's
Merciless current! and yonder, afar on the prairies, the camp-fires

169

Gleam through the night; and the cloud of dust in the gray of the
     daybreak
Marks not the buffalo's track, nor the Mandan's dexterous horse-
     race;
It is a caravan, whitening the desert where dwell the Camanches!
Ha! how the breath of these Saxons and Celts, like the blast of the
     east-wind,
Drifts evermore to the west the scanty smokes of thy wigwams!

SONGS

THE DAY IS DONE

The day is done, and the darkness
  Falls from the wings of Night,
As a feather is wafted downward
  From an eagle in his flight.

I see the lights of the village
  Gleam through the rain and the mist,
And a feeling of sadness comes o'er me
  That my soul cannot resist:

A feeling of sadness and longing,
  That is not akin to pain,
And resembles sorrow only
  As the mist resembles the rain.

Come, read to me some poem,
  Some simple and heartfelt lay,
That shall soothe this restless feeling,
  And banish the thoughts of day.

Not from the grand old masters,
  Not from the bards sublime,
Whose distant footsteps echo
  Through the corridors of Time.

For, like strains of martial music,
  Their mighty thoughts suggest
Life's endless toil and endeavor;
  And to-night I long for rest.

Read from some humbler poet,
  Whose songs gushed from his heart,
As showers from the clouds of summer,
  Or tears from the eyelids start;

Who, through long days of labor,
  And nights devoid of ease,
Still heard in his soul the music

Of wonderful melodies.

Such songs have power to quiet
  The restless pulse of care,
And come like the benediction
  That follows after prayer.

Then read from the treasured volume
  The poem of thy choice,
And lend to the rhyme of the poet
  The beauty of thy voice.

And the night shall be filled with music
  And the cares, that infest the day,
Shall fold their tents, like the Arabs,
  And as silently steal away.

AFTERNOON IN FEBRUARY

The day is ending,
The night is descending;
The marsh is frozen,
The river dead.

Through clouds like ashes
The red sun flashes
On village windows
That glimmer red.

The snow recommences;
The buried fences
Mark no longer
The road o'er the plain;

While through the meadows,
Like fearful shadows,
Slowly passes
A funeral train.

The bell is pealing,
And every feeling
Within me responds
To the dismal knell;

Shadows are trailing,
My heart is bewailing
And tolling within
Like a funeral bell.

TO AN OLD DANISH SONG-BOOK

Welcome, my old friend,
Welcome to a foreign fireside,
While the sullen gales of autumn
Shake the windows.

The ungrateful world
Has, it seems, dealt harshly with thee,
Since, beneath the skies of Denmark,
First I met thee.

There are marks of age,
There are thumb-marks on thy margin,
Made by hands that clasped thee rudely,
At the alehouse.

Soiled and dull thou art;
Yellow are thy time-worn pages,
As the russet, rain-molested
Leaves of autumn.

Thou art stained with wine
Scattered from hilarious goblets,
As the leaves with the libations
Of Olympus.

Yet dost thou recall
Days departed, half-forgotten,
When in dreamy youth I wandered
By the Baltic, —

When I paused to hear
The old ballad of King Christian
Shouted from suburban taverns
In the twilight.

Thou recallest bards,
Who in solitary chambers,
And with hearts by passion wasted,
Wrote thy pages.

Thou recallest homes
Where thy songs of love and friendship
Made the gloomy Northern winter
Bright as summer.

Once some ancient Scald,
In his bleak, ancestral Iceland,
Chanted staves of these old ballads
To the Vikings.

Once in Elsinore,
At the court of old King Hamlet
Yorick and his boon companions
Sang these ditties.

Once Prince Frederick's Guard
Sang them in their smoky barracks;—
Suddenly the English cannon
Joined the chorus!

Peasants in the field,
Sailors on the roaring ocean,
Students, tradesmen, pale mechanics,
All have sung them.

Thou hast been their friend;
They, alas! have left thee friendless!
Yet at least by one warm fireside
Art thou welcome.

And, as swallows build
In these wide, old-fashioned chimneys,
So thy twittering songs shall nestle
In my bosom,—

Quiet, close, and warm,
Sheltered from all molestation,
And recalling by their voices
Youth and travel.

WALTER VON DER VOGELWEID

Vogelweid the Minnesinger,
  When he left this world of ours,
Laid his body in the cloister,
  Under Wurtzburg's minster towers.

And he gave the monks his treasures,
  Gave them all with this behest:
They should feed the birds at noontide
  Daily on his place of rest;

Saying, "From these wandering minstrels
  I have learned the art of song;
Let me now repay the lessons
  They have taught so well and long."

Thus the bard of love departed;
  And, fulfilling his desire,
On his tomb the birds were feasted
  By the children of the choir.

Day by day, o'er tower and turret,
  In foul weather and in fair,
Day by day, in vaster numbers,
  Flocked the poets of the air.

On the tree whose heavy branches
  Overshadowed all the place,
On the pavement, on the tombstone,
  On the poet's sculptured face,

On the cross-bars of each window,
  On the lintel of each door,
They renewed the War of Wartburg,
  Which the bard **had** fought before.

There they sang **their** merry carols,
  Sang their lauds **on every** side;
And the name **their** voices uttered
  Was the name of Vogelweid.

Till at length the portly abbot
  Murmured, "Why this waste of food?
Be it changed to loaves henceforward
  For our tasting brotherhood."

Then in vain o'er tower and turret,
  From the walls and woodland nests,
When the minster bells rang noontide,
  Gathered the unwelcome guests.

Then in vain, with cries discordant,
  Clamorous round the Gothic spire,
Screamed the feathered Minnesingers
  For the children of the choir.

Time has long effaced the inscriptions
  On the cloister's funeral stones,
And tradition only tells us
  Where repose the poet's bones.

But around the vast cathedral,
  By sweet echoes multiplied,
Still the birds repeat the legend,
  And the name of Vogelweid.

DRINKING SONG

INSCRIPTION FOR AN ANTIQUE PITCHER

Come, old friend! sit down and listen!
  From the pitcher, placed between us,
How the waters laugh and glisten
  In the head of old Silenus!

Old Silenus, bloated, drunken,
  Led by his inebriate Satyrs;
On his breast his head is sunken,
  Vacantly he leers and chatters.

Fauns with youthful Bacchus follow;
  Ivy crowns that brow supernal
As the forehead of Apollo,
  And possessing youth eternal.

Round about him, fair Bacchantes,
  Bearing cymbals, flutes, and thyrses,
Wild from Naxian groves, or Zante's
  Vineyards, sing delirious verses.

Thus he won, through all the nations,
  Bloodless victories, and the farmer
Bore, as trophies and oblations,
  Vines for banners, ploughs for armor.

Judged by no o'erzealous rigor,
  Much this mystic throng expresses:
Bacchus was the type of vigor,
  And Silenus of excesses.

These are ancient ethnic revels,
  Of a faith long since forsaken;
Now the Satyrs, changed to devils,
  Frighten mortals wine-o'ertaken.

Now to rivulets from the mountains
  Point the rods of fortune-tellers;
Youth perpetual dwells in fountains, —

Not in flasks, and casks, and cellars.

Claudius, though he sang of flagons
  And huge tankards filled with Rhenish,
From that fiery blood of dragons
  Never would his own replenish.

Even Redi, though he chaunted
  Bacchus in the Tuscan valleys,
Never drank the wine he vaunted
  In his dithyrambic sallies.

Then with water fill the pitcher
  Wreathed about with classic fables;
Ne'er Falernian threw a richer
  Light upon Lucullus' tables.

Come, old friend, sit down and listen
  As it passes thus between us,
How its wavelets laugh and glisten
  In the head of old Silenus!

THE OLD CLOCK ON THE STAIRS

L'eternite est une pendule, dont le balancier dit et redit sans cesse ces deux mots seulement dans le silence des tombeaux: "Toujours! jamais! Jamais! toujours!" —JACQUES BRIDAINE.

Somewhat back from the village street
Stands the old-fashioned country-seat.
Across its antique portico
Tall poplar-trees their shadows throw;
And from its station in the hall
An ancient timepiece says to all,—
      "Forever—never!
      Never—forever!"

Half-way up the stairs it stands,
And points and beckons with its hands
From its case of massive oak,
Like a monk, who, under his cloak,
Crosses himself, and sighs, alas!
With sorrowful voice to all who pass,—
      "Forever—never!
      Never—forever!"

By day its voice is low and light;
But in the silent dead of night,
Distinct as a passing footstep's fall,
It echoes along the vacant hall,
Along the ceiling, along the floor,
And seems to say, at each chamber-door,—
      "Forever—never!
      Never—forever!"

Through days of sorrow and of mirth,
Through days of death and days of birth,
Through every swift vicissitude
Of changeful time, unchanged it has stood,
And as if, like God, it all things saw,

It calmly repeats those words of awe, —
    "Forever—never!
    Never—forever!"

In that mansion used to be
Free-hearted Hospitality;
His great fires up the chimney roared;
The stranger feasted at his board;
But, like the skeleton at the feast,
That warning timepiece never ceased, —
    "Forever—never!
    Never—forever!"

There groups of merry children played,
There youths and maidens dreaming strayed;
O precious hours! O golden prime,
And affluence of love and time!
Even as a Miser counts his gold,
Those hours the ancient timepiece told, —
    "Forever—never!
    Never—forever!"

From that chamber, clothed in white,
The bride came forth on her wedding night;
There, in that silent room below,
The dead lay in his shroud of snow;
And in the hush that followed the prayer,
Was heard the old clock on the stair, —
    "Forever—never!
    Never—forever!"

All are scattered now and fled,
Some are married, some are dead;
And when I ask, with throbs of pain.
"Ah! when shall they all meet again?"
As in the days long since gone by,
The ancient timepiece makes reply, —
    "Forever—never!
    Never—forever!"

Never here, forever there,
Where all parting, pain, and care,
And death, and time shall disappear, —

Forever there, but never here!
The horologe of Eternity
Sayeth this incessantly, —
    "Forever—never!
    Never—forever!"

THE ARROW AND THE SONG

I shot an arrow into the air,
It fell to earth, I knew not where;
For, so swiftly it flew, the sight
Could not follow it in its flight.

I breathed a song into the air,
It fell to earth, I knew not where;
For who has sight so keen and strong,
That it can follow the flight of song?

Long, long afterward, in an oak
I found the arrow, still unbroke;
And the song, from beginning to end,
I found again in the heart of a friend.

SONNETS

MEZZO CAMMIN

Half of my life is gone, and I have let
  The years slip from me and have not fulfilled
  The aspiration of my youth, to build
  Some tower of song with lofty parapet.
Not indolence, nor pleasure, nor the fret
  Of restless passions chat would not be stilled,
  But sorrow, and a care that almost killed,
  Kept me from what I may accomplish yet;
Though, half way up the hill, I see the Past
  Lying beneath me with its sounds and sights, —
  A city in the twilight dim and vast,
With smoking roofs, soft bells, and gleaming lights. —
  And hear above me on the autumnal blast
  The cataract of Death far thundering from the heights.

THE EVENING STAR

Lo! in the painted oriel of the West,
  Whose panes the sunken sun incarnadines,
  Like a fair lady at her casement, shines
  The evening star, the star of love and rest!
And then anon she doth herself divest
  Of all her radiant garments, and reclines
  Behind the sombre screen of yonder pines,
  With slumber and soft dreams of love oppressed.
O my beloved, my sweet Hesperus!
  My morning and my evening star of love!
  My best and gentlest lady! even thus,
As that fair planet in the sky above,
  Dost thou retire unto thy rest at night,
  And from thy darkened window fades the light.

AUTUMN

Thou comest, Autumn, heralded by the rain,
  With banners, by great gales incessant fanned,
  Brighter than brightest silks of Samarcand,
  And stately oxen harnessed to thy wain!
Thou standest, like imperial Charlemagne,
  Upon thy bridge of gold; thy royal hand
  Outstretched with benedictions o'er the land,
  Blessing the farms through all thy vast domain!
Thy shield is the red harvest moon, suspended
  So long beneath the heaven's o'er-hanging eaves;
  Thy steps are by the farmer's prayers attended;
Like flames upon an altar shine the sheaves;
  And, following thee, in thy ovation splendid,
  Thine almoner, the wind, scatters the golden leaves!

DANTE

Tuscan, that wanderest through the realms of gloom,
  With thoughtful pace, and sad, majestic eyes,
  Stern thoughts and awful from thy soul arise,
  Like Farinata from his fiery tomb.
Thy sacred song is like the trump of doom;
  Yet in thy heart what human sympathies,
  What soft compassion glows, as in the skies
  The tender stars their clouded lamps relume!
Methinks I see thee stand, with pallid cheeks,
  By Fra Hilario in his diocese,
  As up the convent-walls, in golden streaks,
The ascending sunbeams mark the day's decrease;
  And, as he asks what there the stranger seeks,
  Thy voice along the cloister whispers, "Peace!"

CURFEW

I.

Solemnly, mournfully,
  Dealing its dole,
The Curfew Bell
  Is beginning to toll.

Cover the embers,
  And put out the light;
Toil comes with the morning,
  And rest with the night.

Dark grow the windows,
  And quenched is the fire;
Sound fades into silence, —
  All footsteps retire.

No voice in the chambers,
  No sound in the hall!
Sleep and oblivion
  Reign over all!

II.

The book is completed,
  And closed, like the day;
And the hand that has written it
  Lays it away.

Dim grow its fancies;
  Forgotten they lie;
Like coals in the ashes,
  They darken and die.

Song sinks into silence,
  The story is told,
The windows are darkened,
  The hearth-stone is cold.

Darker and darker
  The black shadows fall;
Sleep and oblivion
  Reign over all.

EVANGELINE

A TALE OF ACADIE

This is the forest primeval. The murmuring pines and the hemlocks,
Bearded with moss, and in garments green, indistinct in the twilight,
Stand like Druids of eld, with voices sad and prophetic,
Stand like harpers hoar, with beards that rest on their bosoms.
Loud from its rocky caverns, the deep-voiced neighboring ocean
Speaks, and in accents disconsolate answers the wail of the forest.

This is the forest primeval; but where are the hearts that beneath it
Leaped like the roe, when he hears in the woodland the voice of the huntsman?
Where is the thatch-roofed village, the home of Acadian farmers, —
Men whose lives glided on like rivers that water the woodlands,
Darkened by shadows of earth, but reflecting an image of heaven?
Waste are those pleasant farms, and the farmers forever departed!
Scattered like dust and leaves, when the mighty blasts of October
Seize them, and whirl them aloft, and sprinkle them far o'er the ocean.
Naught but tradition remains of the beautiful village of Grand-Pré.

Ye who believe in affection that hopes, and endures, and is patient,
Ye who believe in the beauty and strength of woman's devotion,
List to the mournful tradition, still sung by the pines of the forest;
List to a Tale of Love in Acadie, home of the happy.

Part the First

I

In the Acadian land, on the shores of the Basin of Minas,
Distant, secluded, still, the little village of Grand-Pré
Lay in the fruitful valley. Vast meadows stretched to the eastward,
Giving the village its name, and pasture to flocks without number.
Dikes, that the hands of the farmers had raised with labor incessant,
Shut out the turbulent tides; but at stated seasons the flood-gates

Opened, and welcomed the sea to wander at will o'er the meadows.
West and south there were fields of flax, and orchards and cornfields
Spreading afar and unfenced o'er the plain; and away to the northward
Blomidon rose, and the forests old, and aloft on the mountains
Sea-fogs pitched their tents, and mists from the mighty Atlantic
Looked on the happy valley, but ne'er from their station descended.
There, in the midst of its farms, reposed the Acadian village.
Strongly built were the houses, with frames of oak and of hemlock,
Such as the peasants of Normandy built in the reign of the Henries.
Thatched were the roofs, with dormer-windows; and gables projecting
Over the basement below protected and shaded the doorway.
There in the tranquil evenings of summer, when brightly the sunset
Lighted the village street, and gilded the vanes on the chimneys,
Matrons and maidens sat in snow-white caps and in kirtles
Scarlet and blue and green, with distaffs spinning the golden
Flax for the gossiping looms, whose noisy shuttles within doors
Mingled their sounds with the whir of the wheels and the songs of the maidens.
Solemnly down the street came the parish priest, and the children
Paused in their play to kiss the hand he extended to bless them.
Reverend walked he among them; and up rose matrons and maidens,
Hailing his slow approach with words of affectionate welcome.
Then came the laborers home from the field, and serenely the sun sank
Down to his rest, and twilight prevailed. Anon from the belfry
Softly the Angelus sounded, and over the roofs of the village
Columns of pale blue smoke, like clouds of incense ascending,
Rose from a hundred hearths, the homes of peace and contentment.
Thus dwelt together in love these simple Acadian farmers, —
Dwelt in the love of God and of man. Alike were they free from
Fear, that reigns with the tyrant, and envy, the vice of republics.
Neither locks had they to their doors, nor bars to their windows;
But their dwellings were open as day and the hearts of the owners;
There the richest was poor, and the poorest lived in abundance.

Somewhat apart from the village, and nearer the Basin of Minas,
Benedict Bellefontaine, the wealthiest farmer of Grand-Pré,
Dwelt on his goodly acres; and with him, directing his household,
Gentle Evangeline lived, his child, and the pride of the village.
Stalworth and stately in form was the man of seventy winters;
Hearty and hale was he, an oak that is covered with snow-flakes;
White as the snow were his locks, and his cheeks as brown as the oak-leaves.
Fair was she to behold, that maiden of seventeen summers.
Black were her eyes as the berry that grows on the thorn by the wayside,
Black, yet how softly they gleamed beneath the brown shade of her tresses!
Sweet was her breath as the breath of kine that feed in the meadows.
When in the harvest heat she bore to the reapers at noontide
Flagons of home-brewed ale, ah! fair in sooth was the maiden.
Fair was she when, on Sunday morn, while the bell from its turret
Sprinkled with holy sounds the air, as the priest with his hyssop
Sprinkles the congregation, and scatters blessings upon them,
Down the long street she passed, with her chaplet of beads and her missal,
Wearing her Norman cap, and her kirtle of blue, and the ear-rings,
Brought in the olden time from France, and since, as an heirloom,
Handed down from mother to child, through long generations.
But a celestial brightness—a more ethereal beauty—
Shone on her face and encircled her form, when, after confession,
Homeward serenely she walked with God's benediction upon her.
When she had passed, it seemed like the ceasing of exquisite music.

Firmly builded with rafters of oak, the house of the farmer
Stood on the side of a hill commanding the sea; and a shady
Sycamore grew by the door, with a woodbine wreathing around it.
Rudely carved was the porch, with seats beneath; and a footpath
Led through an orchard wide, and disappeared in the meadow.
Under the sycamore-tree were hives overhung by a penthouse,
Such as the traveller sees in regions remote by the roadside,
Built o'er a box for the poor, or the blessed image of Mary.
Farther down, on the slope of the hill, was the well with its moss-grown
Bucket, fastened with iron, and near it a trough for the horses.
Shielding the house from storms, on the north, were the barns and the farm-yard.
There stood the broad-wheeled wains and the antique ploughs and the harrows;
There were the folds for the sheep; and there, in his feathered seraglio,

Strutted the lordly turkey, and crowed the cock, with the selfsame
Voice that in ages of old had startled the penitent Peter.
Bursting with hay were the barns, themselves a village. In each one
Far o'er the gable projected a roof of thatch; and a staircase,
Under the sheltering eaves, led up to the odorous corn-loft.
There too the dove-cot stood, with its meek and innocent inmates
Murmuring ever of love; while above in the variant breezes
Numberless noisy weathercocks rattled and sang of mutation.

Thus, at peace with God and the world, the farmer of Grand-Pré
Lived on his sunny farm, and Evangeline governed his household.
Many a youth, as he knelt in church and opened his missal,
Fixed his eyes upon her as the saint of his deepest devotion;
Happy was he who might touch her hand or the hem of her garment!
Many a suitor came to her door, by the darkness befriended,
And, as he knocked and waited to hear the sound of her footsteps,
Knew not which beat the louder, his heart or the knocker of iron;
Or at the joyous feast of the Patron Saint of the village,
Bolder grew, and pressed her hand in the dance as he whispered
Hurried words of love, that seemed a part of the music.
But, among all who came, young Gabriel only was welcome;
Gabriel Lajeunesse. the son of Basil the blacksmith,
Who was a mighty man in the village, and honored of all men;
For, since the birth of time, throughout all ages and nations,
Has the craft of the smith been held in repute by the people.
Basil was Benedict's friend. Their children from earliest childhood
Grew up together as brother and sister; and Father Felician,
Priest and pedagogue both in the village, had taught them their letters
Out of the selfsame book, with the hymns of the church and the plain-song.
But when the hymn was sung, and the daily lesson completed,
Swiftly they hurried away to the forge of Basil the blacksmith.
There at the door they stood, with wondering eyes to behold him
Take in his leathern lap the hoof of the horse as a plaything,
Nailing the shoe in its place; while near him the tire of the cart-wheel
Lay like a fiery snake, coiled round in a circle of cinders.
Oft on autumnal eves, when without in the gathering darkness
Bursting with light seemed the smithy, through every cranny and crevice,
Warm by the forge within they watched the laboring bellows,

And as its panting ceased, and the sparks expired in the ashes,
Merrily laughed, and said they were nuns going into the chapel.
Oft on sledges in winter, as swift as the swoop of the eagle,
Down the hillside bounding, they glided away o'er the meadow.
Oft in the barns they climbed to the populous nests on the rafters,
Seeking with eager eyes that wondrous stone, which the swallow
Brings from the shore of the sea to restore the sight of its fledglings;
Lucky was he who found that stone in the nest of the swallow!
Thus passed a few swift years, and they no longer were children.
He was a valiant youth, and his face, like the face of the morning,
Gladdened the earth with its light, and ripened thought into action.
She was a woman now, with the heart and hopes of a woman.
"Sunshine of Saint Eulalie" was she called; for that was the sunshine
Which, as the farmers believed, would load their orchards with apples;
She, too, would bring to her husband's house delight and abundance,
Filling it with love and the ruddy faces of children.

II

Now had the season returned, when the nights grow colder and longer,
And the retreating sun the sign of the Scorpion enters.
Birds of passage sailed through the leaden air, from the ice-bound,
Desolate northern bays to the shores of tropical islands.
Harvests were gathered in; and wild with the winds of September
Wrestled the trees of the forest, as Jacob of old with the angel.
All the signs foretold a winter long and inclement.
Bees, with prophetic instinct of want, had hoarded their honey
Till the hives overflowed; and the Indian hunters asserted
Cold would the winter be, for thick was the fur of the foxes.
Such was the advent of autumn. Then followed that beautiful season,
Called by the pious Acadian peasants the Summer of All-Saints!
Filled was the air with a dreamy and magical light; and the landscape
Lay as if new-created in all the freshness of childhood.
Peace seemed to reign upon earth, and the restless heart of the ocean
Was for a moment consoled. All sounds were in harmony blended.
Voices of children at play, the crowing of cocks in the farm-yards,
Whir of wings in the drowsy air, and the cooing of pigeons,

All were subdued and low as the murmurs of love, and the great sun
Looked with the eye of love through the golden vapors around him;
While arrayed in its robes of russet and scarlet and yellow,
Bright with the sheen of the dew, each glittering tree of the forest
Flashed like the plane-tree the Persian adorned with mantles and jewels.

Now recommenced the reign of rest and affection and stillness.
Day with its burden and heat had departed, and twilight descending
Brought back the evening star to the sky, and the herds to the homestead.
Pawing the ground they came, and resting their necks on each other,
And with their nostrils distended inhaling the freshness of evening.
Foremost, bearing the bell, Evangeline's beautiful heifer,
Proud of her snow-white hide, and the ribbon that waved from her collar,
Quietly paced and slow, as if conscious of human affection.
Then came the shepherd back with his bleating flocks from the seaside,
Where was their favorite pasture. Behind them followed the watch-dog,
Patient, full of importance, and grand in the pride of his instinct,
Walking from side to side with a lordly air, and superbly
Waving his bushy tail, and urging forward the stragglers;
Regent of flocks was he when the shepherd slept; their protector,
When from the forest at night, through the starry silence the wolves howled.
Late, with the rising moon, returned the wains from the marshes,
Laden with briny hay, that filled the air with its odor.
Cheerily neighed the steeds, with dew on their manes and their fetlocks,
While aloft on their shoulders the wooden and ponderous saddles,
Painted with brilliant dyes, and adorned with tassels of crimson,
Nodded in bright array, like hollyhocks heavy with blossoms.
Patiently stood the cows meanwhile, and yielded their udders
Unto the milkmaid's hand; whilst loud and in regular cadence
Into the sounding pails the foaming streamlets descended.
Lowing of cattle and peals of laughter were heard in the farm-yard,
Echoed back by the barns. Anon they sank into stillness;
Heavily closed, with a jarring sound, the valves of the barn-doors,
Rattled the wooden bars, and all for a season was silent.

In-doors, warm by the wide-mouthed fireplace, idly the farmer
Sat in his elbow-chair and watched how the flames and the smoke-wreaths
Struggled together like foes in a burning city. Behind him,

Nodding and mocking along the wall, with gestures fantastic,
Darted his own huge shadow, and vanished away into darkness.
Faces, clumsily carved in oak, on the back of his arm-chair
Laughed in the flickering light; and the pewter plates on the dresser
Caught and reflected the flame, as shields of armies the sunshine.
Fragments of song the old man sang, and carols of Christmas,
Such as at home, in the olden time, his fathers before him
Sang in their Norman orchards and bright Burgundian vineyards.
Close at her father's side was the gentle Evangeline seated,
Spinning flax for the loom, that stood in the corner behind her.
Silent awhile were its treadles, at rest was its diligent shuttle,
While the monotonous drone of the wheel, like the drone of a bagpipe,
Followed the old man's song and united the fragments together.
As in a church, when the chant of the choir at intervals ceases,
Footfalls are heard in the aisles, or words of the priest at the altar,
So, in each pause of the song, with measured motion the clock clicked.

Thus as they sat, there were footsteps heard, and, suddenly lifted,
Sounded the wooden latch, and the door swung back on its hinges.
Benedict knew by the hob-nailed shoes it was Basil the blacksmith,
And by her beating heart Evangeline knew who was with him.
"Welcome!" the farmer exclaimed, as their footsteps paused on the threshold,
"Welcome, Basil, my friend! Come, take thy place on the settle
Close by the chimney-side, which is always empty without thee;
Take from the shelf overhead thy pipe and the box of tobacco;
Never so much thyself art thou as when through the curling
Smoke of the pipe or the forge thy friendly and jovial face gleams
Round and red as the harvest moon through the mist of the marshes."
Then, with a smile of content, thus answered Basil the blacksmith,
Taking with easy air the accustomed seat by the fireside:—
"Benedict Bellefontaine, thou hast ever thy jest and thy ballad!
Ever in cheerfullest mood art thou, when others are filled with
Gloomy forebodings of ill, and see only ruin before them.
Happy art thou, as if every day thou hadst picked up a horseshoe."
Pausing a moment, to take the pipe that Evangeline brought him,
And with a coal from the embers had lighted, he slowly continued:—
"Four days now are passed since the English ships at their anchors
Ride in the Gaspereau's mouth, with their cannon pointed against

us.
What their design may be is unknown; but all are commanded
On the morrow to meet in the church, where his Majesty's mandate
Will be proclaimed as law in the land. Alas! in the mean time
Many surmises of evil alarm the hearts of the people."
Then made answer the farmer: "Perhaps some friendlier purpose
Brings these ships to our shores. Perhaps the harvests in England
By untimely rains or untimelier heat have been blighted,
And from our bursting barns they would feed their cattle and children."
"Not so thinketh the folk in the village," said, warmly, the blacksmith,
Shaking his head, as in doubt; then, heaving a sigh, he continued:—
"Louisburg is not forgotten, nor Beau Séjour, nor Port Royal,
Many already have fled to the forest, and lurk on its outskirts,
Waiting with anxious hearts the dubious fate of tomorrow.
Arms have been taken from us, and warlike weapons of all kinds;
Nothing is left but the blacksmith's sledge and the scythe of the
mower."
Then with a pleasant smile made answer the jovial farmer:—
"Safer are we unarmed, in the midst of our flocks and our cornfields,
Safer within these peaceful dikes, besieged by the ocean,
Than our fathers in forts, besieged by the enemy's cannon.
Fear no evil, my friend, and to-night may no shadow of sorrow
Fall on this house and hearth; for this is the night of the contract.
Built are the house and the barn. The merry lads of the village
Strongly have built them and well; and, breaking the glebe round about them,
Filled the barn with hay, and the house with food for a twelvemonth.
René Leblanc will be here anon, with his papers and inkhorn.
Shall we not then be glad, and rejoice in the joy of our children?"
As apart by the window she stood, with her hand in her lover's,
Blushing Evangeline heard the words that her father had spoken,
And, as they died on his lips, the worthy notary entered.

III

Bent like a laboring oar, that toils in the surf of the ocean,
Bent, but not broken, by age was the form of the notary public;
Shocks of yellow hair, like the silken floss of the maize, hung

197

Over his shoulders; his forehead was high; and glasses with horn bows
Sat astride on his nose, with a look of wisdom supernal.
Father of twenty children was he, and more than a hundred
Children's children rode on his knee, and heard his great watch tick.
Four long years in the times of the war had he languished a captive,
Suffering much in an old French fort as the friend of the English.
Now, though warier grown, without all guile or suspicion,
Ripe in wisdom was he, but patient, and simple, and childlike.
He was beloved by all, and most of all by the children;
For he told them tales of the Loup-garou in the forest,
And of the goblin that came in the night to water the horses,
And of the white Létiche, the ghost of a child who unchristened
Died, and was doomed to haunt unseen the chambers of children;
And how on Christmas eve the oxen talked in the stable,
And how the fever was cured by a spider shut up in a nutshell,
And of the marvellous powers of four-leaved clover and horseshoes,
With whatsoever else was writ in the lore of the village.
Then up rose from his seat by the fireside Basil the blacksmith,
Knocked from his pipe the ashes, and slowly extending his right hand,
"Father Leblanc," he exclaimed, "thou hast heard the talk in the village,
And, perchance, canst tell us some news of these ships and their errand."
Then with modest demeanor made answer the notary public, —
"Gossip enough have I heard, in sooth, yet am never the wiser;
And what their errand may be I know not better than others.
Yet am I not of those who imagine some evil intention
Brings them here, for we are at peace; and why then molest us?"
"God's name!" shouted the hasty and somewhat irascible
            blacksmith;
"Must we in all things look for the how, and the why, and the wherefore?
Daily injustice is done, and might is the right of the strongest!"
But without heeding his warmth, continued the notary public, —
"Man is unjust, but God is just; and finally justice
Triumphs; and well I remember a story, that often consoled me,
When as a captive I lay in the old French fort at Port Royal."
This was the old man's favorite tale, and he loved to repeat it
When his neighbors complained that any injustice was done them.
"Once in an ancient city, whose name I no longer remember,
Raised aloft on a column, a brazen statue of Justice

198

Stood in the public square, upholding the scales in its left hand,
And in its right a sword, as an emblem that justice presided
Over the laws of the land, and the hearts and homes of the people.
Even the birds had built their nests in the scales of the balance,
Having no fear of the sword that flashed in the sunshine above them.
But in the course of time the laws of the land were corrupted;
Might took the place of right, and the weak were oppressed, and the mighty
Ruled with an iron rod. Then it chanced in a nobleman's palace
That a necklace of pearls was lost, and erelong a suspicion
Fell on an orphan girl who lived as a maid in the household.
She, after form of trial condemned to die on the scaffold,
Patiently met her doom at the foot of the statue of Justice.
As to her Father in heaven her innocent spirit ascended,
Lo! o'er the city a tempest rose; and the bolts of the thunder
Smote the statue of bronze, and hurled in wrath from its left hand
Down on the pavement below the clattering scales of the balance,
And in the hollow thereof was found the nest of a magpie,
Into whose clay-built walls the necklace of pearls was inwoven."
Silenced, but not convinced, when the story was ended, the blacksmith
Stood like a man who fain would speak, but findeth no language;
All his thoughts were congealed into lines on his face, as the vapors
Freeze in fantastic shapes on the window-panes in the winter.

Then Evangeline lighted the brazen lamp on the table,
Filled, till it overflowed, the pewter tankard with home-brewed
Nut-brown ale, that was famed for its strength in the village of Grand-Pré;
While from his pocket the notary drew his papers and inkhorn,
Wrote with a steady hand the date and the age of the parties,
Naming the dower of the bride in flocks of sheep and in cattle.
Orderly all things proceeded, and duly and well were completed,
And the great seal of the law was set like a sun on the margin.
Then from his leathern pouch the farmer threw on the table
Three times the old man's fee in solid pieces of silver;
And the notary rising, and blessing the bride and the bridegroom,
Lifted aloft the tankard of ale and drank to their welfare.
Wiping the foam from his lip, he solemnly bowed and departed,
While in silence the others sat and mused by the fireside,
Till Evangeline brought the draught-board out of its corner.

Soon was the game begun. In friendly contention the old men
Laughed at each lucky hit, or unsuccessful manoeuvre,
Laughed when a man was crowned, or a breach was made in the king-row.
Meanwhile apart, in the twilight gloom of a window's embrasure,
Sat the lovers, and whispered together, beholding the moon rise
Over the pallid sea, and the silvery mists of the meadows.
Silently one by one, in the infinite meadows of heaven,
Blossomed the lovely stars, the forget-me-nots of the angels.

Thus was the evening passed. Anon the bell from the belfry
Rang out the hour of nine, the village curfew, and straightway
Rose the guests and departed; and silence reigned in the household.
Many a farewell word and sweet good-night on the door-step
Lingered long in Evangeline's heart, and filled it with gladness.
Carefully then were covered the embers that glowed on the hearth-stone,
And on the oaken stairs resounded the tread of the farmer.
Soon with a soundless step the foot of Evangeline followed.
Up the staircase moved a luminous space in the darkness,
Lighted less by the lamp than the shining face of the maiden.
Silent she passed the hall, and entered the door of her chamber.
Simple that chamber was, with its curtains of white, and its clothes-press
Ample and high, on whose spacious shelves were carefully folded
Linen and woollen stuffs, by the hand of Evangeline woven.
This was the precious dower she would bring to her husband in marriage,
Better than flocks and herds, being proofs of her skill as a housewife.
Soon she extinguished her lamp, for the mellow and radiant moonlight
Streamed through the windows, and lighted the room, till the heart of the maiden
Swelled and obeyed its power, like the tremulous tides of the ocean.
Ah! she was fair, exceeding fair to behold, as she stood with
Naked snow-white feet on the gleaming floor of her chamber!
Little she dreamed that below, among the trees of the orchard,
Waited her lover and watched for the gleam of her lamp and her shadow.
Yet were her thoughts of him, and at times a feeling of sadness
Passed o'er her soul, as the sailing shade of clouds in the moonlight
Flitted across the floor and darkened the room for a moment.
And, as she gazed from the window, she saw serenely the moon pass
Forth from the folds of a cloud, and one star follow her footsteps,

As out of Abraham's tent young Ishmael wandered with Hagar!

IV

Pleasantly rose next morn the sun on the village of Grand-Pré.
Pleasantly gleamed in the soft, sweet air the Basin of Minas,
Where the ships, with their wavering shadows, were riding at anchor.
Life had long been astir in the village, and clamorous labor
Knocked with its hundred hands at the golden gates of the morning.
Now from the country around, from the farms and neighboring hamlets,
Came in their holiday dresses the blithe Acadian peasants.
Many a glad good-morrow and jocund laugh from the young folk
Made the bright air brighter, as up from the numerous meadows,
Where no path could be seen but the track of wheels in the greensward,
Group after group appeared, and joined, or passed on the highway.
Long ere noon, in the village all sounds of labor were silenced.
Thronged were the streets with people; and noisy groups at the house-doors
Sat in the cheerful sun, and rejoiced and gossiped together.
Every house was an inn, where all were welcomed and feasted;
For with this simple people, who lived like brothers together,
All things were held in common, and what one had was another's.
Yet under Benedict's roof hospitality seemed more abundant:
For Evangeline stood among the guests of her father;
Bright was her face with smiles, and words of welcome and gladness
Fell from her beautiful lips, and blessed the cup as she gave it.

Under the open sky, in the odorous air of the orchard,
Stript of its golden fruit, was spread the feast of betrothal.
There in the shade of the porch were the priest and the notary seated;
There good Benedict sat, and sturdy Basil the blacksmith.
Not far withdrawn from these, by the cider-press and the beehives,
Michael the fiddler was placed, with the gayest of hearts and of waistcoats.
Shadow and light from the leaves alternately played on his snow-white
Hair, as it waved in the wind; and the jolly face of the fiddler
Glowed like a living coal when the ashes are blown from the embers.
Gayly the old man sang to the vibrant sound of his fiddle,
Tous les Bourgeois de Chartres, and *Le Carillon de Dunquerque*,
And anon with his wooden shoes beat time to the music.

Merrily, merrily whirled the wheels of the dizzying dances
Under the orchard-trees and down the path to the meadows;
Old folk and young together, and children mingled among them.
Fairest of all the maids was Evangeline, Benedict's daughter!
Noblest of all the youths was Gabriel, son of the blacksmith!

So passed the morning away. And lo! with a summons sonorous
Sounded the bell from its tower, and over the meadows a drum beat.
Thronged erelong was the church with men. Without, in the churchyard,
Waited the women. They stood by the graves, and hung on the headstones
Garlands of autumn-leaves and evergreens fresh from the forest.
Then came the guard from the ships, and marching proudly among them
Entered the sacred portal. With loud and dissonant clangor
Echoed the sound of their brazen drums from ceiling and
casement, —
Echoed a moment only, and slowly the ponderous portal
Closed, and in silence the crowd awaited the will of the soldiers.
Then uprose their commander, and spake from the steps of the altar,
Holding aloft in his hands, with its seals, the royal commission.
"You are convened this day," he said, "by his Majesty's orders.
Clement and kind has he been; but how you have answered his kindness,
Let your own hearts reply! To my natural make and my temper
Painful the task is I do, which to you I know must be grievous.
Yet must I bow and obey, and deliver the will of our monarch;
Namely, that all your lands, and dwellings, and cattle of all kinds
Forfeited be to the crown; and that you yourselves from this province
Be transported to other lands. God grant you may dwell there
Ever as faithful subjects, a happy and peaceable people!
Prisoners now I declare you; for such is his Majesty's pleasure!"
As, when the air is serene in sultry solstice of summer,
Suddenly gathers a storm, and the deadly sling of the hailstones
Beats down the farmer's corn in the field and shatters his windows,
Hiding the sun, and strewing the ground with thatch from the house-roofs,
Bellowing fly the herds, and seek to break their enclosures;
So on the hearts of the people descended the words of the speaker.
Silent a moment they stood in speechless wonder, and then rose
Louder and ever louder a wail of sorrow and anger,
And, by one impulse moved, they madly rushed to the door-way.

Vain was the hope of escape; and cries and fierce imprecations
Rang through the house of prayer; and high o'er the heads of the others
Rose, with his arms uplifted, the figure of Basil the blacksmith,
As, on a stormy sea, a spar is tossed by the billows.
Flushed was his face and distorted with passion; and wildly he
shouted,—
"Down with the tyrants of England! we never have sworn them allegiance!
Death to these foreign soldiers, who seize on our homes and our harvests!"
More he fain would have said, but the merciless hand of a soldier
Smote him upon the mouth, and dragged him down to the pavement.

In the midst of the strife and tumult of angry contention,
Lo! the door of the chancel opened, and Father Felician
Entered, with serious mien, and ascended the steps of the altar.
Raising his reverend hand, with a gesture he awed into silence
All that clamorous throng; and thus he spake to his people;
Deep were his tones and solemn; in accents measured and mournful
Spake he, as, after the tocsin's alarum, distinctly the clock strikes.
"What is this that ye do, my children? what madness has seized you?
Forty years of my life have I labored among you, and taught you,
Not in word alone, but in deed, to love one another!
Is this the fruit of my toils, of my vigils and prayers and privations?
Have you so soon forgotten all lessons of love and forgiveness?
This is the house of the Prince of Peace, and would you profane it
Thus with violent deeds and hearts overflowing with hatred?
Lo! where the crucified Christ from his cross is gazing upon you!
See! in those sorrowful eyes what meekness and holy compassion!
Hark! how those lips still repeat the prayer, 'O Father, forgive them!'
Let us repeat that prayer in the hour when the wicked assail us,
Let us repeat it now, and say, 'O Father, forgive them!'"
Few were his words of rebuke, but deep in the hearts of his people
Sank they, and sobs of contrition succeeded the passionate outbreak,
While they repeated his prayer, and said, "O Father, forgive them!"

Then came the evening service. The tapers gleamed from the altar.
Fervent and deep was the voice of the priest, and the people responded,
Not with their lips alone, but their hearts; and the Ave Maria
Sang they, and fell on their knees, and their souls, with devotion translated,

Rose on the ardor of prayer, like Elijah ascending to heaven.

Meanwhile had spread in the village the tidings of ill, and on all sides
Wandered, wailing, from house to house the women and children.
Long at her father's door Evangeline stood, with her right hand
Shielding her eyes from the level rays of the sun, that, descending,
Lighted the village street with mysterious splendor, and roofed each
Peasant's cottage with golden thatch, and emblazoned its windows.
Long within had been spread the snow-white cloth on the table;
There stood the wheaten loaf, and the honey fragrant with wild-flowers;
There stood the tankard of ale, and the cheese fresh brought from the dairy,
And, at the head of the board, the great arm-chair of the farmer.
Thus did Evangeline wait at her father's door, as the sunset
Threw the long shadows of trees o'er the broad ambrosial meadows.
Ah! on her spirit within a deeper shadow had fallen,
And from the fields of her soul a fragrance celestial ascended, —
Charity, meekness, love, and hope, and forgiveness, and patience!
Then, all-forgetful of self, she wandered into the village,
Cheering with looks and words the mournful hearts of the women,
As o'er the darkening fields with lingering steps they departed,
Urged by their household cares, and the weary feet of their children.
Down sank the great red sun, and in golden, glimmering vapors
Veiled the light of his face, like the Prophet descending from Sinai.
Sweetly over the village the bell of the Angelus sounded.

Meanwhile, amid the gloom, by the church Evangeline lingered.
All was silent within; and in vain at the door and the windows
Stood she, and listened and looked, till, overcome by emotion,
"Gabriel!" cried she aloud with tremulous voice; but no answer
Came from the graves of the dead, nor the gloomier grave of the living.
Slowly at length she returned to the tenantless house of her father.
Smouldered the fire on the hearth, on the board was the supper untasted,
Empty and drear was each room, and haunted with phantoms of terror.
Sadly echoed her step on the stair and the floor of her chamber.
In the dead of the night she heard the disconsolate rain fall
Loud on the withered leaves of the sycamore-tree by the window.
Keenly the lightning flashed; and the voice of the echoing thunder
Told her that God was in heaven, and governed the world he created!

Then she remembered the tale she had heard of the justice of Heaven;
Soothed was her troubled soul, and she peacefully slumbered till morning.

V

Four times the sun had risen and set; and now on the fifth day
Cheerily called the cock to the sleeping maids of the farm-house.
Soon o'er the yellow fields, in silent and mournful procession,
Came from the neighboring hamlets and farms the Acadian women,
Driving in ponderous wains their household goods to the sea-shore,
Pausing and looking back to gaze once more on their dwellings,
Ere they were shut from sight by the winding road and the woodland.
Close at their sides their children ran, and urged on the oxen,
While in their little hands they clasped some fragments of playthings.

Thus to the Gaspereau's mouth they hurried; and there on the sea-beach
Piled in confusion lay the household goods of the peasants.
All day long between the shore and the ships did the boats ply;
All day long the wains came laboring down from the village.
Late in the afternoon, when the sun was near to his setting,
Echoed far o'er the fields came the roll of drums from the churchyard.
Thither the women and children thronged. On a sudden the church-doors
Opened, and forth came the guard, and marching in gloomy procession
Followed the long-imprisoned, but patient, Acadian farmers.
Even as pilgrims, who journey afar from their homes and their country,
Sing as they go, and in singing forget they are weary and wayworn,
So with songs on their lips the Acadian peasants descended
Down from the church to the shore, amid their wives and their daughters.
Foremost the young men came; and, raising together their voices,
Sang with tremulous lips a chant of the Catholic Missions:—
"Sacred heart of the Saviour! O inexhaustible fountain!
Fill our hearts this day with strength and submission and patience!"
Then the old men, as they marched, and the women that stood by the wayside
Joined in the sacred psalm, and the birds in the sunshine above them
Mingled their notes therewith, like voices of spirits departed.

Half-way down to the shore Evangeline waited in silence,
Not overcome with grief, but strong in the hour of affliction,—

Calmly and sadly she waited, until the procession approached her,
And she beheld the face of Gabriel pale with emotion.
Tears then filled her eyes, and, eagerly running to meet him,
Clasped she his hands, and laid her head on his shoulder, and
whispered,—
"Gabriel! be of good cheer! for if we love one another
Nothing, in truth, can harm us, whatever mischances may happen!"
Smiling she spake these words; then suddenly paused, for her father
Saw she slowly advancing. Alas! how changed was his aspect!
Gone was the glow from his cheek, and the fire from his eye, and his footstep
Heavier seemed with the weight of the heavy heart in his bosom.
But with a smile and a sigh, she clasped his neck and embraced him,
Speaking words of endearment where words of comfort availed not.
Thus to the Gaspereau's mouth moved on that mournful procession.

There disorder prevailed, and the tumult and stir of embarking.
Busily plied the freighted boats; and in the confusion
Wives were torn from their husbands, and mothers, too late, saw their children
Left on the land, extending their arms, with wildest entreaties.
So unto separate ships were Basil and Gabriel carried,
While in despair on the shore Evangeline stood with her father.
Half the task was not done when the sun went down, and the twilight
Deepened and darkened around; and in haste the refluent ocean
Fled away from the shore, and left the line of the sand-beach
Covered with waifs of the tide, with kelp and the slippery sea-weed.
Farther back in the midst of the household goods and the wagons,
Like to a gypsy camp, or a leaguer after a battle,
All escape cut off by the sea, and the sentinels near them,
Lay encamped for the night the houseless Acadian farmers.
Back to its nethermost caves retreated the bellowing ocean,
Dragging adown the beach the rattling pebbles, and leaving
Inland and far up the shore the stranded boats of the sailors.
Then, as the night descended, the herds returned from their pastures;
Sweet was the moist still air with the odor of milk from their udders;
Lowing they waited, and long, at the well-known bars of the farm-
yard,—
Waited and looked in vain for the voice and the hand of the milk-maid.
Silence reigned in the streets; from the church no Angelus sounded,

Rose no smoke from the roofs, and gleamed no lights from the windows.

But on the shores meanwhile the evening fires had been kindled,
Built of the drift-wood thrown on the sands from wrecks in the tempest.
Round them shapes of gloom and sorrowful faces were gathered,
Voices of women were heard, and of men, and the crying of children.
Onward from fire to fire, as from hearth to hearth in his parish,
Wandered the faithful priest, consoling and blessing and cheering,
Like unto shipwrecked Paul on Melita's desolate sea-shore.
Thus he approached the place where Evangeline sat with her father,
And in the flickering light beheld the face of the old man,
Haggard and hollow and wan, and without either thought or emotion,
E'en as the face of a clock from which the hands have been taken.
Vainly Evangeline strove with words and caresses to cheer him,
Vainly offered him food; yet he moved not, he looked not, he spake not,
But, with a vacant stare, ever gazed at the flickering fire-light.
"*Benedicite*!" murmured the priest, in tones of compassion.
More he fain would have said, but his heart was full, and his accents
Faltered and paused on his lips, as the feet of a child on a threshold,
Hushed by the scene he beholds, and the awful presence of sorrow.
Silently, therefore, he laid his hand on the head of the maiden,
Raising his tearful eyes to the silent stars that above them
Moved on their way, unperturbed by the wrongs and sorrows of mortals.
Then sat he down at her side, and they wept together in silence.

Suddenly rose from the south a light, as in autumn the blood-red
Moon climbs the crystal walls of heaven, and o'er the horizon
Titan-like stretches its hundred hands upon mountain and meadow,
Seizing the rocks and the rivers and piling huge shadows together.
Broader and ever broader it gleamed on the roofs of the village,
Gleamed on the sky and sea, and the ships that lay in the roadstead.
Columns of shining smoke uprose, and flashes of flame were
Thrust through their folds and withdrawn, like the quivering hands of a martyr.
Then as the wind seized the gleeds and the burning thatch, and, uplifting,
Whirled them aloft through the air, at once from a hundred house-tops
Started the sheeted smoke with flashes of flame intermingled.

These things beheld in dismay the crowd on the shore and on shipboard.

Speechless at first they stood, then cried aloud in their anguish,
"We shall behold no more our homes in the village of Grand-Pré!"
Loud on a sudden the cocks began to crow in the farm-yards,
Thinking the day had dawned; and anon the lowing of cattle
Came on the evening breeze, by the barking of dogs interrupted.
Then rose a sound of dread, such as startles the sleeping encampments
Far in the western prairies or forests that skirt the Nebraska,
When the wild horses affrighted sweep by with the speed of the whirlwind,
Or the loud bellowing herds of buffaloes rush to the river.
Such was the sound that arose on the night, as the herds and the horses
Broke through their folds and fences, and madly rushed o'er the meadows.

Overwhelmed with the sight, yet speechless, the priest and the maiden
Gazed on the scene of terror that reddened and widened before them;
And as they turned at length to speak to their silent companion,
Lo! from his seat he had fallen, and stretched abroad on the sea-shore
Motionless lay his form, from which the soul had departed.
Slowly the priest uplifted the lifeless head, and the maiden
Knelt at her father's side, and wailed aloud in her terror.
Then in a swoon she sank, and lay with her head on his bosom.
Through the long night she lay in deep, oblivious slumber;
And when she awoke from the trance, she beheld a multitude near her.
Faces of friends she beheld, that were mournfully gazing upon her,
Pallid, with tearful eyes, and looks of saddest compassion.
Still the blaze of the burning village illumined the landscape,
Reddened the sky overhead, and gleamed on the faces around her,
And like the day of doom it seemed to her wavering senses.
Then a familiar voice she heard, as it said to the people,—
"Let us bury him here by the sea. When a happier season
Brings us again to our homes from the unknown land of our exile,
Then shall his sacred dust be piously laid in the churchyard."
Such were the words of the priest. And there in haste by the sea-side,
Having the glare of the burning village for funeral torches,
But without bell or book, they buried the farmer of Grand-Pré.
And as the voice of the priest repeated the service of sorrow,
Lo! with a mournful sound, like the voice of a vast congregation,
Solemnly answered the sea, and mingled its roar with the dirges.
'T was the returning tide, that afar from the waste of the ocean,

With the first dawn of the day, came heaving and hurrying landward.
Then recommenced once more the stir and noise of embarking;
And with the ebb of the tide the ships sailed out of the harbor,
Leaving behind them the dead on the shore, and the village in ruins.

THE SEASIDE AND THE FIRESIDE

DEDICATION

As one who, walking in the twilight gloom,
  Hears round about him voices as it darkens,
And seeing not the forms from which they come,
  Pauses from time to time, and turns and hearkens;

So walking here in twilight, O my friends!
  I hear your voices, softened by the distance,
And pause, and turn to listen, as each sends
  His words of friendship, comfort, and assistance.

If any thought of mine, or sung or told,
  Has ever given delight or consolation,
Ye have repaid me back a thousand-fold,
  By every friendly sign and salutation.

Thanks for the sympathies that ye have shown!
  Thanks for each kindly word, each silent token,
That teaches me, when seeming most alone,
  Friends are around us, though no word be spoken.

Kind messages, that pass from land to land;
  Kind letters, that betray the heart's deep history,
In which we feel the pressure of a hand, —
  One touch of fire, — and all the rest is mystery!

The pleasant books, that silently among
  Our household treasures take familiar places,
And are to us as if a living tongue
  Spice from the printed leaves or pictured faces!

Perhaps on earth I never shall behold,
  With eye of sense, your outward form and semblance;
Therefore to me ye never will grow old,
  But live forever young in my remembrance.

Never grow old, nor change, nor pass away!
  Your gentle voices will flow on forever,
When life grows bare and tarnished with decay,

As through a leafless landscape flows a river.

Not chance of birth or place has made us friends,
  Being oftentimes of different tongues and nations,
But the endeavor for the selfsame ends,
  With the same hopes, and fears, and aspirations.

Therefore I hope to join your seaside walk,
  Saddened, and mostly silent, with emotion;
Not interrupting with intrusive talk
  The grand, majestic symphonies of ocean.

Therefore I hope, as no unwelcome guest,
  At your warm fireside, when the lamps are lighted,
To have my place reserved among the rest,
  Nor stand as one unsought and uninvited!

BY THE SEASIDE

THE BUILDING OF THE SHIP

"Build me straight, O worthy Master!
  Stanch and strong, a goodly vessel,
That shall laugh at all disaster,
  And with wave and whirlwind wrestle!"

The merchant's word
Delighted the Master heard;
For his heart was in his work, and the heart
Giveth grace unto every Art.

A quiet smile played round his lips,
As the eddies and dimples of the tide
Play round the bows of ships,
That steadily at anchor ride.
And with a voice that was full of glee,
He answered, "Erelong we will launch
A vessel as goodly, and strong, and stanch,
As ever weathered a wintry sea!"
And first with nicest skill and art,
Perfect and finished in every part,
A little model the Master wrought,
Which should be to the larger plan
What the child is to the man,
Its counterpart in miniature;
That with a hand more swift and sure
The greater labor might be brought
To answer to his inward thought.
And as he labored, his mind ran o'er
The various ships that were built of yore,
And above them all, and strangest of all
Towered the Great Harry, crank and tall,
Whose picture was hanging on the wall,
With bows and stern raised high in air,
And balconies hanging here and there,
And signal lanterns and flags afloat,
And eight round towers, like those that frown
From some old castle, looking down
Upon the drawbridge and the moat.

And he said with a smile, "Our ship, I wis,
Shall be of another form than this!"
It was of another form, indeed;
Built for freight, and yet for speed,
A beautiful and gallant craft;
Broad in the beam, that the stress of the blast,
Pressing down upon sail and mast,
Might not the sharp bows overwhelm;
Broad in the beam, but sloping aft
With graceful curve and slow degrees,
That she might be docile to the helm,
And that the currents of parted seas,
Closing behind, with mighty force,
Might aid and not impede her course.

In the ship-yard stood the Master,
  With the model of the vessel,
That should laugh at all disaster,
  And with wave and whirlwind wrestle!

Covering many a rood of ground,
Lay the timber piled around;
Timber of chestnut, and elm, and oak,
And scattered here and there, with these,
The knarred and crooked cedar knees;
Brought from regions far away,
From Pascagoula's sunny bay,
And the banks of the roaring Roanoke!
Ah! what a wondrous thing it is
To note how many wheels of toil
One thought, one word, can set in motion!
There's not a ship that sails the ocean,
But every climate, every soil,
Must bring its tribute, great or small,
And help to build the wooden wall!

The sun was rising o'er the sea,
And long the level shadows lay,
As if they, too, the beams would be
Of some great, airy argosy.
Framed and launched in a single day.
That silent architect, the sun,
Had hewn and laid them every one,

Ere the work of man was yet begun.
Beside the Master, when he spoke,
A youth, against an anchor leaning,
Listened, to catch his slightest meaning.
Only the long waves, as they broke
In ripples on the pebbly beach,
Interrupted the old man's speech.

Beautiful they were, in sooth,
The old man and the fiery youth!
The old man, in whose busy brain
Many a ship that sailed the main
Was modelled o'er and o'er again;—
The fiery youth, who was to be
the heir of his dexterity,
The heir of his house, and his daughter's hand,
When he had built and launched from land
What the elder head had planned.

"Thus," said he, "will we build this ship!
Lay square the blocks upon the slip,
And follow well this plan of mine.
Choose the timbers with greatest care;
Of all that is unsound beware;
For only what is sound and strong
to this vessel stall belong.
Cedar of Maine and Georgia pine
Here together shall combine.
A goodly frame, and a goodly fame,
And the UNION be her name!
For the day that gives her to the sea
Shall give my daughter unto thee!"

The Master's word
Enraptured the young man heard;
And as he turned his face aside,
With a look of joy and a thrill of pride,
Standing before
Her father's door,
He saw the form of his promised bride.
The sun shone on her golden hair,
And her cheek was glowing fresh and fair,
With the breath of morn and the soft sea air.

Like a beauteous barge was she,
Still at rest on the sandy beach,
Just beyond the billow's reach;
But he
Was the restless, seething, stormy sea!
Ah, how skilful grows the hand
That obeyeth Love's command!
It is the heart, and not the brain,
That to the highest doth attain,
And he who followeth Love's behest
Far excelleth all the rest!

Thus with the rising of the sun
Was the noble task begun
And soon throughout the ship-yard's bounds
Were heard the intermingled sounds
Of axes and of mallets, plied
With vigorous arms on every side;
Plied so deftly and so well,
That, ere the shadows of evening fell,
The keel of oak for a noble ship,
Scarfed and bolted, straight and strong
Was lying ready, and stretched along
The blocks, well placed upon the slip.
Happy, thrice happy, every one
Who sees his labor well begun,
And not perplexed and multiplied,
By idly waiting for time and tide!

And when the hot, long day was o'er,
The young man at the Master's door
Sat with the maiden calm and still.
And within the porch, a little more
Removed beyond the evening chill,
The father sat, and told them tales
Of wrecks in the great September gales,
Of pirates coasting the Spanish Main,
And ships that never came back again,
The chance and change of a sailor's life,
Want and plenty, rest and strife,
His roving fancy, like the wind,
That nothing can stay and nothing can bind,
And the magic charm of foreign lands,

With shadows of palms, and shining sands,
Where the tumbling surf,
O'er the coral reefs of Madagascar,
Washes the feet of the swarthy Lascar,
As he lies alone and asleep on the turf.
And the trembling maiden held her breath
At the tales of that awful, pitiless sea,
With all its terror and mystery,
The dim, dark sea, so like unto Death,
That divides and yet unites mankind!
And whenever the old man paused, a gleam
From the bowl of his pipe would awhile illume
The silent group in the twilight gloom,
And thoughtful faces, as in a dream;
And for a moment one might mark
What had been hidden by the dark,
That the head of the maiden lay at rest,
Tenderly, on the young man's breast!

Day by day the vessel grew,
With timbers fashioned strong and true,
Stemson and keelson and sternson-knee,
Till, framed with perfect symmetry,
A skeleton ship rose up to view!
And around the bows and along the side
The heavy hammers and mallets plied,
Till after many a week, at length,
Wonderful for form and strength,
Sublime in its enormous bulk,
Loomed aloft the shadowy hulk!
And around it columns of smoke, up-wreathing.
Rose from the boiling, bubbling, seething
Caldron, that glowed,
And overflowed
With the black tar, heated for the sheathing.
And amid the clamors
Of clattering hammers,
He who listened heard now and then
The song of the Master and his men:—

"Build me straight, O worthy Master.
  Stanch and strong, a goodly vessel,
That shall laugh at all disaster,

And with wave and whirlwind wrestle!"

With oaken brace and copper band,
Lay the rudder on the sand,
That, like a thought, should have control
Over the movement of the whole;
And near it the anchor, whose giant hand
Would reach down and grapple with the land,
And immovable and fast
Hold the great ship against the bellowing blast!
And at the bows an image stood,
By a cunning artist carved in wood,
With robes of white, that far behind
Seemed to be fluttering in the wind.
It was not shaped in a classic mould,
Not like a Nymph or Goddess of old,
Or Naiad rising from the water,
But modelled from the Master's daughter!
On many a dreary and misty night,
'T will be seen by the rays of the signal light,
Speeding along through the rain and the dark,
Like a ghost in its snow-white sark,
The pilot of some phantom bark,
Guiding the vessel, in its flight,
By a path none other knows aright!
Behold, at last,
Each tall and tapering mast
Is swung into its place;
Shrouds and stays
Holding it firm and fast!

Long ago,
In the deer-haunted forests of Maine,
When upon mountain and plain
Lay the snow,
They fell,—those lordly pines!
Those grand, majestic pines!
'Mid shouts and cheers
The jaded steers,
Panting beneath the goad,
Dragged down the weary, winding road
Those captive kings so straight and tall,
To be shorn of their streaming hair,

217

And, naked and bare,
To feel the stress and the strain
Of the wind and the reeling main,
Whose roar
Would remind them forevermore
Of their native forests they should not see again.

And everywhere
The slender, graceful spars
Poise aloft in the air,
And at the mast-head,
White, blue, and red,
A flag unrolls the stripes and stars.
Ah! when the wanderer, lonely, friendless,
In foreign harbors shall behold
That flag unrolled,
'T will be as a friendly hand
Stretched out from his native land,
Filling his heart with memories sweet and endless!

All is finished! and at length
Has come the bridal day
Of beauty and of strength.
To-day the vessel shall be launched!
With fleecy clouds the sky is blanched,
And o'er the bay,
Slowly, in all his splendors dight,
The great sun rises to behold the sight.

The ocean old,
Centuries old,
Strong as youth, and as uncontrolled,
Paces restless to and fro,
Up and down the sands of gold.
His beating heart is not at rest;
And far and wide,
With ceaseless flow,
His beard of snow
Heaves with the heaving of his breast.
He waits impatient for his bride.
There she stands,
With her foot upon the sands,
Decked with flags and streamers gay,

In honor of her marriage day,
Her snow-white signals fluttering, blending,
Round her like a veil descending,
Ready to be
The bride of the gray old sea.

On the deck another bride
Is standing by her lover's side.
Shadows from the flags and shrouds,
Like the shadows cast by clouds,
Broken by many a sunny fleck,
Fall around them on the deck.

The prayer is said,
The service read,
The joyous bridegroom bows his head;
And in tear's the good old Master
Shakes the brown hand of his son,
Kisses his daughter's glowing cheek
In silence, for he cannot speak,
And ever faster
Down his own the tears begin to run.
The worthy pastor—
The shepherd of that wandering flock,
That has the ocean for its wold,
That has the vessel for its fold,
Leaping ever from rock to rock—
Spake, with accents mild and clear,
Words of warning, words of cheer,
But tedious to the bridegroom's ear.
He knew the chart
Of the sailor's heart,
All its pleasures and its griefs,
All its shallows and rocky reefs,
All those secret currents, that flow
With such resistless undertow,
And lift and drift, with terrible force,
The will from its moorings and its course.
Therefore he spake, and thus said he:—
"Like unto ships far off at sea,
Outward or homeward bound, are we.
Before, behind, and all around,
Floats and swings the horizon's bound,

Seems at its distant rim to rise
And climb the crystal wall of the skies,
And then again to turn and sink,
As if we could slide from its outer brink.
Ah! it is not the sea,
It is not the sea that sinks and shelves,
But ourselves
That rock and rise
With endless and uneasy motion,
Now touching the very skies,
Now sinking into the depths of ocean.
Ah! if our souls but poise and swing
Like the compass in its brazen ring,
Ever level and ever true
To the toil and the task we have to do,
We shall sail securely, and safely reach
The Fortunate Isles, on whose shining beach
The sights we see, and the sounds we hear,
Will be those of joy and not of fear!"

Then the Master,
With a gesture of command,
Waved his hand;
And at the word,
Loud and sudden there was heard,
All around them and below,
The sound of hammers, blow on blow,
Knocking away the shores and spurs.
And see! she stirs!
She starts, — she moves, — she seems to feel
The thrill of life along her keel,
And, spurning with her foot the ground,
With one exulting, joyous bound,
She leaps into the ocean's arms!

And lo! from the assembled crowd
There rose a shout, prolonged and loud,
That to the ocean seemed to say,
"Take her, O bridegroom, old and gray,
Take her to thy protecting arms,
With all her youth and all her charms!"

How beautiful she is! How fair

She lies within those arms, that press
Her form with many a soft caress
Of tenderness and watchful care!
Sail forth into the sea, O ship!
Through wind and wave, right onward steer!
The moistened eye, the trembling lip,
Are not the signs of doubt or fear.

Sail forth into the sea of life,
O gentle, loving, trusting wife,
And safe from all adversity
Upon the bosom of that sea
Thy comings and thy goings be!
For gentleness and love and trust
Prevail o'er angry wave and gust;
And in the wreck of noble lives
Something immortal still survives!

Thou, too, sail on, O Ship of State!
Sail on, O UNION, strong and great!
Humanity with all its fears,
With all the hopes of future years,
Is hanging breathless on thy fate!
We know what Master laid thy keel,
What Workmen wrought thy ribs of steel,
Who made each mast, and sail, and rope,
What anvils rang, what hammers beat,
In what a forge and what a heat
Were shaped the anchors of thy hope!
Fear not each sudden sound and shock,
'T is of the wave and not the rock;
'T is but the flapping of the sail,
And not a rent made by the gale!
In spite of rock and tempest's roar,
In spite of false lights on the shore,
Sail on, nor fear to breast the sea
Our hearts, our hopes, are all with thee,
Our hearts, our hopes, our prayers, our tears,
Our faith triumphant o'er our fears,
Are all with thee,—are all with thee!

SEAWEED

When descends on the Atlantic
  The gigantic
Storm-wind of the equinox,
Landward in his wrath he scourges
  The toiling surges,
Laden with seaweed from the rocks:

From Bermuda's reefs; from edges
  Of sunken ledges,
In some far-off, bright Azore;
From Bahama, and the dashing,
  Silver-flashing
Surges of San Salvador;

From the tumbling surf, that buries
  The Orkneyan skerries,
Answering the hoarse Hebrides;
And from wrecks of ships, and drifting
  Spars, uplifting
On the desolate, rainy seas; —

Ever drifting, drifting, drifting
  On the shifting
Currents of the restless main;
Till in sheltered coves, and reaches
  Of sandy beaches,
All have found repose again.

So when storms of wild emotion
  Strike the ocean
Of the poet's soul, erelong
From each cave and rocky fastness,
  In its vastness,
Floats some fragment of a song:

Front the far-off isles enchanted,
  Heaven has planted
With the golden fruit of Truth;
From the flashing surf, whose vision
  Gleams Elysian

In the tropic clime of Youth;

From the strong Will, and the Endeavor
    That forever
Wrestle with the tides of Fate
From the wreck of Hopes far-scattered,
    Tempest-shattered,
Floating waste and desolate; —

Ever drifting, drifting, drifting
    On the shifting
Currents of the restless heart;
Till at length in books recorded,
    They, like hoarded
Household words, no more depart.

CHRYSAOR

Just above yon sandy bar,
  As the day grows fainter and dimmer,
Lonely and lovely, a single star
  Lights the air with a dusky glimmer

Into the ocean faint and far
  Falls the trail of its golden splendor,
And the gleam of that single star
  Is ever refulgent, soft, and tender.

Chrysaor, rising out of the sea,
  Showed thus glorious and thus emulous,
Leaving the arms of Callirrhoe,
  Forever tender, soft, and tremulous.

Thus o'er the ocean faint and far
  Trailed the gleam of his falchion brightly;
Is it a God, or is it a star
  That, entranced, I gaze on nightly!

THE SECRET OF THE SEA

Ah! what pleasant visions haunt me
  As I gaze upon the sea!
All the old romantic legends,
  All my dreams, come back to me.

Sails of silk and ropes of sandal,
  Such as gleam in ancient lore;
And the singing of the sailors,
  And the answer from the shore!

Most of all, the Spanish ballad
  Haunts me oft, and tarries long,
Of the noble Count Arnaldos
  And the sailor's mystic song.

Like the long waves on a sea-beach,
  Where the sand as silver shines,
With a soft, monotonous cadence,
  Flow its unrhymed lyric lines:—

Telling how the Count Arnaldos,
  With his hawk upon his hand,
Saw a fair and stately galley,
  Steering onward to the land;—

How he heard the ancient helmsman
  Chant a song so wild and clear,
That the sailing sea-bird slowly
  Poised upon the mast to hear,

Till his soul was full of longing,
  And he cried, with impulse strong,—
"Helmsman! for the love of heaven,
  Teach me, too, that wondrous song!"

"Wouldst thou,"—so the helmsman answered,
  "Learn the secret of the sea?
Only those who brave its dangers
  Comprehend its mystery!"

In each sail that skims the horizon,
  In each landward-blowing breeze,
I behold that stately galley,
  Hear those mournful melodies;

Till my soul is full of longing
  For the secret of the sea,
And the heart of the great ocean
  Sends a thrilling pulse through me.

TWILIGHT

The twilight is sad and cloudy,
  The wind blows wild and free,
And like the wings of sea-birds
  Flash the white caps of the sea.

But in the fisherman's cottage
  There shines a ruddier light,
And a little face at the window
  Peers out into the night.

Close, close it is pressed to the window,
  As if those childish eyes
Were looking into the darkness,
  To see some form arise.

And a woman's waving shadow
  Is passing to and fro,
Now rising to the ceiling,
  Now bowing and bending low.

What tale do the roaring ocean,
  And the night-wind, bleak and wild,
As they beat at the crazy casement,
  Tell to that little child?

And why do the roaring ocean,
  And the night-wind, wild and bleak,
As they beat at the heart of the mother,
  Drive the color from her cheek?

SIR HUMPHREY GILBERT

Southward with fleet of ice
  Sailed the corsair Death;
Wild and fast blew the blast,
  And the east-wind was his breath.

His lordly ships of ice
  Glisten in the sun;
On each side, like pennons wide,
  Flashing crystal streamlets run.

His sails of white sea-mist
  Dripped with silver rain;
But where he passed there were cast
  Leaden shadows o'er the main.

Eastward from Campobello
  Sir Humphrey Gilbert sailed;
Three days or more seaward he bore,
  Then, alas! the land-wind failed.

Alas! the land-wind failed,
  And ice-cold grew the night;
And nevermore, on sea or shore,
  Should Sir Humphrey see the light.

He sat upon the deck,
  The Book was in his hand
"Do not fear! Heaven is as near,"
  He said, "by water as by land!"

In the first watch of the night,
  Without a signal's sound,
Out of the sea, mysteriously,
  The fleet of Death rose all around.

The moon and the evening star
  Were hanging in the shrouds;
Every mast, as it passed,
  Seemed to rake the passing clouds.

They grappled with their prize,
  At midnight black and cold!
As of a rock was the shock;
  Heavily the ground-swell rolled.

Southward through day and dark,
  They drift in close embrace,
With mist and rain, o'er the open main;
  Yet there seems no change of place.

Southward, forever southward,
  They drift through dark and day;
And like a dream, in the Gulf-Stream
  Sinking, vanish all away.

THE LIGHTHOUSE

The rocky ledge runs far into the sea,
  And on its outer point, some miles away,
The Lighthouse lifts its massive masonry,
  A pillar of fire by night, of cloud by day.

Even at this distance I can see the tides,
  Upheaving, break unheard along its base,
A speechless wrath, that rises and subsides
  In the white lip and tremor of the face.

And as the evening darkens, lo! how bright,
  Through the deep purple of the twilight air,
Beams forth the sudden radiance of its light
  With strange, unearthly splendor in the glare!

Not one alone; from each projecting cape
  And perilous reef along the ocean's verge,
Starts into life a dim, gigantic shape,
  Holding its lantern o'er the restless surge.

Like the great giant Christopher it stands
  Upon the brink of the tempestuous wave,
Wading far out among the rocks and sands,
  The night-o'ertaken mariner to save.

And the great ships sail outward and return,
  Bending and bowing o'er the billowy swells,
And ever joyful, as they see it burn,
  They wave their silent welcomes and farewells.

They come forth from the darkness, and their sails
  Gleam for a moment only in the blaze,
And eager faces, as the light unveils,
  Gaze at the tower, and vanish while they gaze.

The mariner remembers when a child,
  On his first voyage, he saw it fade and sink;
And when, returning from adventures wild,
  He saw it rise again o'er ocean's brink.

Steadfast, serene, immovable, the same
  Year after year, through all the silent night
Burns on forevermore that quenchless flame,
  Shines on that inextinguishable light!

It sees the ocean to its bosom clasp
  The rocks and sea-sand with the kiss of peace;
It sees the wild winds lift it in their grasp,
  And hold it up, and shake it like a fleece.

The startled waves leap over it; the storm
  Smites it with all the scourges of the rain,
And steadily against its solid form
  Press the great shoulders of the hurricane.

The sea-bird wheeling round it, with the din
  Of wings and winds and solitary cries,
Blinded and maddened by the light within,
  Dashes himself against the glare, and dies.

A new Prometheus, chained upon the rock,
  Still grasping in his hand the fire of Jove,
It does not hear the cry, nor heed the shock,
  But hails the mariner with words of love.

"Sail on!" it says, "sail on, ye stately ships!
  And with your floating bridge the ocean span;
Be mine to guard this light from all eclipse,
  Be yours to bring man nearer unto man!"

THE FIRE OF DRIFT-WOOD

DEVEREUX FARM, NEAR MARBLEHEAD

We sat within the farm-house old,
  Whose windows, looking o'er the bay,
Gave to the sea-breeze, damp and cold,
  An easy entrance, night and day.

Not far away we saw the port,
  The strange, old-fashioned, silent town,
The lighthouse, the dismantled fort,
  The wooden houses, quaint and brown.

We sat and talked until the night,
  Descending, filled the little room;
Our faces faded from the sight,
  Our voices only broke the gloom.

We spake of many a vanished scene,
  Of what we once had thought and said,
Of what had been, and might have been,
  And who was changed, and who was dead;

And all that fills the hearts of friends,
  When first they feel, with secret pain,
Their lives thenceforth have separate ends,
  And never can be one again;

The first slight swerving of the heart,
  That words are powerless to express,
And leave it still unsaid in part,
  Or say it in too great excess.

The very tones in which we spake
  Had something strange, I could but mark;
The leaves of memory seemed to make
  A mournful rustling in the dark.

Oft died the words upon our lips,
  As suddenly, from out the fire
Built of the wreck of stranded ships,

The flames would leap and then expire.

And, as their splendor flashed and failed,
  We thought of wrecks upon the main,
Of ships dismasted, that were hailed
  And sent no answer back again.

The windows, rattling in their frames,
  The ocean, roaring up the beach,
The gusty blast, the bickering flames,
  All mingled vaguely in our speech.

Until they made themselves a part
  Of fancies floating through the brain,
The long-lost ventures of the heart,
  That send no answers back again.

O flames that glowed! O hearts that yearned!
  They were indeed too much akin,
The drift-wood fire without that burned,
  The thoughts that burned and glowed within.

BY THE FIRESIDE

RESIGNATION

There is no flock, however watched and tended,
  But one dead lamb is there!
There is no fireside, howsoe'er defended,
  But has one vacant chair!

The air is full of farewells to the dying,
  And mournings for the dead;
The heart of Rachel, for her children crying,
  Will not be comforted!

Let us be patient! These severe afflictions
  Not from the ground arise,
But oftentimes celestial benedictions
  Assume this dark disguise.

We see but dimly through the mists and vapors;
  Amid these earthly damps
What seem to us but sad, funereal tapers
  May be heaven's distant lamps.

There is no Death! What seems so is transition;
  This life of mortal breath
Is but a suburb of the life elysian,
  Whose portal we call Death.

She is not dead, — the child of our affection, —
  But gone unto that school
Where she no longer needs our poor protection,
  And Christ himself doth rule.

In that great cloister's stillness and seclusion,
  By guardian angels led,
Safe from temptation, safe from sin's pollution,
  She lives, whom we call dead.

Day after day we think what she is doing
  In those bright realms of air;
Year after year, her tender steps pursuing,

Behold her grown more fair.

Thus do we walk with her, and keep unbroken
  The bond which nature gives,
Thinking that our remembrance, though unspoken,
  May reach her where she lives.

Not as a child shall we again behold her;
  For when with raptures wild
In our embraces we again enfold her,
  She will not be a child;

But a fair maiden, in her Father's mansion,
  Clothed with celestial grace;
And beautiful with all the soul's expansion
  Shall we behold her face.

And though at times impetuous with emotion
  And anguish long suppressed,
The swelling heart heaves moaning like the ocean,
  That cannot be at rest, —

We will be patient, and assuage the feeling
  We may not wholly stay;
By silence sanctifying, not concealing,
  The grief that must have way.

THE BUILDERS

All are architects of Fate,
  Working in these walls of Time;
Some with massive deeds and great,
  Some with ornaments of rhyme.

Nothing useless is, or low;
  Each thing in its place is best;
And what seems but idle show
  Strengthens and supports the rest.

For the structure that we raise,
  Time is with materials filled;
Our to-days and yesterdays
  Are the blocks with which we build.

Truly shape and fashion these;
  Leave no yawning gaps between;
Think not, because no man sees,
  Such things will remain unseen.

In the elder days of Art,
  Builders wrought with greatest care
Each minute and unseen part;
  For the Gods see everywhere.

Let us do our work as well,
  Both the unseen and the seen;
Make the house, where Gods may dwell,
  Beautiful, entire, and clean.

Else our lives are incomplete,
  Standing in these walls of Time,
Broken stairways, where the feet
  Stumble as they seek to climb.

Build to-day, then, strong and sure,
  With a firm and ample base;
And ascending and secure
  Shall to-morrow find its place.

Thus alone can we attain
  To those turrets, where the eye
Sees the world as one vast plain,
  And one boundless reach of sky.

SAND OF THE DESERT IN AN HOUR-GLASS

A handful of red sand, from the hot clime
  Of Arab deserts brought,
Within this glass becomes the spy of Time,
  The minister of Thought.

How many weary centuries has it been
  About those deserts blown!
How many strange vicissitudes has seen,
  How many histories known!

Perhaps the camels of the Ishmaelite
  Trampled and passed it o'er,
When into Egypt from the patriarch's sight
  His favorite son they bore.

Perhaps the feet of Moses, burnt and bare,
  Crushed it beneath their tread;
Or Pharaoh's flashing wheels into the air
  Scattered it as they sped;

Or Mary, with the Christ of Nazareth
  Held close in her caress,
Whose pilgrimage of hope and love and faith
  Illumed the wilderness;

Or anchorites beneath Engaddi's palms
  Pacing the Dead Sea beach,
And singing slow their old Armenian psalms
  In half-articulate speech;

Or caravans, that from Bassora's gate
  With westward steps depart;
Or Mecca's pilgrims, confident of Fate,
  And resolute in heart!

These have passed over it, or may have passed!
  Now in this crystal tower
Imprisoned by some curious hand at last,
  It counts the passing hour,

And as I gaze, these narrow walls expand;
  Before my dreamy eye
Stretches the desert with its shifting sand,
  Its unimpeded sky.

And borne aloft by the sustaining blast,
  This little golden thread
Dilates into a column high and vast,
  A form of fear and dread.

And onward, and across the setting sun,
  Across the boundless plain,
The column and its broader shadow run,
  Till thought pursues in vain.

The vision vanishes! These walls again
  Shut out the lurid sun,
Shut out the hot, immeasurable plain;
  The half-hour's sand is run!

THE OPEN WINDOW

The old house by the lindens
  Stood silent in the shade,
And on the gravelled pathway
  The light and shadow played.

I saw the nursery windows
  Wide open to the air;
But the faces of the children,
  They were no longer there.

The large Newfoundland house-dog
  Was standing by the door;
He looked for his little playmates,
  Who would return no more.

They walked not under the lindens,
  They played not in the hall;
But shadow, and silence, and sadness
  Were hanging over all.

The birds sang in the branches,
  With sweet, familiar tone;
But the voices of the children
  Will be heard in dreams alone!

And the boy that walked beside me,
  He could not understand
Why closer in mine, ah! closer,
  I pressed his warm, soft hand!

KING WITLAF'S DRINKING-HORN

Witlaf, a king of the Saxons,
  Ere yet his last he breathed,
To the merry monks of Croyland
  His drinking-horn bequeathed, —

That, whenever they sat at their revels,
  And drank from the golden bowl,
They might remember the donor,
  And breathe a prayer for his soul.

So sat they once at Christmas,
  And bade the goblet pass;
In their beards the red wine glistened
  Like dew-drops in the grass.

They drank to the soul of Witlaf,
  They drank to Christ the Lord,
And to each of the Twelve Apostles,
  Who had preached his holy word.

They drank to the Saints and Martyrs
  Of the dismal days of yore,
And as soon as the horn was empty
  They remembered one Saint more.

And the reader droned from the pulpit
  Like the murmur of many bees,
The legend of good Saint Guthlac,
  And Saint Basil's homilies;

Till the great bells of the convent,
  From their prison in the tower,
Guthlac and Bartholomaeus,
  Proclaimed the midnight hour.

And the Yule-log cracked in the chimney,
  And the Abbot bowed his head,
And the flamelets flapped and flickered,
  But the Abbot was stark and dead.

Yet still in his pallid fingers
  He clutched the golden bowl,
In which, like a pearl dissolving,
  Had sunk and dissolved his soul.

But not for this their revels
  The jovial monks forbore,
For they cried, "Fill high the goblet!
  We must drink to one Saint more!"

GASPAR BECERRA

By his evening fire the artist
  Pondered o'er his secret shame;
Baffled, weary, and disheartened,
  Still he mused, and dreamed of fame.

'T was an image of the Virgin
  That had tasked his utmost skill;
But, alas! his fair ideal
  Vanished and escaped him still.

From a distant Eastern island
  Had the precious wood been brought
Day and night the anxious master
  At his toil untiring wrought;

Till, discouraged and desponding,
  Sat he now in shadows deep,
And the day's humiliation
  Found oblivion in sleep.

Then a voice cried, "Rise, O master!
  From the burning brand of oak
Shape the thought that stirs within thee!"
  And the startled artist woke,—

Woke, and from the smoking embers
  Seized and quenched the glowing wood;
And therefrom he carved an image,
  And he saw that it was good.

O thou sculptor, painter, poet!
  Take this lesson to thy heart:
That is best which lieth nearest;
  Shape from that thy work of art.

PEGASUS IN POUND

Once into a quiet village,
  Without haste and without heed,
In the golden prime of morning,
  Strayed the poet's winged steed.

It was Autumn, and incessant
  Piped the quails from shocks and sheaves,
And, like living coals, the apples
  Burned among the withering leaves.

Loud the clamorous bell was ringing
  From its belfry gaunt and grim;
'T was the daily call to labor,
  Not a triumph meant for him.

Not the less he saw the landscape,
  In its gleaming vapor veiled;
Not the less he breathed the odors
  That the dying leaves exhaled.

Thus, upon the village common,
  By the school-boys he was found;
And the wise men, in their wisdom,
  Put him straightway into pound.

Then the sombre village crier,
  Ringing loud his brazen bell,
Wandered down the street proclaiming
  There was an estray to sell.

And the curious country people,
  Rich and poor, and young and old,
Came in haste to see this wondrous
  Winged steed, with mane of gold.

Thus the day passed, and the evening
  Fell, with vapors cold and dim;
But it brought no food nor shelter,
  Brought no straw nor stall, for him.

Patiently, and still expectant,
  Looked he through the wooden bars,
Saw the moon rise o'er the landscape,
  Saw the tranquil, patient stars;

Till at length the bell at midnight
  Sounded from its dark abode,
And, from out a neighboring farm-yard
  Loud the cock Alectryon crowed.

Then, with nostrils wide distended,
  Breaking from his iron chain,
And unfolding far his pinions,
  To those stars he soared again.

On the morrow, when the village
  Woke to all its toil and care,
Lo! the strange steed had departed,
  And they knew not when nor where.

But they found, upon the greensward
  Where his straggling hoofs had trod,
Pure and bright, a fountain flowing
  From the hoof-marks in the sod.

From that hour, the fount unfailing
  Gladdens the whole region round,
Strengthening all who drink its waters,
  While it soothes them with its sound.

TEGNER'S DRAPA

I heard a voice, that cried,
"Balder the Beautiful
Is dead, is dead!"
And through the misty air
Passed like the mournful cry
Of sunward sailing cranes.

I saw the pallid corpse
Of the dead sun
Borne through the Northern sky.
Blasts from Niffelheim
Lifted the sheeted mists
Around him as he passed.

And the voice forever cried,
"Balder the Beautiful
Is dead, is dead!"
And died away
Through the dreary night,
In accents of despair.

Balder the Beautiful,
God of the summer sun,
Fairest of all the Gods!
Light from his forehead beamed,
Runes were upon his tongue,
As on the warrior's sword.

All things in earth and air
Bound were by magic spell
Never to do him harm;
Even the plants and stones;
All save the mistletoe,
The sacred mistletoe!

Hoeder, the blind old God,
Whose feet are shod with silence,
Pierced through that gentle breast
With his sharp spear, by fraud
Made of the mistletoe,

The accursed mistletoe!

They laid him in his ship,
With horse and harness,
As on a funeral pyre.
Odin placed
A ring upon his finger,
And whispered in his ear.

They launched the burning ship!
It floated far away
Over the misty sea,
Till like the sun it seemed,
Sinking beneath the waves.
Balder returned no more!

So perish the old Gods!
But out of the sea of Time
Rises a new land of song,
Fairer than the old.
Over its meadows green
Walk the young bards and sing.

Build it again,
O ye bards,
Fairer than before!
Ye fathers of the new race,
Feed upon morning dew,
Sing the new Song of Love!

The law of force is dead!
The law of love prevails!
Thor, the thunderer,
Shall rule the earth no more,
No more, with threats,
Challenge the meek Christ.

Sing no more,
O ye bards of the North,
Of Vikings and of Jarls!
Of the days of Eld
Preserve the freedom only,
Not the deeds of blood!

SONNET

ON MRS. KEMBLE'S READINGS FROM SHAKESPEARE

O precious evenings! all too swiftly sped!
  Leaving us heirs to amplest heritages
  Of all the best thoughts of the greatest sages,
  And giving tongues unto the silent dead!
How our hearts glowed and trembled as she read,
  Interpreting by tones the wondrous pages
  Of the great poet who foreruns the ages,
  Anticipating all that shall be said!
O happy Reader! having for thy text
  The magic book, whose Sibylline leaves have caught
  The rarest essence of all human thought!
O happy Poet! by no critic vext!
  How must thy listening spirit now rejoice
  To be interpreted by such a voice!

THE SINGERS

God sent his Singers upon earth
With songs of sadness and of mirth,
That they might touch the hearts of men,
And bring them back to heaven again.

The first, a youth, with soul of fire,
Held in his hand a golden lyre;
Through groves he wandered, and by streams,
Playing the music of our dreams.

The second, with a bearded face,
Stood singing in the market-place,
And stirred with accents deep and loud
The hearts of all the listening crowd.

A gray old man, the third and last,
Sang in cathedrals dim and vast,
While the majestic organ rolled
Contrition from its mouths of gold.

And those who heard the Singers three
Disputed which the best might be;
For still their music seemed to start
Discordant echoes in each heart,

But the great Master said, "I see
No best in kind, but in degree;
I gave a various gift to each,
To charm, to strengthen, and to teach.

"These are the three great chords of might,
And he whose ear is tuned aright
Will hear no discord in the three,
But the most perfect harmony."

SUSPIRIA

Take them, O Death! and bear away
  Whatever thou canst call thine own!
Thine image, stamped upon this clay,
  Doth give thee that, but that alone!

Take them, O Grave! and let them lie
  Folded upon thy narrow shelves,
As garments by the soul laid by,
  And precious only to ourselves!

Take them, O great Eternity!
  Our little life is but a gust
That bends the branches of thy tree,
  And trails its blossoms in the dust!

HYMN

FOR MY BROTHER'S ORDINATION

Christ to the young man said: "Yet one thing more;
  If thou wouldst perfect be,
Sell all thou hast and give it to the poor,
  And come and follow me!"

Within this temple Christ again, unseen,
  Those sacred words hath said,
And his invisible hands to-day have been
  Laid on a young man's head.

And evermore beside him on his way
  The unseen Christ shall move,
That he may lean upon his arm and say,
  "Dost thou, dear Lord, approve?"

Beside him at the marriage feast shall be,
  To make the scene more fair;
Beside him in the dark Gethsemane
  Of pain and midnight prayer.

O holy trust! O endless sense of rest!
  Like the beloved John
To lay his head upon the Saviour's breast,
  And thus to journey on!

THE SONG OF HIAWATHA
<Notes from HIAWATHA follow>

INTRODUCTION

Should you ask me, whence these stories?
Whence these legends and traditions,
With the odors of the forest
With the dew and damp of meadows,
With the curling smoke of wigwams,
With the rushing of great rivers,
With their frequent repetitions,
And their wild reverberations
As of thunder in the mountains?
  I should answer, I should tell you,
"From the forests and the prairies,
From the great lakes of the Northland,
From the land of the Ojibways,
From the land of the Dacotahs,
From the mountains, moors, and fen-lands
Where the heron, the Shuh-shuh-gah,
Feeds among the reeds and rushes.
I repeat them as I heard them
From the lips of Nawadaha,
The musician, the sweet singer."
  Should you ask where Nawadaha
Found these songs so wild and wayward,
Found these legends and traditions,
I should answer, I should tell you,
"In the bird's-nests of the forest,
In the lodges of the beaver,
In the hoof-prints of the bison,
In the eyry of the eagle!
  "All the wild-fowl sang them to him,
In the moorlands and the fen-lands,
In the melancholy marshes;
Chetowaik, the plover, sang them,
Mahng, the loon, the wild-goose, Wawa,
The blue heron, the Shuh-shuh-gah,
And the grouse, the Mushkodasa!"
  If still further you should ask me,
Saying, "Who was Nawadaha?

Tell us of this Nawadaha,"
I should answer your inquiries
Straightway in such words as follow.
  "In the vale of Tawasentha,
In the green and silent valley,
By the pleasant water-courses,
Dwelt the singer Nawadaha.
Round about the Indian village
Spread the meadows and the corn-fields,
And beyond them stood the forest,
Stood the groves of singing pine-trees,
Green in Summer, white in Winter,
Ever sighing, ever singing.
  "And the pleasant water-courses,
You could trace them through the valley,
By the rushing in the Spring-time,
By the alders in the Summer,
By the white fog in the Autumn,
By the black line in the Winter;
And beside them dwelt the singer,
In the vale of Tawasentha,
In the green and silent valley.
  "There he sang of Hiawatha,
Sang the Song of Hiawatha,
Sang his wondrous birth and being,
How he prayed and how he fasted,
How he lived, and toiled, and suffered,
That the tribes of men might prosper,
That he might advance his people!"
  Ye who love the haunts of Nature,
Love the sunshine of the meadow,
Love the shadow of the forest,
Love the wind among the branches,
And the rain-shower and the snow-storm,
And the rushing of great rivers
Through their palisades of pine-trees,
And the thunder in the mountains,
Whose innumerable echoes
Flap like eagles in their eyries;—
Listen to these wild traditions,
To this Song of Hiawatha!
  Ye who love a nation's legends,
Love the ballads of a people,

That like voices from afar off
Call to us to pause and listen,
Speak in tones so plain and childlike,
Scarcely can the ear distinguish
Whether they are sung or spoken;—
Listen to this Indian Legend,
To this Song of Hiawatha!
  Ye whose hearts are fresh and simple,
Who have faith in God and Nature,
Who believe that in all ages
Every human heart is human,
That in even savage bosoms
There are longings, yearnings, strivings
For the good they comprehend not,
That the feeble hands and helpless,
Groping blindly in the darkness,
Touch God's right hand in that darkness
And are lifted up and strengthened;—
Listen to this simple story,
To this Song of Hiawatha!
  Ye, who sometimes, in your rambles
Through the green lanes of the country,
Where the tangled barberry-bushes
Hang their tufts of crimson berries
Over stone walls gray with mosses,
Pause by some neglected graveyard,
For a while to muse, and ponder
On a half-effaced inscription,
Written with little skill of song-craft,
Homely phrases, but each letter
Full of hope and yet of heart-break,
Full of all the tender pathos
Of the Here and the Hereafter;—
Stay and read this rude inscription,
Read this Song of Hiawatha!

I

THE PEACE-PIPE

On the Mountains of the Prairie,
On the great Red Pipe-stone Quarry,
Gitche Manito, the mighty,

254

He the Master of Life, descending,
On the red crags of the quarry
Stood erect, and called the nations,
Called the tribes of men together.
  From his footprints flowed a river,
Leaped into the light of morning,
O'er the precipice plunging downward
Gleamed like Ishkoodah, the comet.
And the Spirit, stooping earthward,
With his finger on the meadow
Traced a winding pathway for it,
Saying to it, "Run in this way!"
  From the red stone of the quarry
With his hand he broke a fragment,
Moulded it into a pipe-head,
Shaped and fashioned it with figures;
From the margin of the river
Took a long reed for a pipe-stem,
With its dark green leaves upon it;
Filled the pipe with bark of willow,
With the bark of the red willow;
Breathed upon the neighboring forest,
Made its great boughs chafe together,
Till in flame they burst and kindled;
And erect upon the mountains,
Gitche Manito, the mighty,
Smoked the calumet, the Peace-Pipe,
As a signal to the nations.
  And the smoke rose slowly, slowly,
Through the tranquil air of morning,
First a single line of darkness,
Then a denser, bluer vapor,
Then a snow-white cloud unfolding,
Like the tree-tops of the forest,
Ever rising, rising, rising,
Till it touched the top of heaven,
Till it broke against the heaven,
And rolled outward all around it.
  From the Vale of Tawasentha,
From the Valley of Wyoming,
From the groves of Tuscaloosa,
From the far-off Rocky Mountains,
From the Northern lakes and rivers

All the tribes beheld the signal,
Saw the distant smoke ascending,
The Pukwana of the Peace-Pipe.
  And the Prophets of the nations
Said: "Behold it, the Pukwana!
By the signal of the Peace-Pipe,
Bending like a wand of willow,
Waving like a hand that beckons,
Gitche Manito, the mighty,
Calls the tribes of men together,
Calls the warriors to his council!"
  Down the rivers, o'er the prairies,
Came the warriors of the nations,
Came the Delawares and Mohawks,
Came the Choctaws and Camanches,
Came the Shoshonies and Blackfeet,
Came the Pawnees and Omahas,
Came the Mandans and Dacotahs,
Came the Hurons and Ojibways,
All the warriors drawn together
By the signal of the Peace-Pipe,
To the Mountains of the Prairie,
To the great Red Pipe-stone Quarry.
  And they stood there on the meadow,
With their weapons and their war-gear,
Painted like the leaves of Autumn,
Painted like the sky of morning,
Wildly glaring at each other;
In their faces stern defiance,
In their hearts the feuds of ages,
The hereditary hatred,
The ancestral thirst of vengeance.
  Gitche Manito, the mighty,
The creator of the nations,
Looked upon them with compassion,
With paternal love and pity;
Looked upon their wrath and wrangling
But as quarrels among children,
But as feuds and fights of children!
  Over them he stretched his right hand,
To subdue their stubborn natures,
To allay their thirst and fever,
By the shadow of his right hand;

Spake to them with voice majestic
As the sound of far-off waters,
Falling into deep abysses,
Warning, chiding, spake in this wise:—
  "O my children! my poor children!
Listen to the words of wisdom,
Listen to the words of warning,
From the lips of the Great Spirit,
From the Master of Life, who made you!
  "I have given you lands to hunt in,
I have given you streams to fish in,
I have given you bear and bison,
I have given you roe and reindeer,
I have given you brant and beaver,
Filled the marshes full of wild-fowl,
Filled the rivers full of fishes:
Why then are you not contented?
Why then will you hunt each other?
  "I am weary of your quarrels,
Weary of your wars and bloodshed,
Weary of your prayers for vengeance,
Of your wranglings and dissensions;
All your strength is in your union,
All your danger is in discord;
Therefore be at peace henceforward,
And as brothers live together.
  "I will send a Prophet to you,
A Deliverer of the nations,
Who shall guide you and shall teach you,
Who shall toil and suffer with you.
If you listen to his counsels,
You will multiply and prosper;
If his warnings pass unheeded,
You will fade away and perish!
  "Bathe now in the stream before you,
Wash the war-paint from your faces,
Wash the blood-stains from your fingers,
Bury your war-clubs and your weapons,
Break the red stone from this quarry,
Mould and make it into Peace-Pipes,
Take the reeds that grow beside you,
Deck them with your brightest feathers,
Smoke the calumet together,

And as brothers live henceforward!"
  Then upon the ground the warriors
Threw their cloaks and shirts of deer-skin,
Threw their weapons and their war-gear,
Leaped into the rushing river,
Washed the war-paint from their faces.
Clear above them flowed the water,
Clear and limpid from the footprints
Of the Master of Life descending;
Dark below them flowed the water,
Soiled and stained with streaks of crimson,
As if blood were mingled with it!
  From the river came the warriors,
Clean and washed from all their war-paint;
On the banks their clubs they buried,
Buried all their warlike weapons.
Gitche Manito, the mighty,
The Great Spirit, the creator,
Smiled upon his helpless children!
  And in silence all the warriors
Broke the red stone of the quarry,
Smoothed and formed it into Peace-Pipes,
Broke the long reeds by the river,
Decked them with their brightest feathers,
And departed each one homeward,
While the Master of Life, ascending,
Through the opening of cloud-curtains,
Through the doorways of the heaven,
Vanished from before their faces,
In the smoke that rolled around him,
The Pukwana of the Peace-Pipe!

                    II

The Four Winds

"Honor be to Mudjekeewis!"
Cried the warriors, cried the old men,
When he came in triumph homeward
With the sacred Belt of Wampum,
From the regions of the North-Wind,
From the kingdom of Wabasso,
From the land of the White Rabbit.

He had stolen the Belt of Wampum
From the neck of Mishe-Mokwa,
From the Great Bear of the mountains,
From the terror of the nations,
As he lay asleep and cumbrous
On the summit of the mountains,
Like a rock with mosses on it,
Spotted brown and gray with mosses.
  Silently he stole upon him,
Till the red nails of the monster
Almost touched him, almost scared him,
Till the hot breath of his nostrils
Warmed the hands of Mudjekeewis,
As he drew the Belt of Wampum
Over the round ears, that heard not,
Over the small eyes, that saw not,
Over the long nose and nostrils,
The black muffle of the nostrils,
Out of which the heavy breathing
Warmed the hands of Mudjekeewis.
  Then he swung aloft his war-club,
Shouted loud and long his war-cry,
Smote the mighty Mishe-Mokwa
In the middle of the forehead,
Right between the eyes he smote him.
  With the heavy blow bewildered,
Rose the Great Bear of the mountains;
But his knees beneath him trembled,
And he whimpered like a woman,
As he reeled and staggered forward,
As he sat upon his haunches;
And the mighty Mudjekeewis,
Standing fearlessly before him,
Taunted him in loud derision,
Spake disdainfully in this wise:—
  "Hark you, Bear! you are a coward;
And no Brave, as you pretended;
Else you would not cry and whimper
Like a miserable woman!
Bear! you know our tribes are hostile,
Long have been at war together;
Now you find that we are strongest,
You go sneaking in the forest,

You go hiding in the mountains!
Had you conquered me in battle
Not a groan would I have uttered;
But you, Bear! sit here and whimper,
And disgrace your tribe by crying,
Like a wretched Shaugodaya,
Like a cowardly old woman!"
  Then again he raised his war-club,
Smote again the Mishe-Mokwa
In the middle of his forehead,
Broke his skull, as ice is broken
When one goes to fish in Winter.
Thus was slain the Mishe-Mokwa,
He the Great Bear of the mountains,
He the terror of the nations.
  "Honor be to Mudjekeewis!"
With a shout exclaimed the people,
"Honor be to Mudjekeewis!
Henceforth he shall be the West-Wind,
And hereafter and forever
Shall he hold supreme dominion
Over all the winds of heaven.
Call him no more Mudjekeewis,
Call him Kabeyun, the West-Wind!"
  Thus was Mudjekeewis chosen
Father of the Winds of Heaven.
For himself he kept the West-Wind,
Gave the others to his children;
Unto Wabun gave the East-Wind,
Gave the South to Shawondasee,
And the North-Wind, wild and cruel,
To the fierce Kabibonokka.
  Young and beautiful was Wabun;
He it was who brought the morning,
He it was whose silver arrows
Chased the dark o'er hill and valley;
He it was whose cheeks were painted
With the brightest streaks of crimson,
And whose voice awoke the village,
Called the deer, and called the hunter.
  Lonely in the sky was Wabun;
Though the birds sang gayly to him,
Though the wild-flowers of the meadow

Filled the air with odors for him,
Though the forests and the rivers
Sang and shouted at his coming,
Still his heart was sad within him,
For he was alone in heaven.
  But one morning, gazing earthward,
While the village still was sleeping,
And the fog lay on the river,
Like a ghost, that goes at sunrise,
He beheld a maiden walking
All alone upon a meadow,
Gathering water-flags and rushes
By a river in the meadow.
  Every morning, gazing earthward,
Still the first thing he beheld there
Was her blue eyes looking at him,
Two blue lakes among the rushes.
And he loved the lonely maiden,
Who thus waited for his coming;
For they both were solitary,
She on earth and he in heaven.
  And he wooed her with caresses,
Wooed her with his smile of sunshine,
With his flattering words he wooed her,
With his sighing and his singing,
Gentlest whispers in the branches,
Softest music, sweetest odors,
Till he drew her to his bosom,
Folded in his robes of crimson,
Till into a star he changed her,
Trembling still upon his bosom;
And forever in the heavens
They are seen together walking,
Wabun and the Wabun-Annung,
Wabun and the Star of Morning.
  But the fierce Kabibonokka
Had his dwelling among icebergs,
In the everlasting snow-drifts,
In the kingdom of Wabasso,
In the land of the White Rabbit.
He it was whose hand in Autumn
Painted all the trees with scarlet,
Stained the leaves with red and yellow;

He it was who sent the snow-flake,
Sifting, hissing through the forest,
Froze the ponds, the lakes, the rivers,
Drove the loon and sea-gull southward,
Drove the cormorant and curlew
To their nests of sedge and sea-tang
In the realms of Shawondasee.
  Once the fierce Kabibonokka
Issued from his lodge of snow-drifts
From his home among the icebergs,
And his hair, with snow besprinkled,
Streamed behind him like a river,
Like a black and wintry river,
As he howled and hurried southward,
Over frozen lakes and moorlands.
  There among the reeds and rushes
Found he Shingebis, the diver,
Trailing strings of fish behind him,
O'er the frozen fens and moorlands,
Lingering still among the moorlands,
Though his tribe had long departed
To the land of Shawondasee.
  Cried the fierce Kabibonokka,
"Who is this that dares to brave me?
Dares to stay in my dominions,
When the Wawa has departed,
When the wild-goose has gone southward,
And the heron, the Shuh-shuh-gah,
Long ago departed southward?
I will go into his wigwam,
I will put his smouldering fire out!"
  And at night Kabibonokka,
To the lodge came wild and wailing,
Heaped the snow in drifts about it,
Shouted down into the smoke-flue,
Shook the lodge-poles in his fury,
Flapped the curtain of the door-way.
Shingebis, the diver, feared not,
Shingebis, the diver, cared not;
Four great logs had he for firewood,
One for each moon of the winter,
And for food the fishes served him.
By his blazing fire he sat there,

Warm and merry, eating, laughing,
Singing, "O Kabibonokka,
You are but my fellow-mortal!"
    Then Kabibonokka entered,
And though Shingebis, the diver,
Felt his presence by the coldness,
Felt his icy breath upon him,
Still he did not cease his singing,
Still he did not leave his laughing,
Only turned the log a little,
Only made the fire burn brighter,
Made the sparks fly up the smoke-flue.
    From Kabibonokka's forehead,
From his snow-besprinkled tresses,
Drops of sweat fell fast and heavy,
Making dints upon the ashes,
As along the eaves of lodges,
As from drooping boughs of hemlock,
Drips the melting snow in spring-time,
Making hollows in the snow-drifts.
    Till at last he rose defeated,
Could not bear the heat and laughter,
Could not bear the merry singing,
But rushed headlong through the door-way,
Stamped upon the crusted snow-drifts,
Stamped upon the lakes and rivers,
Made the snow upon them harder,
Made the ice upon them thicker,
Challenged Shingebis, the diver,
To come forth and wrestle with him,
To come forth and wrestle naked
On the frozen fens and moorlands.
    Forth went Shingebis, the diver,
Wrestled all night with the North-Wind,
Wrestled naked on the moorlands
With the fierce Kabibonokka,
Till his panting breath grew fainter,
Till his frozen grasp grew feebler,
Till he reeled and staggered backward,
And retreated, baffled, beaten,
To the kingdom of Wabasso,
To the land of the White Rabbit,
Hearing still the gusty laughter,

Hearing Shingebis, the diver,
Singing, "O Kabibonokka,
You are but my fellow-mortal!"
  Shawondasee, fat and lazy,
Had his dwelling far to southward,
In the drowsy, dreamy sunshine,
In the never-ending Summer.
He it was who sent the wood-birds,
Sent the robin, the Opechee,
Sent the bluebird, the Owaissa,
Sent the Shawshaw, sent the swallow,
Sent the wild-goose, Wawa, northward,
Sent the melons and tobacco,
And the grapes in purple clusters.
  From his pipe the smoke ascending
Filled the sky with haze and vapor,
Filled the air with dreamy softness,
Gave a twinkle to the water,
Touched the rugged hills with smoothness,
Brought the tender Indian Summer
To the melancholy north-land,
In the dreary Moon of Snow-shoes.
  Listless, careless Shawondasee!
In his life he had one shadow,
In his heart one sorrow had he.
Once, as he was gazing northward,
Far away upon a prairie
He beheld a maiden standing,
Saw a tall and slender maiden
All alone upon a prairie;
Brightest green were all her garments,
And her hair was like the sunshine.
  Day by day he gazed upon her,
Day by day he sighed with passion,
Day by day his heart within him
Grew more hot with love and longing
For the maid with yellow tresses.
But he was too fat and lazy
To bestir himself and woo her;
Yes, too indolent and easy
To pursue her and persuade her;
So he only gazed upon her,
Only sat and sighed with passion

For the maiden of the prairie.
  Till one morning, looking northward,
He beheld her yellow tresses
Changed and covered o'er with whiteness,
Covered as with whitest snow-flakes.
"Ah! my brother from the North-land,
From the kingdom of Wabasso,
From the land of the White Rabbit!
You have stolen the maiden from me,
You have laid your hand upon her,
You have wooed and won my maiden,
With your stories of the North-land!"
  Thus the wretched Shawondasee
Breathed into the air his sorrow;
And the South-Wind o'er the prairie
Wandered warm with sighs of passion,
With the sighs of Shawondasee,
Till the air seemed full of snow-flakes,
Full of thistle-down the prairie,
And the maid with hair like sunshine
Vanished from his sight forever;
Never more did Shawondasee
See the maid with yellow tresses!
  Poor, deluded Shawondasee!
'T was no woman that you gazed at,
'T was no maiden that you sighed for,
'T was the prairie dandelion
That through all the dreamy Summer
You had gazed at with such longing,
You had sighed for with such passion,
And had puffed away forever,
Blown into the air with sighing.
Ah! deluded Shawondasee!
  Thus the Four Winds were divided;
Thus the sons of Mudjekeewis
Had their stations in the heavens,
At the corners of the heavens;
For himself the West-Wind only
Kept the mighty Mudjekeewis.

III

HIAWATHA'S CHILDHOOD

Downward through the evening twilight,
In the days that are forgotten,
In the unremembered ages,
From the full moon fell Nokomis,
Fell the beautiful Nokomis,
She a wife, but not a mother.
  She was sporting with her women,
Swinging in a swing of grape-vines,
When her rival, the rejected,
Full of jealousy and hatred,
Cut the leafy swing asunder,
Cut in twain the twisted grape-vines,
And Nokomis fell affrighted
Downward through the evening twilight,
On the Muskoday, the meadow,
On the prairie full of blossoms.
"See! a star falls!" said the people;
"From the sky a star is falling!"
  There among the ferns and mosses,
There among the prairie lilies,
On the Muskoday, the meadow,
In the moonlight and the starlight,
Fair Nokomis bore a daughter.
And she called her name Wenonah,
As the first-born of her daughters.
And the daughter of Nokomis
Grew up like the prairie lilies,
Grew a tall and slender maiden,
With the beauty of the moonlight,
With the beauty of the starlight.
  And Nokomis warned her often,
Saying oft, and oft repeating,
"Oh, beware of Mudjekeewis,
Of the West-Wind, Mudjekeewis;
Listen not to what he tells you;
Lie not down upon the meadow,
Stoop not down among the lilies,
Lest the West-Wind come and harm you!"
  But she heeded not the warning,

Heeded not those words of wisdom,
And the West-Wind came at evening,
Walking lightly o'er the prairie,
Whispering to the leaves and blossoms,
Bending low the flowers and grasses,
Found the beautiful Wenonah,
Lying there among the lilies,
Wooed her with his words of sweetness,
Wooed her with his soft caresses,
Till she bore a son in sorrow,
Bore a son of love and sorrow.
  Thus was born my Hiawatha,
Thus was born the child of wonder;
But the daughter of Nokomis,
Hiawatha's gentle mother,
In her anguish died deserted
By the West-Wind, false and faithless,
By the heartless Mudjekeewis.
  For her daughter long and loudly
Wailed and wept the sad Nokomis;
"Oh that I were dead!" she murmured,
"Oh that I were dead, as thou art!
No more work, and no more weeping,
Wahonowin! Wahonowin!"
  By the shores of Gitche Gumee,
By the shining Big-Sea-Water,
Stood the wigwam of Nokomis,
Daughter of the Moon, Nokomis.
Dark behind it rose the forest,
Rose the black and gloomy pine-trees,
Rose the firs with cones upon them;
Bright before it beat the water,
Beat the clear and sunny water,
Beat the shining Big-Sea-Water.
  There the wrinkled old Nokomis
Nursed the little Hiawatha,
Rocked him in his linden cradle,
Bedded soft in moss and rushes,
Safely bound with reindeer sinews;
Stilled his fretful wail by saying,
"Hush! the Naked Bear will hear thee!"
Lulled him into slumber, singing,
"Ewa-yea! my little owlet!

Who is this, that lights the wigwam?
With his great eyes lights the wigwam?
Ewa-yea! my little owlet!"
  Many things Nokomis taught him
Of the stars that shine in heaven;
Showed him Ishkoodah, the comet,
Ishkoodah, with fiery tresses;
Showed the Death-Dance of the spirits,
Warriors with their plumes and war-clubs,
Flaring far away to northward
In the frosty nights of Winter;
Showed the broad white road in heaven,
Pathway of the ghosts, the shadows,
Running straight across the heavens,
Crowded with the ghosts, the shadows.
  At the door on summer evenings
Sat the little Hiawatha;
Heard the whispering of the pine-trees,
Heard the lapping of the water,
Sounds of music, words of wonder;
'Minne-wawa!" said the Pine-trees,
Mudway-aushka!" said the water.
  Saw the fire-fly, Wah-wah-taysee,
Flitting through the dusk of evening,
With the twinkle of its candle
Lighting up the brakes and bushes,
And he sang the song of children,
Sang the song Nokomis taught him:
"Wah-wah-taysee, little fire-fly,
Little, flitting, white-fire insect,
Little, dancing, white-fire creature,
Light me with your little candle,
Ere upon my bed I lay me,
Ere in sleep I close my eyelids!"
  Saw the moon rise from the water
Rippling, rounding from the water,
Saw the flecks and shadows on it,
Whispered, "What is that, Nokomis?"
And the good Nokomis answered:
"Once a warrior, very angry,
Seized his grandmother, and threw her
Up into the sky at midnight;
Right against the moon he threw her;

'T is her body that you see there."
　Saw the rainbow in the heaven,
In the eastern sky, the rainbow,
Whispered, "What is that, Nokomis?"
And the good Nokomis answered:
"'T is the heaven of flowers you see there;
All the wild-flowers of the forest,
All the lilies of the prairie,
When on earth they fade and perish,
Blossom in that heaven above us."
　When he heard the owls at midnight,
Hooting, laughing in the forest,
"What is that?" he cried in terror,
"What is that," he said, "Nokomis?"
And the good Nokomis answered:
"That is but the owl and owlet,
Talking in their native language,
Talking, scolding at each other."
　Then the little Hiawatha
Learned of every bird its language,
Learned their names and all their secrets,
How they built their nests in Summer,
Where they hid themselves in Winter,
Talked with them whene'er he met them,
Called them "Hiawatha's Chickens."
　Of all beasts he learned the language,
Learned their names and all their secrets,
How the beavers built their lodges,
Where the squirrels hid their acorns,
How the reindeer ran so swiftly,
Why the rabbit was so timid,
Talked with them whene'er he met them,
Called them "Hiawatha's Brothers."
　Then Iagoo, the great boaster,
He the marvellous story-teller,
He the traveller and the talker,
He the friend of old Nokomis,
Made a bow for Hiawatha;
From a branch of ash he made it,
From an oak-bough made the arrows,
Tipped with flint, and winged with feathers,
And the cord he made of deer-skin.
　Then he said to Hiawatha:

"Go, my son, into the forest,
Where the red deer herd together,
Kill for us a famous roebuck,
Kill for us a deer with antlers!"
  Forth into the forest straightway
All alone walked Hiawatha
Proudly, with his bow and arrows;
And the birds sang round him, o'er him,
"Do not shoot us, Hiawatha!"
Sang the robin, the Opechee,
Sang the bluebird, the Owaissa,
"Do not shoot us, Hiawatha!"
  Up the oak-tree, close beside him,
Sprang the squirrel, Adjidaumo,
In and out among the branches,
Coughed and chattered from the oak-tree,
Laughed, and said between his laughing,
"Do not shoot me, Hiawatha!"
  And the rabbit from his pathway
Leaped aside, and at a distance
Sat erect upon his haunches,
Half in fear and half in frolic,
Saying to the little hunter,
"Do not shoot me, Hiawatha!"
  But he heeded not, nor heard them,
For his thoughts were with the red deer;
On their tracks his eyes were fastened,
Leading downward to the river,
To the ford across the river,
And as one in slumber walked he.
  Hidden in the alder-bushes,
There he waited till the deer came,
Till he saw two antlers lifted,
Saw two eyes look from the thicket,
Saw two nostrils point to windward,
And a deer came down the pathway,
Flecked with leafy light and shadow.
And his heart within him fluttered,
Trembled like the leaves above him,
Like the birch-leaf palpitated,
As the deer came down the pathway.
  Then, upon one knee uprising,
Hiawatha aimed an arrow;

Scarce a twig moved with his motion,
Scarce a leaf was stirred or rustled,
But the wary roebuck started,
Stamped with all his hoofs together,
Listened with one foot uplifted,
Leaped as if to meet the arrow;
Ah! the singing, fatal arrow,
Like a wasp it buzzed and stung him!
  Dead he lay there in the forest,
By the ford across the river;
Beat his timid heart no longer,
But the heart of Hiawatha
Throbbed and shouted and exulted,
As he bore the red deer homeward,
And Iagoo and Nokomis
Hailed his coming with applauses.
  From the red deer's hide Nokomis
Made a cloak for Hiawatha,
From the red deer's flesh Nokomis
Made a banquet to his honor.
All the village came and feasted,
All the guests praised Hiawatha,
Called him Strong-Heart, Soan-ge-taha!
Called him Loon-Heart, Mahn-go-taysee!

IV

HIAWATHA AND MUDJEKEEWIS

Out of childhood into manhood
Now had grown my Hiawatha,
Skilled in all the craft of hunters,
Learned in all the lore of old men,
In all youthful sports and pastimes,
In all manly arts and labors.
  Swift of foot was Hiawatha;
He could shoot an arrow from him,
And run forward with such fleetness,
That the arrow fell behind him!
Strong of arm was Hiawatha;
He could shoot ten arrows upward,
Shoot them with such strength and swiftness,
That the tenth had left the bow-string

Ere the first to earth had fallen!
  He had mittens, Minjekahwun,
Magic mittens made of deer-skin;
When upon his hands he wore them,
He could smite the rocks asunder,
He could grind them into powder.
He had moccasins enchanted,
Magic moccasins of deer-skin;
When he bound them round his ankles,
When upon his feet he tied them,
At each stride a mile he measured!
  Much he questioned old Nokomis
Of his father Mudjekeewis;
Learned from her the fatal secret
Of the beauty of his mother,
Of the falsehood of his father;
And his heart was hot within him,
Like a living coal his heart was.
  Then he said to old Nokomis,
"I will go to Mudjekeewis,
See how fares it with my father,
At the doorways of the West-Wind,
At the portals of the Sunset!"
  From his lodge went Hiawatha,
Dressed for travel, armed for hunting;
Dressed in deer-skin shirt and leggings,
Richly wrought with quills and wampum;
On his head his eagle-feathers,
Round his waist his belt of wampum,
In his hand his bow of ash-wood,
Strung with sinews of the reindeer;
In his quiver oaken arrows,
Tipped with jasper, winged with feathers;
With his mittens, Minjekahwun,
With his moccasins enchanted.
  Warning said the old Nokomis,
"Go not forth, O Hiawatha!
To the kingdom of the West-Wind,
To the realms of Mudjekeewis,
Lest he harm you with his magic,
Lest he kill you with his cunning!"
  But the fearless Hiawatha
Heeded not her woman's warning;

Forth he strode into the forest,
At each stride a mile he measured;
Lurid seemed the sky above him,
Lurid seemed the earth beneath him,
Hot and close the air around him,
Filled with smoke and fiery vapors,
As of burning woods and prairies,
For his heart was hot within him,
Like a living coal his heart was.
  So he journeyed westward, westward,
Left the fleetest deer behind him,
Left the antelope and bison;
Crossed the rushing Esconaba,
Crossed the mighty Mississippi,
Passed the Mountains of the Prairie,
Passed the land of Crows and Foxes,
Passed the dwellings of the Blackfeet,
Came unto the Rocky Mountains,
To the kingdom of the West-Wind,
Where upon the gusty summits
Sat the ancient Mudjekeewis,
Ruler of the winds of heaven.
  Filled with awe was Hiawatha
At the aspect of his father.
On the air about him wildly
Tossed and streamed his cloudy tresses,
Gleamed like drifting snow his tresses,
Glared like Ishkoodah, the comet,
Like the star with fiery tresses.
  Filled with joy was Mudjekeewis
When he looked on Hiawatha,
Saw his youth rise up before him
In the face of Hiawatha,
Saw the beauty of Wenonah
From the grave rise up before him.
  "Welcome!" said he, "Hiawatha,
To the kingdom of the West-Wind!
Long have I been waiting for you!
Youth is lovely, age is lonely,
Youth is fiery, age is frosty;
You bring back the days departed,
You bring back my youth of passion,
And the beautiful Wenonah!"

Many days they talked together,
Questioned, listened, waited, answered;
Much the mighty Mudjekeewis
Boasted of his ancient prowess,
Of his perilous adventures,
His indomitable courage,
His invulnerable body.
   Patiently sat Hiawatha,
Listening to his father's boasting;
With a smile he sat and listened,
Uttered neither threat nor menace,
Neither word nor look betrayed him,
But his heart was hot within him,
Like a living coal his heart was.
   Then he said, "O Mudjekeewis,
Is there nothing that can harm you?
Nothing that you are afraid of?"
And the mighty Mudjekeewis,
Grand and gracious in his boasting,
Answered, saying, "There is nothing,
Nothing but the black rock yonder,
Nothing but the fatal Wawbeek!"
   And he looked at Hiawatha
With a wise look and benignant,
With a countenance paternal,
Looked with pride upon the beauty
Of his tall and graceful figure,
Saying, "O my Hiawatha!
Is there anything can harm you?
Anything you are afraid of?"
   But the wary Hiawatha
Paused awhile, as if uncertain,
Held his peace, as if resolving,
And then answered, "There is nothing,
Nothing but the bulrush yonder,
Nothing but the great Apukwa!"
   And as Mudjekeewis, rising,
Stretched his hand to pluck the bulrush,
Hiawatha cried in terror,
Cried in well-dissembled terror,
"Kago! kago! do not touch it!"
"Ah, kaween!" said Mudjekeewis,
"No indeed, I will not touch it!"

Then they talked of other matters;
First of Hiawatha's brothers,
First of Wabun, of the East-Wind,
Of the South-Wind, Shawondasee,
Of the North, Kabibonokka;
Then of Hiawatha's mother,
Of the beautiful Wenonah,
Of her birth upon the meadow,
Of her death, as old Nokomis
Had remembered and related.
 And he cried, "O Mudjekeewis,
It was you who killed Wenonah,
Took her young life and her beauty,
Broke the Lily of the Prairie,
Trampled it beneath your footsteps;
You confess it! you confess it!"
And the mighty Mudjekeewis
Tossed upon the wind his tresses,
Bowed his hoary head in anguish,
With a silent nod assented.
 Then up started Hiawatha,
And with threatening look and gesture
Laid his hand upon the black rock,
On the fatal Wawbeek laid it,
With his mittens, Minjekahwun,
Rent the jutting crag asunder,
Smote and crushed it into fragments,
Hurled them madly at his father,
The remorseful Mudjekeewis,
For his heart was hot within him,
Like a living coal his heart was.
 But the ruler of the West-Wind
Blew the fragments backward from him,
With the breathing of his nostrils,
With the tempest of his anger,
Blew them back at his assailant;
Seized the bulrush, the Apukwa,
Dragged it with its roots and fibres
From the margin of the meadow,
From its ooze the giant bulrush;
Long and loud laughed Hiawatha!
 Then began the deadly conflict,
Hand to hand among the mountains;

From his eyry screamed the eagle,
The Keneu, the great war-eagle,
Sat upon the crags around them,
Wheeling flapped his wings above them.
  Like a tall tree in the tempest
Bent and lashed the giant bulrush;
And in masses huge and heavy
Crashing fell the fatal Wawbeek;
Till the earth shook with the tumult
And confusion of the battle,
And the air was full of shoutings,
And the thunder of the mountains,
Starting, answered, "Baim-wawa!"
  Back retreated Mudjekeewis,
Rushing westward o'er the mountains,
Stumbling westward down the mountains,
Three whole days retreated fighting,
Still pursued by Hiawatha
To the doorways of the West-Wind,
To the portals of the Sunset,
To the earth's remotest border,
Where into the empty spaces
Sinks the sun, as a flamingo
Drops into her nest at nightfall,
In the melancholy marshes.
  "Hold!" at length cried Mudjekeewis,
"Hold, my son, my Hiawatha!
'T is impossible to kill me,
For you cannot kill the immortal.
I have put you to this trial,
But to know and prove your courage;
Now receive the prize of valor!
  "Go back to your home and people,
Live among them, toil among them,
Cleanse the earth from all that harms it,
Clear the fishing-grounds and rivers,
Slay all monsters and magicians,
All the Wendigoes, the giants,
All the serpents, the Kenabeeks,
As I slew the Mishe-Mokwa,
Slew the Great Bear of the mountains.
  "And at last when Death draws near you,
When the awful eyes of Pauguk

Glare upon you in the darkness,
I will share my kingdom with you,
Ruler shall you be thenceforward
Of the Northwest-Wind, Keewaydin,
Of the home-wind, the Keewaydin."
  Thus was fought that famous battle
In the dreadful days of Shah-shah,
In the days long since departed,
In the kingdom of the West-Wind.
Still the hunter sees its traces
Scattered far o'er hill and valley;
Sees the giant bulrush growing
By the ponds and water-courses,
Sees the masses of the Wawbeek
Lying still in every valley.
  Homeward now went Hiawatha;
Pleasant was the landscape round him,
Pleasant was the air above him,
For the bitterness of anger
Had departed wholly from him,
From his brain the thought of vengeance,
From his heart the burning fever.
  Only once his pace he slackened,
Only once he paused or halted,
Paused to purchase heads of arrows
Of the ancient Arrow-maker,
In the land of the Dacotahs,
Where the Falls of Minnehaha
Flash and gleam among the oak-trees,
Laugh and leap into the valley.
  There the ancient Arrow-maker
Made his arrow-heads of sandstone,
Arrow-heads of chalcedony,
Arrow-heads of flint and jasper,
Smoothed and sharpened at the edges,
Hard and polished, keen and costly.
  With him dwelt his dark-eyed daughter,
Wayward as the Minnehaha,
With her moods of shade and sunshine,
Eyes that smiled and frowned alternate,
Feet as rapid as the river,
Tresses flowing like the water,
And as musical a laughter;

And he named her from the river,
From the water-fall he named her,
Minnehaha, Laughing Water.
  Was it then for heads of arrows,
Arrow-heads of chalcedony,
Arrow-heads of flint and jasper,
That my Hiawatha halted
In the land of the Dacotahs?
  Was it not to see the maiden,
See the face of Laughing Water
Peeping from behind the curtain,
Hear the rustling of her garments
From behind the waving curtain,
As one sees the Minnehaha
Gleaming, glancing through the branches,
As one hears the Laughing Water
From behind its screen of branches?
  Who shall say what thoughts and visions
Fill the fiery brains of young men?
Who shall say what dreams of beauty
Filled the heart of Hiawatha?
All he told to old Nokomis,
When he reached the lodge at sunset,
Was the meeting with his father,
Was his fight with Mudjekeewis;
Not a word he said of arrows,
Not a word of Laughing Water.

V

HIAWATHA'S FASTING

You shall hear how Hiawatha
Prayed and fasted in the forest,
Not for greater skill in hunting,
Not for greater craft in fishing,
Not for triumphs in the battle,
And renown among the warriors,
But for profit of the people,
For advantage of the nations.
  First he built a lodge for fasting,
Built a wigwam in the forest,
By the shining Big-Sea-Water,

In the blithe and pleasant Spring-time,
In the Moon of Leaves he built it,
And, with dreams and visions many,
Seven whole days and nights he fasted.
  On the first day of his fasting
Through the leafy woods he wandered;
Saw the deer start from the thicket,
Saw the rabbit in his burrow,
Heard the pheasant, Bena, drumming,
Heard the squirrel, Adjidaumo,
Rattling in his hoard of acorns,
Saw the pigeon, the Omeme,
Building nests among the pine-trees,
And in flocks the wild-goose, Wawa,
Flying to the fen-lands northward,
Whirring, wailing far above him.
"Master of Life!" he cried, desponding,
"Must our lives depend on these things?"
  On the next day of his fasting
By the river's brink he wandered,
Through the Muskoday, the meadow,
Saw the wild rice, Mahnomonee,
Saw the blueberry, Meenahga,
And the strawberry, Odahmin,
And the gooseberry, Shahbomin,
And the grape-vine, the Bemahgut,
Trailing o'er the alder-branches,
Filling all the air with fragrance!
"Master of Life!" he cried, desponding,
"Must our lives depend on these things?"
  On the third day of his fasting
By the lake he sat and pondered,
By the still, transparent water;
Saw the sturgeon, Nahma, leaping,
Scattering drops like beads of wampum,
Saw the yellow perch, the Sahwa,
Like a sunbeam in the water,
Saw the pike, the Maskenozha,
And the herring, Okahahwis,
And the Shawgashee, the crawfish!
"Master of Life!" he cried, desponding,
"Must our lives depend on these things?"
  On the fourth day of his fasting

In his lodge he lay exhausted;
From his couch of leaves and branches
Gazing with half-open eyelids,
Full of shadowy dreams and visions,
On the dizzy, swimming landscape,
On the gleaming of the water,
On the splendor of the sunset.
  And he saw a youth approaching,
Dressed in garments green and yellow,
Coming through the purple twilight,
Through the splendor of the sunset;
Plumes of green bent o'er his forehead,
And his hair was soft and golden.
  Standing at the open doorway,
Long he looked at Hiawatha,
Looked with pity and compassion
On his wasted form and features,
And, in accents like the sighing
Of the South-Wind in the tree-tops,
Said he, "O my Hiawatha!
All your prayers are heard in heaven,
For you pray not like the others;
Not for greater skill in hunting,
Not for greater craft in fishing,
Not for triumph in the battle,
Nor renown among the warriors,
But for profit of the people,
For advantage of the nations.
  "From the Master of Life descending,
I, the friend of man, Mondamin,
Come to warn you and instruct you,
How by struggle and by labor
You shall gain what you have prayed for.
Rise up from your bed of branches,
Rise, O youth, and wrestle with me!"
  Faint with famine, Hiawatha
Started from his bed of branches,
From the twilight of his wigwam
Forth into the flush of sunset
Came, and wrestled with Mondamin;
At his touch he felt new courage
Throbbing in his brain and bosom,
Felt new life and hope and vigor

Run through every nerve and fibre.
  So they wrestled there together
In the glory of the sunset,
And the more they strove and struggled,
Stronger still grew Hiawatha;
Till the darkness fell around them,
And the heron, the Shuh-shuh-gah,
From her nest among the pine-trees,
Gave a cry of lamentation,
Gave a scream of pain and famine.
  "'T is enough!" then said Mondamin,
Smiling upon Hiawatha,
"But tomorrow, when the sun sets,
I will come again to try you."
And he vanished, and was seen not;
Whether sinking as the rain sinks,
Whether rising as the mists rise,
Hiawatha saw not, knew not,
Only saw that he had vanished,
Leaving him alone and fainting,
With the misty lake below him,
And the reeling stars above him.
  On the morrow and the next day,
When the sun through heaven descending,
Like a red and burning cinder
From the hearth of the Great Spirit,
Fell into the western waters,
Came Mondamin for the trial,
For the strife with Hiawatha;
Came as silent as the dew comes,
From the empty air appearing,
Into empty air returning,
Taking shape when earth it touches,
But invisible to all men
In its coming and its going.
  Thrice they wrestled there together
In the glory of the sunset,
Till the darkness fell around them,
Till the heron, the Shuh-shuh-gah,
From her nest among the pine-trees,
Uttered her loud cry of famine,
And Mondamin paused to listen.
  Tall and beautiful he stood there,

In his garments green and yellow;
To and fro his plumes above him,
Waved and nodded with his breathing,
And the sweat of the encounter
Stood like drops of dew upon him.
 And he cried, "O Hiawatha!
Bravely have you wrestled with me,
Thrice have wrestled stoutly with me,
And the Master of Life, who sees us,
He will give to you the triumph!"
 Then he smiled, and said: "To-morrow
Is the last day of your conflict,
Is the last day of your fasting.
You will conquer and o'ercome me;
Make a bed for me to lie in,
Where the rain may fall upon me,
Where the sun may come and warm me;
Strip these garments, green and yellow,
Strip this nodding plumage from me,
Lay me in the earth, and make it
Soft and loose and light above me.
 "Let no hand disturb my slumber,
Let no weed nor worm molest me,
Let not Kahgahgee, the raven,
Come to haunt me and molest me,
Only come yourself to watch me,
Till I wake, and start, and quicken,
Till I leap into the sunshine."
 And thus saying, he departed;
Peacefully slept Hiawatha,
But he heard the Wawonaissa,
Heard the whippoorwill complaining,
Perched upon his lonely wigwam;
Heard the rushing Sebowisha,
Heard the rivulet rippling near him,
Talking to the darksome forest;
Heard the sighing of the branches,
As they lifted and subsided
At the passing of the night-wind,
Heard them, as one hears in slumber
Far-off murmurs, dreamy whispers:
Peacefully slept Hiawatha.
 On the morrow came Nokomis,

On the seventh day of his fasting,
Came with food for Hiawatha,
Came imploring and bewailing,
Lest his hunger should o'ercome him,
Lest his fasting should be fatal.
  But he tasted not, and touched not,
Only said to her, "Nokomis,
Wait until the sun is setting,
Till the darkness falls around us,
Till the heron, the Shuh-shuh-gah,
Crying from the desolate marshes,
Tells us that the day is ended."
  Homeward weeping went Nokomis,
Sorrowing for her Hiawatha,
Fearing lest his strength should fail him,
Lest his fasting should be fatal.
He meanwhile sat weary waiting
For the coming of Mondamin,
Till the shadows, pointing eastward,
Lengthened over field and forest,
Till the sun dropped from the heaven,
Floating on the waters westward,
As a red leaf in the Autumn
Falls and floats upon the water,
Falls and sinks into its bosom.
  And behold! the young Mondamin,
With his soft and shining tresses,
With his garments green and yellow,
With his long and glossy plumage,
Stood and beckoned at the doorway.
And as one in slumber walking,
Pale and haggard, but undaunted,
From the wigwam Hiawatha
Came and wrestled with Mondamin.
  Round about him spun the landscape,
Sky and forest reeled together,
And his strong heart leaped within him,
As the sturgeon leaps and struggles
In a net to break its meshes.
Like a ring of fire around him
Blazed and flared the red horizon,
And a hundred suns seemed looking
At the combat of the wrestlers.

Suddenly upon the greensward
All alone stood Hiawatha,
Panting with his wild exertion,
Palpitating with the struggle;
And before him breathless, lifeless,
Lay the youth, with hair dishevelled,
Plumage torn, and garments tattered,
Dead he lay there in the sunset.
  And victorious Hiawatha
Made the grave as he commanded,
Stripped the garments from Mondamin,
Stripped his tattered plumage from him,
Laid him in the earth, and made it
Soft and loose and light above him;
And the heron, the Shuh-shuh-gah,
From the melancholy moorlands,
Gave a cry of lamentation,
Gave a cry of pain and anguish!
  Homeward then went Hiawatha
To the lodge of old Nokomis,
And the seven days of his fasting
Were accomplished and completed.
But the place was not forgotten
Where he wrestled with Mondamin;
Nor forgotten nor neglected
Was the grave where lay Mondamin,
Sleeping in the rain and sunshine,
Where his scattered plumes and garments
Faded in the rain and sunshine.
  Day by day did Hiawatha
Go to wait and watch beside it;
Kept the dark mould soft above it,
Kept it clean from weeds and insects,
Drove away, with scoffs and shoutings,
Kahgahgee, the king of ravens.
  Till at length a small green feather
From the earth shot slowly upward,
Then another and another,
And before the Summer ended
Stood the maize in all its beauty,
With its shining robes about it,
And its long, soft, yellow tresses;
And in rapture Hiawatha

Cried aloud, "It is Mondamin!
Yes, the friend of man, Mondamin!"
  Then he called to old Nokomis
And Iagoo, the great boaster,
Showed them where the maize was growing,
Told them of his wondrous vision,
Of his wrestling and his triumph,
Of this new gift to the nations,
Which should be their food forever.
  And still later, when the Autumn
Changed the long, green leaves to yellow,
And the soft and juicy kernels
Grew like wampum hard and yellow,
Then the ripened ears he gathered,
Stripped the withered husks from off them,
As he once had stripped the wrestler,
Gave the first Feast of Mondamin,
And made known unto the people
This new gift of the Great Spirit.

VI

HIAWATHA'S FRIENDS

Two good friends had Hiawatha,
Singled out from all the others,
Bound to him in closest union,
And to whom he gave the right hand
Of his heart, in joy and sorrow;
Chibiabos, the musician,
And the very strong man, Kwasind.
  Straight between them ran the pathway,
Never grew the grass upon it;
Singing birds, that utter falsehoods,
Story-tellers, mischief-makers,
Found no eager ear to listen,
Could not breed ill-will between them,
For they kept each other's counsel,
Spake with naked hearts together,
Pondering much and much contriving
How the tribes of men might prosper.
  Most beloved by Hiawatha
Was the gentle Chibiabos,

He the best of all musicians,
He the sweetest of all singers.
Beautiful and childlike was he,
Brave as man is, soft as woman,
Pliant as a wand of willow,
Stately as a deer with antlers.
  When he sang, the village listened;
All the warriors gathered round him,
All the women came to hear him;
Now he stirred their souls to passion,
Now he melted them to pity.
  From the hollow reeds he fashioned
Flutes so musical and mellow,
That the brook, the Sebowisha,
Ceased to murmur in the woodland,
That the wood-birds ceased from singing,
And the squirrel, Adjidaumo,
Ceased his chatter in the oak-tree,
And the rabbit, the Wabasso,
Sat upright to look and listen.
  Yes, the brook, the Sebowisha,
Pausing, said, "O Chibiabos,
Teach my waves to flow in music,
Softly as your words in singing!"
  Yes, the bluebird, the Owaissa,
Envious, said, "O Chibiabos,
Teach me tones as wild and wayward,
Teach me songs as full of frenzy!"
  Yes, the robin, the Opechee,
Joyous, said, "O Chibiabos,
Teach me tones as sweet and tender,
Teach me songs as full of gladness!"
  And the whippoorwill, Wawonaissa,
Sobbing, said, "O Chibiabos,
Teach me tones as melancholy,
Teach me songs as full of sadness!"
  All the many sounds of nature
Borrowed sweetness from his singing;
All the hearts of men were softened
By the pathos of his music;
For he sang of peace and freedom,
Sang of beauty, love, and longing;
Sang of death, and life undying

In the Islands of the Blessed,
In the kingdom of Ponemah,
In the land of the Hereafter.
  Very dear to Hiawatha
Was the gentle Chibiabos,
He the best of all musicians,
He the sweetest of all singers;
For his gentleness he loved him,
And the magic of his singing.
  Dear, too, unto Hiawatha
Was the very strong man, Kwasind,
He the strongest of all mortals,
He the mightiest among many;
For his very strength he loved him,
For his strength allied to goodness.
  Idle in his youth was Kwasind,
Very listless, dull, and dreamy,
Never played with other children,
Never fished and never hunted,
Not like other children was he;
But they saw that much he fasted,
Much his Manito entreated,
Much besought his Guardian Spirit.
  "Lazy Kwasind!" said his mother,
"In my work you never help me!
In the Summer you are roaming
Idly in the fields and forests;
In the Winter you are cowering
O'er the firebrands in the wigwam!
In the coldest days of Winter
I must break the ice for fishing;
With my nets you never help me!
At the door my nets are hanging,
Dripping, freezing with the water;
Go and wring them, Yenadizze!
Go and dry them in the sunshine!"
  Slowly, from the ashes, Kwasind
Rose, but made no angry answer;
From the lodge went forth in silence,
Took the nets, that hung together,
Dripping, freezing at the doorway;
Like a wisp of straw he wrung them,
Like a wisp of straw he broke them,

Could not wring them without breaking,
Such the strength was in his fingers.
    "Lazy Kwasind!" said his father,
"In the hunt you never help me;
Every bow you touch is broken,
Snapped asunder every arrow;
Yet come with me to the forest,
You shall bring the hunting homeward."
    Down a narrow pass they wandered,
Where a brooklet led them onward,
Where the trail of deer and bison
Marked the soft mud on the margin,
Till they found all further passage
Shut against them, barred securely
By the trunks of trees uprooted,
Lying lengthwise, lying crosswise,
And forbidding further passage.
    "We must go back," said the old man,
"O'er these logs we cannot clamber;
Not a woodchuck could get through them,
Not a squirrel clamber o'er them!"
And straightway his pipe he lighted,
And sat down to smoke and ponder.
But before his pipe was finished,
Lo! the path was cleared before him;
All the trunks had Kwasind lifted,
To the right hand, to the left hand,
Shot the pine-trees swift as arrows,
Hurled the cedars light as lances.
    "Lazy Kwasind!" said the young men,
As they sported in the meadow:
"Why stand idly looking at us,
Leaning on the rock behind you?
Come and wrestle with the others,
Let us pitch the quoit together!"
    Lazy Kwasind made no answer,
To their challenge made no answer,
Only rose, and slowly turning,
Seized the huge rock in his fingers,
Tore it from its deep foundation,
Poised it in the air a moment,
Pitched it sheer into the river,
Sheer into the swift Pauwating,

288

Where it still is seen in Summer.
  Once as down that foaming river,
Down the rapids of Pauwating,
Kwasind sailed with his companions,
In the stream he saw a beaver,
Saw Ahmeek, the King of Beavers,
Struggling with the rushing currents,
Rising, sinking in the water.
  Without speaking, without pausing,
Kwasind leaped into the river,
Plunged beneath the bubbling surface,
Through the whirlpools chased the beaver,
Followed him among the islands,
Stayed so long beneath the water,
That his terrified companions
Cried, "Alas! good-by to Kwasind!
We shall never more see Kwasind!"
But he reappeared triumphant,
And upon his shining shoulders
Brought the beaver, dead and dripping,
Brought the King of all the Beavers.
  And these two, as I have told you,
Were the friends of Hiawatha,
Chibiabos, the musician,
And the very strong man, Kwasind.
Long they lived in peace together,
Spake with naked hearts together,
Pondering much and much contriving
How the tribes of men might prosper.

        VII

HIAWATHA'S SAILING

"Give me of your bark, O Birch-tree!
Of your yellow bark, O Birch-tree!
Growing by the rushing river,
Tall and stately in the valley!
I a light canoe will build me,
Build a swift Cheemaun for sailing,
That shall float on the river,
Like a yellow leaf in Autumn,
Like a yellow water-lily!

"Lay aside your cloak, O Birch-tree!
Lay aside your white-skin wrapper,
For the Summer-time is coming,
And the sun is warm in heaven,
And you need no white-skin wrapper!"
 Thus aloud cried Hiawatha
In the solitary forest,
By the rushing Taquamenaw,
When the birds were singing gayly,
In the Moon of Leaves were singing,
And the sun, from sleep awaking,
Started up and said, "Behold me!
Gheezis, the great Sun, behold me!"
 And the tree with all its branches
Rustled in the breeze of morning,
Saying, with a sigh of patience,
"Take my cloak, O Hiawatha!"
 With his knife the tree he girdled;
Just beneath its lowest branches,
Just above the roots, he cut it,
Till the sap came oozing outward;
Down the trunk, from top to bottom,
Sheer he cleft the bark asunder,
With a wooden wedge he raised it,
Stripped it from the trunk unbroken.
 "Give me of your boughs, O Cedar!
Of your strong and pliant branches,
My canoe to make more steady,
Make more strong and firm beneath me!"
 Through the summit of the Cedar
Went a sound, a cry of horror,
Went a murmur of resistance;
But it whispered, bending downward,
'Take my boughs, O Hiawatha!"
 Down he hewed the boughs of cedar,
Shaped them straightway to a framework,
Like two bows he formed and shaped them,
Like two bended bows together.
 "Give me of your roots, O Tamarack!
Of your fibrous roots, O Larch-tree!
My canoe to bind together,
So to bind the ends together
That the water may not enter,

That the river may not wet me!"
  And the Larch, with all its fibres,
Shivered in the air of morning,
Touched his forehead with its tassels,
Slid, with one long sigh of sorrow.
"Take them all, O Hiawatha!"
  From the earth he tore the fibres,
Tore the tough roots of the Larch-tree,
Closely sewed the bark together,
Bound it closely to the frame-work.
  "Give me of your balm, O Fir-tree!
Of your balsam and your resin,
So to close the seams together
That the water may not enter,
That the river may not wet me!"
  And the Fir-tree, tall and sombre,
Sobbed through all its robes of darkness,
Rattled like a shore with pebbles,
Answered wailing, answered weeping,
"Take my balm, O Hiawatha!"
  And he took the tears of balsam,
Took the resin of the Fir-tree,
Smeared therewith each seam and fissure,
Made each crevice safe from water.
  "Give me of your quills, O Hedgehog!
All your quills, O Kagh, the Hedgehog!
I will make a necklace of them,
Make a girdle for my beauty,
And two stars to deck her bosom!"
  From a hollow tree the Hedgehog
With his sleepy eyes looked at him,
Shot his shining quills, like arrows,
Saying with a drowsy murmur,
Through the tangle of his whiskers,
"Take my quills, O Hiawatha!"
  From the ground the quills he gathered,
All the little shining arrows,
Stained them red and blue and yellow,
With the juice of roots and berries;
Into his canoe he wrought them,
Round its waist a shining girdle,
Round its bows a gleaming necklace,
On its breast two stars resplendent.

Thus the Birch Canoe was builded
In the valley, by the river,
In the bosom of the forest;
And the forest's life was in it,
All its mystery and its magic,
All the lightness of the birch-tree,
All the toughness of the cedar,
All the larch's supple sinews;
And it floated on the river
Like a yellow leaf in Autumn,
Like a yellow water-lily.
  Paddles none had Hiawatha,
Paddles none he had or needed,
For his thoughts as paddles served him,
And his wishes served to guide him;
Swift or slow at will he glided,
Veered to right or left at pleasure.
  Then he called aloud to Kwasind,
To his friend, the strong man, Kwasind,
Saying, "Help me clear this river
Of its sunken logs and sand-bars."
  Straight into the river Kwasind
Plunged as if he were an otter,
Dived as if he were a beaver,
Stood up to his waist in water,
To his arm-pits in the river,
Swam and scouted in the river,
Tugged at sunken logs and branches,
With his hands he scooped the sand-bars,
With his feet the ooze and tangle.
  And thus sailed my Hiawatha
Down the rushing Taquamenaw,
Sailed through all its bends and windings,
Sailed through all its deeps and shallows,
While his friend, the strong man, Kwasind,
Swam the deeps, the shallows waded.
  Up and down the river went they,
In and out among its islands,
Cleared its bed of root and sand-bar,
Dragged the dead trees from its channel,
Made its passage safe and certain,
Made a pathway for the people,
From its springs among the mountains,

To the waters of Pauwating,
To the bay of Taquamenaw.

VIII

HIAWATHA'S FISHING

Forth upon the Gitche Gumee,
On the shining Big-Sea-Water,
With his fishing-line of cedar,
Of the twisted bark of cedar,
Forth to catch the sturgeon Nahma,
Mishe-Nahma, King of Fishes,
In his birch canoe exulting
All alone went Hiawatha.
   Through the clear, transparent water
He could see the fishes swimming
Far down in the depths below him;
See the yellow perch, the Sahwa,
Like a sunbeam in the water,
See the Shawgashee, the craw-fish,
Like a spider on the bottom,
On the white and sandy bottom.
   At the stern sat Hiawatha,
With his fishing-line of cedar;
In his plumes the breeze of morning
Played as in the hemlock branches;
On the bows, with tail erected,
Sat the squirrel, Adjidaumo;
In his fur the breeze of morning
Played as in the prairie grasses.
   On the white sand of the bottom
Lay the monster Mishe-Nahma,
Lay the sturgeon, King of Fishes;
Through his gills he breathed the water,
With his fins he fanned and winnowed,
With his tail he swept the sand-floor.
   There he lay in all his armor;
On each side a shield to guard him,
Plates of bone upon his forehead,
Down his sides and back and shoulders
Plates of bone with spines projecting
Painted was he with his war-paints,

Stripes of yellow, red, and azure,
Spots of brown and spots of sable;
And he lay there on the bottom,
Fanning with his fins of purple,
As above him Hiawatha
In his birch canoe came sailing,
With his fishing-line of cedar.
   "Take my bait," cried Hiawatha,
Down into the depths beneath him,
"Take my bait, O Sturgeon, Nahma!
Come up from below the water,
Let us see which is the stronger!"
And he dropped his line of cedar
Through the clear, transparent water,
Waited vainly for an answer,
Long sat waiting for an answer,
And repeating loud and louder,
"Take my bait, O King of Fishes!"
   Quiet lay the sturgeon, Nahma,
Fanning slowly in the water,
Looking up at Hiawatha,
Listening to his call and clamor,
His unnecessary tumult,
Till he wearied of the shouting;
And he said to the Kenozha,
To the pike, the Maskenozha,
"Take the bait of this rude fellow,
Break the line of Hiawatha!"
   In his fingers Hiawatha
Felt the loose line jerk and tighten;
As he drew it in, it tugged so
That the birch canoe stood endwise,
Like a birch log in the water,
With the squirrel, Adjidaumo,
Perched and frisking on the summit.
Full of scorn was Hiawatha
When he saw the fish rise upward,
Saw the pike, the Maskenozha,
Coming nearer, nearer to him,
And he shouted through the water,
"Esa! esa! shame upon you!
You are but the pike, Kenozha,
You are not the fish I wanted,

You are not the King of Fishes!"
  Reeling downward to the bottom
Sank the pike in great confusion,
And the mighty sturgeon, Nahma,
Said to Ugudwash, the sun-fish,
To the bream, with scales of crimson,
"Take the bait of this great boaster,
Break the line of Hiawatha!"
  Slowly upward, wavering, gleaming,
Rose the Ugudwash, the sun-fish,
Seized the line of Hiawatha,
Swung with all his weight upon it,
Made a whirlpool in the water,
Whirled the birch canoe in circles,
Round and round in gurgling eddies,
Till the circles in the water
Reached the far-off sandy beaches,
Till the water-flags and rushes
Nodded on the distant margins.
  But when Hiawatha saw him
Slowly rising through the water,
Lifting up his disk refulgent,
Loud he shouted in derision,
"Esa! esa! shame upon you!
You are Ugudwash, the sun-fish,
You are not the fish I wanted,
You are not the King of Fishes!"
  Slowly downward, wavering, gleaming,
Sank the Ugudwash, the sun-fish,
And again the sturgeon, Nahma,
Heard the shout of Hiawatha,
Heard his challenge of defiance,
The unnecessary tumult,
Ringing far across the water.
  From the white sand of the bottom
Up he rose with angry gesture,
Quivering in each nerve and fibre,
Clashing all his plates of armor,
Gleaming bright with all his war-paint;
In his wrath he darted upward,
Flashing leaped into the sunshine,
Opened his great jaws, and swallowed
Both canoe and Hiawatha.

Down into that darksome cavern
Plunged the headlong Hiawatha,
As a log on some black river
Shoots and plunges down the rapids,
Found himself in utter darkness,
Groped about in helpless wonder,
Till he felt a great heart beating,
Throbbing in that utter darkness.
  And he smote it in his anger,
With his fist, the heart of Nahma,
Felt the mighty King of Fishes
Shudder through each nerve and fibre,
Heard the water gurgle round him
As he leaped and staggered through it,
Sick at heart, and faint and weary.
  Crosswise then did Hiawatha
Drag his birch-canoe for safety,
Lest from out the jaws of Nahma,
In the turmoil and confusion,
Forth he might be hurled and perish.
And the squirrel, Adjidaumo,
Frisked and chatted very gayly,
Toiled and tugged with Hiawatha
Till the labor was completed.
  Then said Hiawatha to him,
"O my little friend, the squirrel,
Bravely have you toiled to help me;
Take the thanks of Hiawatha,
And the name which now he gives you;
For hereafter and forever
Boys shall call you Adjidaumo,
Tail-in-air the boys shall call you!"
  And again the sturgeon, Nahma,
Gasped and quivered in the water,
Then was still, and drifted landward
Till he grated on the pebbles,
Till the listening Hiawatha
Heard him grate upon the margin,
Felt him strand upon the pebbles,
Knew that Nahma, King of Fishes,
Lay there dead upon the margin.
  Then he heard a clang and flapping,
As of many wings assembling,

Heard a screaming and confusion,
As of birds of prey contending,
Saw a gleam of light above him,
Shining through the ribs of Nahma,
Saw the glittering eyes of sea-gulls,
Of Kayoshk, the sea-gulls, peering,
Gazing at him through the opening,
Heard them saying to each other,
"'T is our brother, Hiawatha!"
    And he shouted from below them,
Cried exulting from the caverns:
"O ye sea-gulls! O my brothers!
I have slain the sturgeon, Nahma;
Make the rifts a little larger,
With your claws the openings widen,
Set me free from this dark prison,
And henceforward and forever
Men shall speak of your achievements,
Calling you Kayoshk, the sea-gulls,
Yes, Kayoshk, the Noble Scratchers!"
    And the wild and clamorous sea-gulls
Toiled with beak and claws together,
Made the rifts and openings wider
In the mighty ribs of Nahma,
And from peril and from prison,
From the body of the sturgeon,
From the peril of the water,
They released my Hiawatha.
    He was standing near his wigwam,
On the margin of the water,
And he called to old Nokomis,
Called and beckoned to Nokomis,
Pointed to the sturgeon, Nahma,
Lying lifeless on the pebbles,
With the sea-gulls feeding on him.
    "I have slain the Mishe-Nahma,
Slain the King of Fishes!" said he;
"Look! the sea-gulls feed upon him,
Yes, my friends Kayoshk, the sea-gulls;
Drive them not away, Nokomis,
They have saved me from great peril
In the body of the sturgeon,
Wait until their meal is ended,

Till their craws are full with feasting,
Till they homeward fly, at sunset,
To their nests among the marshes;
Then bring all your pots and kettles,
And make oil for us in Winter."
  And she waited till the sun set,
Till the pallid moon, the Night-sun,
Rose above the tranquil water,
Till Kayoshk, the sated sea-gulls,
From their banquet rose with clamor,
And across the fiery sunset
Winged their way to far-off islands,
To their nests among the rushes.
  To his sleep went Hiawatha,
And Nokomis to her labor,
Toiling patient in the moonlight,
Till the sun and moon changed places,
Till the sky was red with sunrise,
And Kayoshk, the hungry sea-gulls,
Came back from the reedy islands,
Clamorous for their morning banquet.
  Three whole days and nights alternate
Old Nokomis and the sea-gulls
Stripped the oily flesh of Nahma,
Till the waves washed through the rib-bones,
Till the sea-gulls came no longer,
And upon the sands lay nothing
But the skeleton of Nahma.

IX

HIAWATHA AND THE PEARL-FEATHER

On the shores of Gitche Gumee,
Of the shining Big-Sea-Water,
Stood Nokomis, the old woman,
Pointing with her finger westward,
O'er the water pointing westward,
To the purple clouds of sunset.
  Fiercely the red sun descending
Burned his way along the heavens,
Set the sky on fire behind him,
As war-parties, when retreating,

Burn the prairies on their war-trail;
And the moon, the Night-sun, eastward,
Suddenly starting from his ambush,
Followed fast those bloody footprints,
Followed in that fiery war-trail,
With its glare upon his features.
  And Nokomis, the old woman,
Pointing with her finger westward,
Spake these words to Hiawatha:
"Yonder dwells the great Pearl-Feather,
Megissogwon, the Magician,
Manito of Wealth and Wampum,
Guarded by his fiery serpents,
Guarded by the black pitch-water.
You can see his fiery serpents,
The Kenabeek, the great serpents,
Coiling, playing in the water;
You can see the black pitch-water
Stretching far away beyond them,
To the purple clouds of sunset!
  "He it was who slew my father,
By his wicked wiles and cunning,
When he from the moon descended,
When he came on earth to seek me.
He, the mightiest of Magicians,
Sends the fever from the marshes,
Sends the pestilential vapors,
Sends the poisonous exhalations,
Sends the white fog from the fen-lands,
Sends disease and death among us!
  "Take your bow, O Hiawatha,
Take your arrows, jasper-headed,
Take your war-club, Puggawaugun,
And your mittens, Minjekahwun,
And your birch-canoe for sailing,
And the oil of Mishe-Nahma,
So to smear its sides, that swiftly
You may pass the black pitch-water;
Slay this merciless magician,
Save the people from the fever
That he breathes across the fen-lands,
And avenge my father's murder!"
  Straightway then my Hiawatha

Armed himself with all his war-gear,
Launched his birch-canoe for sailing;
With his palm its sides he patted,
Said with glee, "Cheemaun, my darling,
O my Birch-canoe! leap forward,
Where you see the fiery serpents,
Where you see the black pitch-water!"
  Forward leaped Cheemaun exulting,
And the noble Hiawatha
Sang his war-song wild and woful,
And above him the war-eagle,
The Keneu, the great war-eagle,
Master of all fowls with feathers,
Screamed and hurtled through the heavens.
  Soon he reached the fiery serpents,
The Kenabeek, the great serpents,
Lying huge upon the water,
Sparkling, rippling in the water,
Lying coiled across the passage,
With their blazing crests uplifted,
Breathing fiery fogs and vapors,
So that none could pass beyond them.
  But the fearless Hiawatha
Cried aloud, and spake in this wise:
"Let me pass my way, Kenabeek,
Let me go upon my journey!"
And they answered, hissing fiercely,
With their fiery breath made answer:
"Back, go back! O Shaugodaya!
Back to old Nokomis, Faint-heart!"
  Then the angry Hiawatha
Raised his mighty bow of ash-tree,
Seized his arrows, jasper-headed,
Shot them fast among the serpents;
Every twanging of the bow-string
Was a war-cry and a death-cry,
Every whizzing of an arrow
Was a death-song of Kenabeek.
  Weltering in the bloody water,
Dead lay all the fiery serpents,
And among them Hiawatha
Harmless sailed, and cried exulting:
"Onward, O Cheemaun, my darling!

Onward to the black pitch-water!"
  Then he took the oil of Nahma,
And the bows and sides anointed,
Smeared them well with oil, that swiftly
He might pass the black pitch-water.
  All night long he sailed upon it,
Sailed upon that sluggish water,
Covered with its mould of ages,
Black with rotting water-rushes,
Rank with flags and leaves of lilies,
Stagnant, lifeless, dreary, dismal,
Lighted by the shimmering moonlight,
And by will-o'-the-wisps illumined,
Fires by ghosts of dead men kindled,
In their weary night-encampments.
  All the air was white with moonlight,
All the water black with shadow,
And around him the Suggema,
The mosquito, sang his war-song,
And the fire-flies, Wah-wah-taysee,
Waved their torches to mislead him;
And the bull-frog, the Dahinda,
Thrust his head into the moonlight,
Fixed his yellow eyes upon him,
Sobbed and sank beneath the surface;
And anon a thousand whistles,
Answered over all the fen-lands,
And the heron, the Shuh-shuh-gah,
Far off on the reedy margin,
Heralded the hero's coming.
  Westward thus fared Hiawatha,
Toward the realm of Megissogwon,
Toward the land of the Pearl-Feather,
Till the level moon stared at him,
In his face stared pale and haggard,
Till the sun was hot behind him,
Till it burned upon his shoulders,
And before him on the upland
He could see the Shining Wigwam
Of the Manito of Wampum,
Of the mightiest of Magicians.
  Then once more Cheemaun he patted,
To his birch-canoe said, "Onward!"

And it stirred in all its fibres,
And with one great bound of triumph
Leaped across the water-lilies,
Leaped through tangled flags and rushes,
And upon the beach beyond them
Dry-shod landed Hiawatha.
  Straight he took his bow of ash-tree,
On the sand one end he rested,
With his knee he pressed the middle,
Stretched the faithful bow-string tighter,
Took an arrow, jasper-headed,
Shot it at the Shining Wigwam,
Sent it singing as a herald,
As a bearer of his message,
Of his challenge loud and lofty:
"Come forth from your lodge, Pearl-Feather!
Hiawatha waits your coming!"
  Straightway from the Shining Wigwam
Came the mighty Megissogwon,
Tall of stature, broad of shoulder,
Dark and terrible in aspect,
Clad from head to foot in wampum,
Armed with all his warlike weapons,
Painted like the sky of morning,
Streaked with crimson, blue, and yellow,
Crested with great eagle-feathers,
Streaming upward, streaming outward.
  "Well I know you, Hiawatha!"
Cried he in a voice of thunder,
In a tone of loud derision.
"Hasten back, O Shaugodaya!
Hasten back among the women,
Back to old Nokomis, Faint-heart!
I will slay you as you stand there,
As of old I slew her father!"
  But my Hiawatha answered,
Nothing daunted, fearing nothing:
"Big words do not smite like war-clubs,
Boastful breath is not a bow-string,
Taunts are not so sharp as arrows,
Deeds are better things than words are,
Actions mightier than boastings!"
  Then began the greatest battle

That the sun had ever looked on,
That the war-birds ever witnessed.
All a Summer's day it lasted,
From the sunrise to the sunset;
For the shafts of Hiawatha
Harmless hit the shirt of wampum,
Harmless fell the blows he dealt it
With his mittens, Minjekahwun,
Harmless fell the heavy war-club;
It could dash the rocks asunder,
But it could not break the meshes
Of that magic shirt of wampum.
  Till at sunset Hiawatha,
Leaning on his bow of ash-tree,
Wounded, weary, and desponding,
With his mighty war-club broken,
With his mittens torn and tattered,
And three useless arrows only,
Paused to rest beneath a pine-tree,
From whose branches trailed the mosses,
And whose trunk was coated over
With the Dead-man's Moccasin-leather,
With the fungus white and yellow.
  Suddenly from the boughs above him
Sang the Mama, the woodpecker:
"Aim your arrows, Hiawatha,
At the head of Megissogwon,
Strike the tuft of hair upon it,
At their roots the long black tresses;
There alone can he be wounded!"
  Winged with feathers, tipped with jasper,
Swift flew Hiawatha's arrow,
Just as Megissogwon, stooping,
Raised a heavy stone to throw it.
Full upon the crown it struck him,
At the roots of his long tresses,
And he reeled and staggered forward,
Plunging like a wounded bison,
Yes, like Pezhekee, the bison,
When the snow is on the prairie.
  Swifter flew the second arrow,
In the pathway of the other,
Piercing deeper than the other,

Wounding sorer than the other;
And the knees of Megissogwon
Shook like windy reeds beneath him,
Bent and trembled like the rushes.
  But the third and latest arrow
Swiftest flew, and wounded sorest,
And the mighty Megissogwon
Saw the fiery eyes of Pauguk,
Saw the eyes of Death glare at him,
Heard his voice call in the darkness;
At the feet of Hiawatha
Lifeless lay the great Pearl-Feather,
Lay the mightiest of Magicians.
  Then the grateful Hiawatha
Called the Mama, the woodpecker,
From his perch among the branches
Of the melancholy pine-tree,
And, in honor of his service,
Stained with blood the tuft of feathers
On the little head of Mama;
Even to this day he wears it,
Wears the tuft of crimson feathers,
As a symbol of his service.
  Then he stripped the shirt of wampum
From the back of Megissogwon,
As a trophy of the battle,
As a signal of his conquest.
On the shore he left the body,
Half on land and half in water,
In the sand his feet were buried,
And his face was in the water.
And above him, wheeled and clamored
The Keneu, the great war-eagle,
Sailing round in narrower circles,
Hovering nearer, nearer, nearer.
  From the wigwam Hiawatha
Bore the wealth of Megissogwon,
All his wealth of skins and wampum,
Furs of bison and of beaver,
Furs of sable and of ermine,
Wampum belts and strings and pouches,
Quivers wrought with beads of wampum,
Filled with arrows, silver-headed.

Homeward then he sailed exulting,
Homeward through the black pitch-water,
Homeward through the weltering serpents,
With the trophies of the battle,
With a shout and song of triumph.
  On the shore stood old Nokomis,
On the shore stood Chibiabos,
And the very strong man, Kwasind,
Waiting for the hero's coming,
Listening to his songs of triumph.
And the people of the village
Welcomed him with songs and dances,
Made a joyous feast, and shouted:
"Honor be to Hiawatha!
He has slain the great Pearl-Feather,
Slain the mightiest of Magicians,
Him, who sent the fiery fever,
Sent the white fog from the fen-lands,
Sent disease and death among us!"
  Ever dear to Hiawatha
Was the memory of Mama!
And in token of his friendship,
As a mark of his remembrance,
He adorned and decked his pipe-stem
With the crimson tuft of feathers,
With the blood-red crest of Mama.
But the wealth of Megissogwon,
All the trophies of the battle,
He divided with his people,
Shared it equally among them.

X

HIAWATHA'S WOOING

"As unto the bow the cord is,
So unto the man is woman;
Though she bends him, she obeys him,
Though she draws him, yet she follows,
Useless each without the other!"
  Thus the youthful Hiawatha
Said within himself and pondered,
Much perplexed by various feelings,

305

Listless, longing, hoping, fearing,
Dreaming still of Minnehaha,
Of the lovely Laughing Water,
In the land of the Dacotahs.
　"Wed a maiden of your people,"
Warning said the old Nokomis;
"Go not eastward, go not westward,
For a stranger, whom we know not!
Like a fire upon the hearth-stone
Is a neighbor's homely daughter,
Like the starlight or the moonlight
Is the handsomest of strangers!"
　Thus dissuading spake Nokomis,
And my Hiawatha answered
Only this: "Dear old Nokomis,
Very pleasant is the firelight,
But I like the starlight better,
Better do I like the moonlight!"
　Gravely then said old Nokomis:
"Bring not here an idle maiden,
Bring not here a useless woman,
Hands unskilful, feet unwilling;
Bring a wife with nimble fingers,
Heart and hand that move together,
Feet that run on willing errands!"
　Smiling answered Hiawatha:
"In the land of the Dacotahs
Lives the Arrow-maker's daughter,
Minnehaha, Laughing Water,
Handsomest of all the women.
I will bring her to your wigwam,
She shall run upon your errands,
Be your starlight, moonlight, firelight,
Be the sunlight of my people!"
　Still dissuading said Nokomis:
"Bring not to my lodge a stranger
From the land of the Dacotahs!
Very fierce are the Dacotahs,
Often is there war between us,
There are feuds yet unforgotten,
Wounds that ache and still may open!"
　Laughing answered Hiawatha:
"For that reason, if no other,

Would I wed the fair Dacotah,
That our tribes might be united,
That old feuds might be forgotten,
And old wounds be healed forever!"
  Thus departed Hiawatha
To the land of the Dacotahs,
To the land of handsome women;
Striding over moor and meadow,
Through interminable forests,
Through uninterrupted silence.
  With his moccasins of magic,
At each stride a mile he measured;
Yet the way seemed long before him,
And his heart outran his footsteps;
And he journeyed without resting,
Till he heard the cataract's laughter,
Heard the Falls of Minnehaha
Calling to him through the silence.
"Pleasant is the sound!" he murmured,
"Pleasant is the voice that calls me!"
  On the outskirts of the forests,
'Twixt the shadow and the sunshine,
Herds of fallow deer were feeding,
But they saw not Hiawatha;
To his bow he whispered, "Fail not!"
To his arrow whispered, "Swerve not!"
Sent it singing on its errand,
To the red heart of the roebuck;
Threw the deer across his shoulder,
And sped forward without pausing.
  At the doorway of his wigwam
Sat the ancient Arrow-maker,
In the land of the Dacotahs,
Making arrow-heads of jasper,
Arrow-heads of chalcedony.
At his side, in all her beauty,
Sat the lovely Minnehaha,
Sat his daughter, Laughing Water,
Plaiting mats of flags and rushes
Of the past the old man's thoughts were,
And the maiden's of the future.
  He was thinking, as he sat there,
Of the days when with such arrows

He had struck the deer and bison,
On the Muskoday, the meadow;
Shot the wild goose, flying southward
On the wing, the clamorous Wawa;
Thinking of the great war-parties,
How they came to buy his arrows,
Could not fight without his arrows.
Ah, no more such noble warriors
Could be found on earth as they were!
Now the men were all like women,
Only used their tongues for weapons!
  She was thinking of a hunter,
From another tribe and country,
Young and tall and very handsome,
Who one morning, in the Spring-time,
Came to buy her father's arrows,
Sat and rested in the wigwam,
Lingered long about the doorway,
Looking back as he departed.
She had heard her father praise him,
Praise his courage and his wisdom;
Would he come again for arrows
To the Falls of Minnehaha?
On the mat her hands lay idle,
And her eyes were very dreamy.
  Through their thoughts they heard a footstep,
Heard a rustling in the branches,
And with glowing cheek and forehead,
With the deer upon his shoulders,
Suddenly from out the woodlands
Hiawatha stood before them.
  Straight the ancient Arrow-maker
Looked up gravely from his labor,
Laid aside the unfinished arrow,
Bade him enter at the doorway,
Saying, as he rose to meet him,
'Hiawatha, you are welcome!"
  At the feet of Laughing Water
Hiawatha laid his burden,
Threw the red deer from his shoulders;
And the maiden looked up at him,
Looked up from her mat of rushes,
Said with gentle look and accent,

"You are welcome, Hiawatha!"
  Very spacious was the wigwam,
Made of deer-skins dressed and whitened,
With the Gods of the Dacotahs
Drawn and painted on its curtains,
And so tall the doorway, hardly
Hiawatha stooped to enter,
Hardly touched his eagle-feathers
As he entered at the doorway.
  Then uprose the Laughing Water,
From the ground fair Minnehaha,
Laid aside her mat unfinished,
Brought forth food and set before them,
Water brought them from the brooklet,
Gave them food in earthen vessels,
Gave them drink in bowls of bass-wood,
Listened while the guest was speaking,
Listened while her father answered,
But not once her lips she opened,
Not a single word she uttered.
  Yes, as in a dream she listened
To the words of Hiawatha,
As he talked of old Nokomis,
Who had nursed him in his childhood,
As he told of his companions,
Chibiabos, the musician,
And the very strong man, Kwasind,
And of happiness and plenty
In the land of the Ojibways,
In the pleasant land and peaceful.
  "After many years of warfare,
Many years of strife and bloodshed,
There is peace between the Ojibways
And the tribe of the Dacotahs."
Thus continued Hiawatha,
And then added, speaking slowly,
"That this peace may last forever,
And our hands be clasped more closely,
And our hearts be more united,
Give me as my wife this maiden,
Minnehaha, Laughing Water,
Loveliest of Dacotah women!"
  And the ancient Arrow-maker

Paused a moment ere he answered,
Smoked a little while in silence,
Looked at Hiawatha proudly,
Fondly looked at Laughing Water,
And made answer very gravely:
"Yes, if Minnehaha wishes;
Let your heart speak, Minnehaha!"
  And the lovely Laughing Water
Seemed more lovely as she stood there,
Neither willing nor reluctant,
As she went to Hiawatha,
Softly took the seat beside him,
While she said, and blushed to say it,
"I will follow you, my husband!"
  This was Hiawatha's wooing!
Thus it was he won the daughter
Of the ancient Arrow-maker,
In the land of the Dacotahs!
  From the wigwam he departed,
Leading with him Laughing Water;
Hand in hand they went together,
Through the woodland and the meadow,
Left the old man standing lonely
At the doorway of his wigwam,
Heard the Falls of Minnehaha
Calling to them from the distance,
Crying to them from afar off,
"Fare thee well, O Minnehaha!"
  And the ancient Arrow-maker
Turned again unto his labor,
Sat down by his sunny doorway,
Murmuring to himself, and saying:
"Thus it is our daughters leave us,
Those we love, and those who love us!
Just when they have learned to help us,
When we are old and lean upon them,
Comes a youth with flaunting feathers,
With his flute of reeds, a stranger
Wanders piping through the village,
Beckons to the fairest maiden,
And she follows where he leads her,
Leaving all things for the stranger!"
  Pleasant was the journey homeward,

Through interminable forests,
Over meadow, over mountain,
Over river, hill, and hollow.
Short it seemed to Hiawatha,
Though they journeyed very slowly,
Though his pace he checked and slackened
To the steps of Laughing Water.
  Over wide and rushing rivers
In his arms he bore the maiden;
Light he thought her as a feather,
As the plume upon his head-gear;
Cleared the tangled pathway for her,
Bent aside the swaying branches,
Made at night a lodge of branches,
And a bed with boughs of hemlock,
And a fire before the doorway
With the dry cones of the pine-tree.
  All the travelling winds went with them,
O'er the meadows, through the forest;
All the stars of night looked at them,
Watched with sleepless eyes their slumber;
From his ambush in the oak-tree
Peeped the squirrel, Adjidaumo,
Watched with eager eyes the lovers;
And the rabbit, the Wabasso,
Scampered from the path before them,
Peering, peeping from his burrow,
Sat erect upon his haunches,
Watched with curious eyes the lovers.
  Pleasant was the journey homeward!
All the birds sang loud and sweetly
Songs of happiness and heart's-ease;
Sang the bluebird, the Owaissa,
"Happy are you, Hiawatha,
Having such a wife to love you!"
Sang the robin, the Opechee,
"Happy are you, Laughing Water,
Having such a noble husband!"
  From the sky the sun benignant
Looked upon them through the branches,
Saying to them, "O my children,
Love is sunshine, hate is shadow,
Life is checkered shade and sunshine,

Rule by love, O Hiawatha!"
  From the sky the moon looked at them,
Filled the lodge with mystic splendors,
Whispered to them, "O my children,
Day is restless, night is quiet,
Man imperious, woman feeble;
Half is mine, although I follow;
Rule by patience, Laughing Water!"
  Thus it was they journeyed homeward;
Thus it was that Hiawatha
To the lodge of old Nokomis
Brought the moonlight, starlight, firelight,
Brought the sunshine of his people,
Minnehaha, Laughing Water,
Handsomest of all the women
In the land of the Dacotahs,
In the land of handsome women.

XI

HIAWATHA'S WEDDING-FEAST

You shall hear how Pau-Puk-Keewis,
How the handsome Yenadizze
Danced at Hiawatha's wedding;
How the gentle Chibiabos,
He the sweetest of musicians,
Sang his songs of love and longing;
How Iagoo, the great boaster,
He the marvellous story-teller,
Told his tales of strange adventure,
That the feast might be more joyous,
That the time might pass more gayly,
And the guests be more contented.
  Sumptuous was the feast Nokomis
Made at Hiawatha's wedding;
All the bowls were made of bass-wood,
White and polished very smoothly,
All the spoons of horn of bison,
Black and polished very smoothly.
  She had sent through all the village
Messengers with wands of willow,
As a sign of invitation,

As a token of the feasting;
And the wedding guests assembled,
Clad in all their richest raiment,
Robes of fur and belts of wampum,
Splendid with their paint and plumage,
Beautiful with beads and tassels.

  First they ate the sturgeon, Nahma,
And the pike, the Maskenozha,
Caught and cooked by old Nokomis;
Then on pemican they feasted,
Pemican and buffalo marrow,
Haunch of deer and hump of bison,
Yellow cakes of the Mondamin,
And the wild rice of the river.

  But the gracious Hiawatha,
And the lovely Laughing Water,
And the careful old Nokomis,
Tasted not the food before them,
Only waited on the others
Only served their guests in silence.

  And when all the guests had finished,
Old Nokomis, brisk and busy,
From an ample pouch of otter,
Filled the red-stone pipes for smoking
With tobacco from the South-land,
Mixed with bark of the red willow,
And with herbs and leaves of fragrance.

  Then she said, "O Pau-Puk-Keewis,
Dance for us your merry dances,
Dance the Beggar's Dance to please us,
That the feast may be more joyous,
That the time may pass more gayly,
And our guests be more contented!"

  Then the handsome Pau-Puk-Keewis,
He the idle Yenadizze,
He the merry mischief-maker,
Whom the people called the Storm-Fool,
Rose among the guests assembled.

  Skilled was he in sports and pastimes,
In the merry dance of snow-shoes,
In the play of quoits and ball-play;
Skilled was he in games of hazard,
In all games of skill and hazard,

313

Pugasaing, the Bowl and Counters,
Kuntassoo, the Game of Plum-stones.
  Though the warriors called him Faint-Heart,
Called him coward, Shaugodaya,
Idler, gambler, Yenadizze,
Little heeded he their jesting,
Little cared he for their insults,
For the women and the maidens
Loved the handsome Pau-Puk-Keewis.
  He was dressed in shirt of doeskin,
White and soft, and fringed with ermine,
All inwrought with beads of wampum;
He was dressed in deer-skin leggings,
Fringed with hedgehog quills and ermine,
And in moccasins of buck-skin,
Thick with quills and beads embroidered.
On his head were plumes of swan's down,
On his heels were tails of foxes,
In one hand a fan of feathers,
And a pipe was in the other.
  Barred with streaks of red and yellow,
Streaks of blue and bright vermilion,
Shone the face of Pau-Puk-Keewis.
From his forehead fell his tresses,
Smooth, and parted like a woman's,
Shining bright with oil, and plaited,
Hung with braids of scented grasses,
As among the guests assembled,
To the sound of flutes and singing,
To the sound of drums and voices,
Rose the handsome Pau-Puk-Keewis,
And began his mystic dances.
  First he danced a solemn measure,
Very slow in step and gesture,
In and out among the pine-trees,
Through the shadows and the sunshine,
Treading softly like a panther.
Then more swiftly and still swifter,
Whirling, spinning round in circles,
Leaping o'er the guests assembled,
Eddying round and round the wigwam,
Till the leaves went whirling with him,
Till the dust and wind together

Swept in eddies round about him.
  Then along the sandy margin
Of the lake, the Big-Sea-Water,
On he sped with frenzied gestures,
Stamped upon the sand, and tossed it
Wildly in the air around him;
Till the wind became a whirlwind,
Till the sand was blown and sifted
Like great snowdrifts o'er the landscape,
Heaping all the shores with Sand Dunes,
Sand Hills of the Nagow Wudjoo!
  Thus the merry Pau-Puk-Keewis
Danced his Beggar's Dance to please them,
And, returning, sat down laughing
There among the guests assembled,
Sat and fanned himself serenely
With his fan of turkey-feathers.
  Then they said to Chibiabos,
To the friend of Hiawatha,
To the sweetest of all singers,
To the best of all musicians,
"Sing to us, O Chibiabos!
Songs of love and songs of longing,
That the feast may be more joyous,
That the time may pass more gayly,
And our guests be more contented!"
  And the gentle Chibiabos
Sang in accents sweet and tender,
Sang in tones of deep emotion,
Songs of love and songs of longing;
Looking still at Hiawatha,
Looking at fair Laughing Water,
Sang he softly, sang in this wise:
  "Onaway! Awake, beloved!
Thou the wild-flower of the forest!
Thou the wild-bird of the prairie!
Thou with eyes so soft and fawn-like!
  "If thou only lookest at me,
I am happy, I am happy,
As the lilies of the prairie,
When they feel the dew upon them!
  "Sweet thy breath is as the fragrance
Of the wild-flowers in the morning,

315

As their fragrance is at evening,
In the Moon when leaves are falling.
  "Does not all the blood within me
Leap to meet thee, leap to meet thee,
As the springs to meet the sunshine,
In the Moon when nights are brightest?
  "Onaway! my heart sings to thee,
Sings with joy when thou art near me,
As the sighing, singing branches
In the pleasant Moon of Strawberries!
  "When thou art not pleased, beloved,
Then my heart is sad and darkened,
As the shining river darkens
When the clouds drop shadows on it!
  "When thou smilest, my beloved,
Then my troubled heart is brightened,
As in sunshine gleam the ripples
That the cold wind makes in rivers.
  "Smiles the earth, and smile the waters,
Smile the cloudless skies above us,
But I lose the way of smiling
When thou art no longer near me!
  "I myself, myself! behold me!
Blood of my beating heart, behold me!
Oh awake, awake, beloved!
Onaway! awake, beloved!"
  Thus the gentle Chibiabos
Sang his song of love and longing;
And Iagoo, the great boaster,
He the marvellous story-teller,
He the friend of old Nokomis,
Jealous of the sweet musician,
Jealous of the applause they gave him,
Saw in all the eyes around him,
Saw in all their looks and gestures,
That the wedding guests assembled
Longed to hear his pleasant stories,
His immeasurable falsehoods.
  Very boastful was Iagoo;
Never heard he an adventure
But himself had met a greater;
Never any deed of daring
But himself had done a bolder;

Never any marvellous story
But himself could tell a stranger.
  Would you listen to his boasting,
Would you only give him credence,
No one ever shot an arrow
Half so far and high as he had;
Ever caught so many fishes,
Ever killed so many reindeer,
Ever trapped so many beaver!
  None could run so fast as he could,
None could dive so deep as he could,
None could swim so far as he could;
None had made so many journeys,
None had seen so many wonders,
As this wonderful Iagoo,
As this marvellous story-teller!
  Thus his name became a by-word
And a jest among the people;
And whene'er a boastful hunter
Praised his own address too highly,
Or a warrior, home returning,
Talked too much of his achievements,
All his hearers cried, "Iagoo!
Here's Iagoo come among us!"
  He it was who carved the cradle
Of the little Hiawatha,
Carved its framework out of linden,
Bound it strong with reindeer sinews;
He it was who taught him later
How to make his bows and arrows,
How to make the bows of ash-tree,
And the arrows of the oak-tree.
So among the guests assembled
At my Hiawatha's wedding
Sat Iagoo, old and ugly,
Sat the marvellous story-teller.
  And they said, "O good Iagoo,
Tell us now a tale of wonder,
Tell us of some strange adventure,
That the feast may be more joyous,
That the time may pass more gayly,
And our guests be more contented!"
  And Iagoo answered straightway,

"You shall hear a tale of wonder,
You shall hear the strange adventures
Of Osseo, the Magician,
From the Evening Star descending."

XII

THE SON OF THE EVENING STAR

Can it be the sun descending
O'er the level plain of water?
Or the Red Swan floating, flying,
Wounded by the magic arrow,
Staining all the waves with crimson,
With the crimson of its life-blood,
Filling all the air with splendor,
With the splendor of its plumage?
  Yes; it is the sun descending,
Sinking down into the water;
All the sky is stained with purple,
All the water flushed with crimson!
No; it is the Red Swan floating,
Diving down beneath the water;
To the sky its wings are lifted,
With its blood the waves are reddened!
  Over it the Star of Evening
Melts and trembles through the purple,
Hangs suspended in the twilight.
No; it is a bead of wampum
On the robes of the Great Spirit
As he passes through the twilight,
Walks in silence through the heavens.
  This with joy beheld Iagoo
And he said in haste: "Behold it!
See the sacred Star of Evening!
You shall hear a tale of wonder,
Hear the story of Osseo,
Son of the Evening Star, Osseo!
  "Once, in days no more remembered,
Ages nearer the beginning,
When the heavens were closer to us,
And the Gods were more familiar,
In the North-land lived a hunter,

318

With ten young and comely daughters,
Tall and lithe as wands of willow;
Only Oweenee, the youngest,
She the wilful and the wayward,
She the silent, dreamy maiden,
Was the fairest of the sisters.
  "All these women married warriors,
Married brave and haughty husbands;
Only Oweenee, the youngest,
Laughed and flouted all her lovers,
All her young and handsome suitors,
And then married old Osseo,
Old Osseo, poor and ugly,
Broken with age and weak with coughing,
Always coughing like a squirrel.
  "Ah, but beautiful within him
Was the spirit of Osseo,
From the Evening Star descended,
Star of Evening, Star of Woman,
Star of tenderness and passion!
All its fire was in his bosom,
All its beauty in his spirit,
All its mystery in his being,
All its splendor in his language!
  "And her lovers, the rejected,
Handsome men with belts of wampum,
Handsome men with paint and feathers.
Pointed at her in derision,
Followed her with jest and laughter.
But she said: 'I care not for you,
Care not for your belts of wampum,
Care not for your paint and feathers,
Care not for your jests and laughter;
I am happy with Osseo!'
  "Once to some great feast invited,
Through the damp and dusk of evening,
Walked together the ten sisters,
Walked together with their husbands;
Slowly followed old Osseo,
With fair Oweenee beside him;
All the others chatted gayly,
These two only walked in silence.
  "At the western sky Osseo

Gazed intent, as if imploring,
Often stopped and gazed imploring
At the trembling Star of Evening,
At the tender Star of Woman;
And they heard him murmur softly,
'Ah, showain nemeshin, Nosa!
Pity, pity me, my father!'
   "'Listen!' said the eldest sister,
'He is praying to his father!
What a pity that the old man
Does not stumble in the pathway,
Does not break his neck by falling!'
And they laughed till all the forest
Rang with their unseemly laughter.
   "On their pathway through the woodlands
Lay an oak, by storms uprooted,
Lay the great trunk of an oak-tree,
Buried half in leaves and mosses,
Mouldering, crumbling, huge and hollow.
And Osseo, when he saw it,
Gave a shout, a cry of anguish,
Leaped into its yawning cavern,
At one end went in an old man,
Wasted, wrinkled, old, and ugly;
From the other came a young man,
Tall and straight and strong and handsome.
   "Thus Osseo was transfigured,
Thus restored to youth and beauty;
But, alas for good Osseo,
And for Oweenee, the faithful!
Strangely, too, was she transfigured.
Changed into a weak old woman,
With a staff she tottered onward,
Wasted, wrinkled, old, and ugly!
And the sisters and their husbands
Laughed until the echoing forest
Rang with their unseemly laughter.
   "But Osseo turned not from her,
Walked with slower step beside her,
Took her hand, as brown and withered
As an oak-leaf is in Winter,
Called her sweetheart, Nenemoosha,
Soothed her with soft words of kindness,

Till they reached the lodge of feasting,
Till they sat down in the wigwam,
Sacred to the Star of Evening,
To the tender Star of Woman.
  "Wrapt in visions, lost in dreaming,
At the banquet sat Osseo;
All were merry, all were happy,
All were joyous but Osseo.
Neither food nor drink he tasted,
Neither did he speak nor listen;
But as one bewildered sat he,
Looking dreamily and sadly,
First at Oweenee, then upward
At the gleaming sky above them.
  "Then a voice was heard, a whisper,
Coming from the starry distance,
Coming from the empty vastness,
Low, and musical, and tender;
And the voice said: 'O Osseo!
O my son, my best beloved!
Broken are the spells that bound you,
All the charms of the magicians,
All the magic powers of evil;
Come to me; ascend, Osseo!
  "'Taste the food that stands before you:
It is blessed and enchanted,
It has magic virtues in it,
It will change you to a spirit.
All your bowls and all your kettles
Shall be wood and clay no longer;
But the bowls be changed to wampum,
And the kettles shall be silver;
They shall shine like shells of scarlet,
Like the fire shall gleam and glimmer.
  "'And the women shall no longer
Bear the dreary doom of labor,
But be changed to birds, and glisten
With the beauty of the starlight,
Painted with the dusky splendors
Of the skies and clouds of evening!'
  "What Osseo heard as whispers,
What as words he comprehended,
Was but music to the others,

Music as of birds afar off,
Of the whippoorwill afar off,
Of the lonely Wawonaissa
Singing in the darksome forest.
  "Then the lodge began to tremble,
Straight began to shake and tremble,
And they felt it rising, rising,
Slowly through the air ascending,
From the darkness of the tree-tops
Forth into the dewy starlight,
Till it passed the topmost branches;
And behold! the wooden dishes
All were changed to shells of scarlet!
And behold! the earthen kettles
All were changed to bowls of silver!
And the roof-poles of the wigwam
Were as glittering rods of silver,
And the roof of bark upon them
As the shining shards of beetles.
  "Then Osseo gazed around him,
And he saw the nine fair sisters,
All the sisters and their husbands,
Changed to birds of various plumage.
Some were jays and some were magpies,
Others thrushes, others blackbirds;
And they hopped, and sang, and twittered,
Perked and fluttered all their feathers,
Strutted in their shining plumage,
And their tails like fans unfolded.
  "Only Oweenee, the youngest,
Was not changed, but sat in silence,
Wasted, wrinkled, old, and ugly,
Looking sadly at the others;
Till Osseo, gazing upward,
Gave another cry of anguish,
Such a cry as he had uttered
By the oak-tree in the forest.
  "Then returned her youth and beauty,
And her soiled and tattered garments
Were transformed to robes of ermine,
And her staff became a feather,
Yes, a shining silver feather!
  "And again the wigwam trembled,

Swayed and rushed through airy currents,
Through transparent cloud and vapor,
And amid celestial splendors
On the Evening Star alighted,
As a snow-flake falls on snow-flake,
As a leaf drops on a river,
As the thistledown on water.
  "Forth with cheerful words of welcome
Came the father of Osseo,
He with radiant locks of silver,
He with eyes serene and tender.
And he said: 'My son, Osseo,
Hang the cage of birds you bring there,
Hang the cage with rods of silver,
And the birds with glistening feathers,
At the doorway of my wigwam.'
  "At the door he hung the bird-cage,
And they entered in and gladly
Listened to Osseo's father,
Ruler of the Star of Evening,
As he said: 'O my Osseo!
I have had compassion on you,
Given you back your youth and beauty,
Into birds of various plumage
Changed your sisters and their husbands;
Changed them thus because they mocked you
In the figure of the old man,
In that aspect sad and wrinkled,
Could not see your heart of passion,
Could not see your youth immortal;
Only Oweenee, the faithful,
Saw your naked heart and loved you.
  "'In the lodge that glimmers yonder,
In the little star that twinkles
Through the vapors, on the left hand,
Lives the envious Evil Spirit,
The Wabeno, the magician,
Who transformed you to an old man.
Take heed lest his beams fall on you,
For the rays he darts around him
Are the power of his enchantment,
Are the arrows that he uses.'
  "Many years, in peace and quiet,

On the peaceful Star of Evening
Dwelt Osseo with his father;
Many years, in song and flutter,
At the doorway of the wigwam,
Hung the cage with rods of silver,
And fair Oweenee, the faithful,
Bore a son unto Osseo,
With the beauty of his mother,
With the courage of his father.
   "And the boy grew up and prospered,
And Osseo, to delight him,
Made him little bows and arrows,
Opened the great cage of silver,
And let loose his aunts and uncles,
All those birds with glossy feathers,
For his little son to shoot at.
   "Round and round they wheeled and darted,
Filled the Evening Star with music,
With their songs of joy and freedom
Filled the Evening Star with splendor,
With the fluttering of their plumage;
Till the boy, the little hunter,
Bent his bow and shot an arrow,
Shot a swift and fatal arrow,
And a bird, with shining feathers,
At his feet fell wounded sorely.
   "But, O wondrous transformation!
'T was no bird he saw before him,
'T was a beautiful young woman,
With the arrow in her bosom!
   "When her blood fell on the planet,
On the sacred Star of Evening,
Broken was the spell of magic,
Powerless was the strange enchantment,
And the youth, the fearless bowman,
Suddenly felt himself descending,
Held by unseen hands, but sinking
Downward through the empty spaces,
Downward through the clouds and vapors,
Till he rested on an island,
On an island, green and grassy,
Yonder in the Big-Sea-Water.
   "After him he saw descending

All the birds with shining feathers,
Fluttering, falling, wafted downward,
Like the painted leaves of Autumn;
And the lodge with poles of silver,
With its roof like wings of beetles,
Like the shining shards of beetles,
By the winds of heaven uplifted,
Slowly sank upon the island,
Bringing back the good Osseo,
Bringing Oweenee, the faithful.
    "Then the birds, again transfigured,
Reassumed the shape of mortals,
Took their shape, but not their stature;
They remained as Little People,
Like the pygmies, the Puk-Wudjies,
And on pleasant nights of Summer,
When the Evening Star was shining,
Hand in hand they danced together
On the island's craggy headlands,
On the sand-beach low and level.
    "Still their glittering lodge is seen there,
On the tranquil Summer evenings,
And upon the shore the fisher
Sometimes hears their happy voices,
Sees them dancing in the starlight!"
    When the story was completed,
When the wondrous tale was ended,
Looking round upon his listeners,
Solemnly Iagoo added:
"There are great men, I have known such,
Whom their people understand not,
Whom they even make a jest of,
Scoff and jeer at in derision.
From the story of Osseo
Let us learn the fate of jesters!"
    All the wedding guests delighted
Listened to the marvellous story,
Listened laughing and applauding,
And they whispered to each other:
"Does he mean himself, I wonder?
And are we the aunts and uncles?"
    Then again sang Chibiabos,
Sang a song of love and longing,

In those accents sweet and tender,
In those tones of pensive sadness,
Sang a maiden's lamentation
For her lover, her Algonquin.
 "When I think of my beloved,
Ah me! think of my beloved,
When my heart is thinking of him,
O my sweetheart, my Algonquin!
 "Ah me! when I parted from him,
Round my neck he hung the wampum,
As a pledge, the snow-white wampum,
O my sweetheart, my Algonquin!
 "I will go with you, he whispered,
Ah me! to your native country;
Let me go with you, he whispered,
O my sweetheart, my Algonquin!
 "Far away, away, I answered,
Very far away, I answered,
Ah me! is my native country,
O my sweetheart, my Algonquin!
 "When I looked back to behold him,
Where we parted, to behold him,
After me he still was gazing,
O my sweetheart, my Algonquin!
 "By the tree he still was standing,
By the fallen tree was standing,
That had dropped into the water,
O my sweetheart, my Algonquin!
 "When I think of my beloved,
Ah me! think of my beloved,
When my heart is thinking of him,
O my sweetheart, my Algonquin!"
 Such was Hiawatha's Wedding,
Such the dance of Pau-Puk-Keewis,
Such the story of Iagoo,
Such the songs of Chibiabos;
Thus the wedding banquet ended,
And the wedding guests departed,
Leaving Hiawatha happy
With the night and Minnehaha.

XIII

BLESSING THE CORNFIELDS

Sing, O Song of Hiawatha,
Of the happy days that followed,
In the land of the Ojibways,
In the pleasant land and peaceful!
Sing the mysteries of Mondamin,
Sing the Blessing of the Cornfields!
  Buried was the bloody hatchet,
Buried was the dreadful war-club,
Buried were all warlike weapons,
And the war-cry was forgotten.
There was peace among the nations;
Unmolested roved the hunters,
Built the birch canoe for sailing,
Caught the fish in lake and river,
Shot the deer and trapped the beaver;
Unmolested worked the women,
Made their sugar from the maple,
Gathered wild rice in the meadows,
Dressed the skins of deer and beaver.
  All around the happy village
Stood the maize-fields, green and shining,
Waved the green plumes of Mondamin,
Waved his soft and sunny tresses,
Filling all the land with plenty.
'T was the women who in Spring-time
Planted the broad fields and fruitful,
Buried in the earth Mondamin;
'T was the women who in Autumn
Stripped the yellow husks of harvest,
Stripped the garments from Mondamin,
Even as Hiawatha taught them.
  Once, when all the maize was planted,
Hiawatha, wise and thoughtful,
Spake and said to Minnehaha,
To his wife, the Laughing Water:
"You shall bless to-night the cornfields,
Draw a magic circle round them,
To protect them from destruction,
Blast of mildew, blight of insect,

Wagemin, the thief of cornfields,
Paimosaid, who steals the maize-ear!
　"In the night, when all is silence,
In the night, when all is darkness,
When the Spirit of Sleep, Nepahwin,
Shuts the doors of all the wigwams,
So that not an ear can hear you,
So that not an eye can see you,
Rise up from your bed in silence,
Lay aside your garments wholly,
Walk around the fields you planted,
Round the borders of the cornfields,
Covered by your tresses only,
Robed with darkness as a garment.
　"Thus the fields shall be more fruitful,
And the passing of your footsteps
Draw a magic circle round them,
So that neither blight nor mildew,
Neither burrowing worm nor insect,
Shall pass o'er the magic circle;
Not the dragon-fly, Kwo-ne-she,
Nor the spider, Subbekashe,
Nor the grasshopper, Pah-puk-keena;
Nor the mighty caterpillar,
Way-muk-kwana, with the bear-skin,
King of all the caterpillars!"
　On the tree-tops near the cornfields
Sat the hungry crows and ravens,
Kahgahgee, the King of Ravens,
With his band of black marauders.
And they laughed at Hiawatha,
Till the tree-tops shook with laughter,
With their melancholy laughter,
At the words of Hiawatha.
"Hear him!" said they; "hear the Wise Man,
Hear the plots of Hiawatha!"
　When the noiseless night descended
Broad and dark o'er field and forest,
When the mournful Wawonaissa
Sorrowing sang among the hemlocks,
And the Spirit of Sleep, Nepahwin,
Shut the doors of all the wigwams,
From her bed rose Laughing Water,

Laid aside her garments wholly,
And with darkness clothed and guarded,
Unashamed and unaffrighted,
Walked securely round the cornfields,
Drew the sacred, magic circle
Of her footprints round the cornfields.
  No one but the Midnight only
Saw her beauty in the darkness,
No one but the Wawonaissa
Heard the panting of her bosom;
Guskewau, the darkness, wrapped her
Closely in his sacred mantle,
So that none might see her beauty,
So that none might boast, "I saw her!"
  On the morrow, as the day dawned,
Kahgahgee, the King of Ravens,
Gathered all his black marauders,
Crows and blackbirds, jays and ravens,
Clamorous on the dusky tree-tops,
And descended, fast and fearless,
On the fields of Hiawatha,
On the grave of the Mondamin.
  "We will drag Mondamin," said they,
"From the grave where he is buried,
Spite of all the magic circles
Laughing Water draws around it,
Spite of all the sacred footprints
Minnehaha stamps upon it!"
  But the wary Hiawatha,
Ever thoughtful, careful, watchful,
Had o'erheard the scornful laughter
When they mocked him from the tree-tops.
"Kaw!" he said, "my friends the ravens!
Kahgahgee, my King of Ravens!
I will teach you all a lesson
That shall not be soon forgotten!"
  He had risen before the daybreak,
He had spread o'er all the cornfields
Snares to catch the black marauders,
And was lying now in ambush
In the neighboring grove of pine-trees,
Waiting for the crows and blackbirds,
Waiting for the jays and ravens.

Soon they came with caw and clamor,
Rush of wings and cry of voices,
To their work of devastation,
Settling down upon the cornfields,
Delving deep with beak and talon,
For the body of Mondamin.
And with all their craft and cunning,
All their skill in wiles of warfare,
They perceived no danger near them,
Till their claws became entangled,
Till they found themselves imprisoned
In the snares of Hiawatha.
From his place of ambush came he,
Striding terrible among them,
And so awful was his aspect
That the bravest quailed with terror.
Without mercy he destroyed them
Right and left, by tens and twenties,
And their wretched, lifeless bodies
Hung aloft on poles for scarecrows
Round the consecrated cornfields,
As a signal of his vengeance,
As a warning to marauders.
Only Kahgahgee, the leader,
Kahgahgee, the King of Ravens,
He alone was spared among them
As a hostage for his people.
With his prisoner-string he bound him,
Led him captive to his wigwam,
Tied him fast with cords of elm-bark
To the ridge-pole of his wigwam.
"Kahgahgee, my raven!" said he,
"You the leader of the robbers,
You the plotter of this mischief,
The contriver of this outrage,
I will keep you, I will hold you,
As a hostage for your people,
As a pledge of good behavior!"
And he left him, grim and sulky,
Sitting in the morning sunshine
On the summit of the wigwam,
Croaking fiercely his displeasure,
Flapping his great sable pinions,

Vainly struggling for his freedom,
Vainly calling on his people!
  Summer passed, and Shawondasee
Breathed his sighs o'er all the landscape,
From the South-land sent his ardor,
Wafted kisses warm and tender;
And the maize-field grew and ripened,
Till it stood in all the splendor
Of its garments green and yellow,
Of its tassels and its plumage,
And the maize-ears full and shining
Gleamed from bursting sheaths of verdure.
  Then Nokomis, the old woman,
Spake, and said to Minnehaha:
"'T is the Moon when leaves are falling;
All the wild-rice has been gathered,
And the maize is ripe and ready;
Let us gather in the harvest,
Let us wrestle with Mondamin,
Strip him of his plumes and tassels,
Of his garments green and yellow!"
  And the merry Laughing Water
Went rejoicing from the wigwam,
With Nokomis, old and wrinkled,
And they called the women round them,
Called the young men and the maidens,
To the harvest of the cornfields,
To the husking of the maize-ear.
  On the border of the forest,
Underneath the fragrant pine-trees,
Sat the old men and the warriors
Smoking in the pleasant shadow.
In uninterrupted silence
Looked they at the gamesome labor
Of the young men and the women;
Listened to their noisy talking,
To their laughter and their singing,
Heard them chattering like the magpies,
Heard them laughing like the blue-jays,
Heard them singing like the robins.
  And whene'er some lucky maiden
Found a red ear in the husking,
Found a maize-ear red as blood is,

331

"Nushka!" cried they all together,
"Nushka! you shall have a sweetheart,
You shall have a handsome husband!"
"Ugh!" the old men all responded
From their seats beneath the pine-trees.
   And whene'er a youth or maiden
Found a crooked ear in husking,
Found a maize-ear in the husking
Blighted, mildewed, or misshapen,
Then they laughed and sang together,
Crept and limped about the cornfields,
Mimicked in their gait and gestures
Some old man, bent almost double,
Singing singly or together:
"Wagemin, the thief of cornfields!
Paimosaid, who steals the maize-ear!"
   Till the cornfields rang with laughter,
Till from Hiawatha's wigwam
Kahgahgee, the King of Ravens,
Screamed and quivered in his anger,
And from all the neighboring tree-tops
Cawed and croaked the black marauders.
"Ugh!" the old men all responded,
From their seats beneath the pine-trees!

XIV

PICTURE-WRITING

In those days said Hiawatha,
"Lo! how all things fade and perish!
From the memory of the old men
Pass away the great traditions,
The achievements of the warriors,
The adventures of the hunters,
All the wisdom of the Medas,
All the craft of the Wabenos,
All the marvellous dreams and visions
Of the Jossakeeds, the Prophets!
   "Great men die and are forgotten,
Wise men speak; their words of wisdom
Perish in the ears that hear them,

Do not reach the generations
That, as yet unborn, are waiting
In the great, mysterious darkness
Of the speechless days that shall be!
    "On the grave-posts of our fathers
Are no signs, no figures painted;
Who are in those graves we know not,
Only know they are our fathers.
Of what kith they are and kindred,
From what old, ancestral Totem,
Be it Eagle, Bear, or Beaver,
They descended, this we know not,
Only know they are our fathers.
    "Face to face we speak together,
But we cannot speak when absent,
Cannot send our voices from us
To the friends that dwell afar off;
Cannot send a secret message,
But the bearer learns our secret,
May pervert it, may betray it,
May reveal it unto others."
    Thus said Hiawatha, walking
In the solitary forest,
Pondering, musing in the forest,
On the welfare of his people.
    From his pouch he took his colors,
Took his paints of different colors,
On the smooth bark of a birch-tree
Painted many shapes and figures,
Wonderful and mystic figures,
And each figure had a meaning,
Each some word or thought suggested.
    Gitche Manito the Mighty,
He, the Master of Life, was painted
As an egg, with points projecting
To the four winds of the heavens.
Everywhere is the Great Spirit,
Was the meaning of this symbol.
    Mitche Manito the Mighty,
He the dreadful Spirit of Evil,
As a serpent was depicted,
As Kenabeek, the great serpent.
Very crafty, very cunning,

Is the creeping Spirit of Evil,
Was the meaning of this symbol.
  Life and Death he drew as circles,
Life was white, but Death was darkened;
Sun and moon and stars he painted,
Man and beast, and fish and reptile,
Forests, mountains, lakes, and rivers.
  For the earth he drew a straight line,
For the sky a bow above it;
White the space between for daytime,
Filled with little stars for night-time;
On the left a point for sunrise,
On the right a point for sunset,
On the top a point for noontide,
And for rain and cloudy weather
Waving lines descending from it.
  Footprints pointing towards a wigwam
Were a sign of invitation,
Were a sign of guests assembling;
Bloody hands with palms uplifted
Were a symbol of destruction,
Were a hostile sign and symbol.
  All these things did Hiawatha
Show unto his wondering people,
And interpreted their meaning,
And he said: "Behold, your grave-posts
Have no mark, no sign, nor symbol,
Go and paint them all with figures;
Each one with its household symbol,
With its own ancestral Totem;
So that those who follow after
May distinguish them and know them."
  And they painted on the grave-posts
On the graves yet unforgotten,
Each his own ancestral Totem,
Each the symbol of his household;
Figures of the Bear and Reindeer,
Of the Turtle, Crane, and Beaver,
Each inverted as a token
That the owner was departed,
That the chief who bore the symbol
Lay beneath in dust and ashes.
  And the Jossakeeds, the Prophets,

The Wabenos, the Magicians,
And the Medicine-men, the Medas,
Painted upon bark and deer-skin
Figures for the songs they chanted,
For each song a separate symbol,
Figures mystical and awful,
Figures strange and brightly colored;
And each figure had its meaning,
Each some magic song suggested.
  The Great Spirit, the Creator,
Flashing light through all the heaven;
The Great Serpent, the Kenabeek,
With his bloody crest erected,
Creeping, looking into heaven;
In the sky the sun, that listens,
And the moon eclipsed and dying;
Owl and eagle, crane and hen-hawk,
And the cormorant, bird of magic;
Headless men, that walk the heavens,
Bodies lying pierced with arrows,
Bloody hands of death uplifted,
Flags on graves, and great war-captains
Grasping both the earth and heaven!
  Such as these the shapes they painted
On the birch-bark and the deer-skin;
Songs of war and songs of hunting,
Songs of medicine and of magic,
All were written in these figures,
For each figure had its meaning,
Each its separate song recorded.
  Nor forgotten was the Love-Song,
The most subtle of all medicines,
The most potent spell of magic,
Dangerous more than war or hunting!
Thus the Love-Song was recorded,
Symbol and interpretation.
  First a human figure standing,
Painted in the brightest scarlet;
'T is the lover, the musician,
And the meaning is, "My painting
Makes me powerful over others."
  Then the figure seated, singing,
Playing on a drum of magic,

And the interpretation, "Listen!
'T is my voice you hear, my singing!"
   Then the same red figure seated
In the shelter of a wigwam,
And the meaning of the symbol,
"I will come and sit beside you
In the mystery of my passion!"
   Then two figures, man and woman,
Standing hand in hand together
With their hands so clasped together
That they seemed in one united,
And the words thus represented
Are, "I see your heart within you,
And your cheeks are red with blushes!"
   Next the maiden on an island,
In the centre of an island;
And the song this shape suggested
Was, "Though you were at a distance,
Were upon some far-off island,
Such the spell I cast upon you,
Such the magic power of passion,
I could straightway draw you to me!"
   Then the figure of the maiden
Sleeping, and the lover near her,
Whispering to her in her slumbers,
Saying, "Though you were far from me
In the land of Sleep and Silence,
Still the voice of love would reach you!"
   And the last of all the figures
Was a heart within a circle,
Drawn within a magic circle;
And the image had this meaning:
"Naked lies your heart before me,
To your naked heart I whisper!"
   Thus it was that Hiawatha,
In his wisdom, taught the people
All the mysteries of painting,
All the art of Picture-Writing,
On the smooth bark of the birch-tree,
On the white skin of the reindeer,
On the grave-posts of the village.

XV

HIAWATHA'S LAMENTATION

In those days the Evil Spirits,
All the Manitos of mischief,
Fearing Hiawatha's wisdom,
And his love for Chibiabos,
Jealous of their faithful friendship,
And their noble words and actions,
Made at length a league against them,
To molest them and destroy them.
  Hiawatha, wise and wary,
Often said to Chibiabos,
"O my brother! do not leave me,
Lest the Evil Spirits harm you!"
Chibiabos, young and heedless,
Laughing shook his coal-black tresses,
Answered ever sweet and childlike,
"Do not fear for me, O brother!
Harm and evil come not near me!"
  Once when Peboan, the Winter,
Roofed with ice the Big-Sea-Water,
When the snow-flakes, whirling downward,
Hissed among the withered oak-leaves,
Changed the pine-trees into wigwams,
Covered all the earth with silence, —
Armed with arrows, shod with snow-shoes,
Heeding not his brother's warning,
Fearing not the Evil Spirits,
Forth to hunt the deer with antlers
All alone went Chibiabos.
  Right across the Big-Sea-Water
Sprang with speed the deer before him.
With the wind and snow he followed,
O'er the treacherous ice he followed,
Wild with all the fierce commotion
And the rapture of the hunting.
  But beneath, the Evil Spirits
Lay in ambush, waiting for him,
Broke the treacherous ice beneath him,
Dragged him downward to the bottom,
Buried in the sand his body.

Unktahee, the god of water,
He the god of the Dacotahs,
Drowned him in the deep abysses
Of the lake of Gitche Gumee.
    From the headlands Hiawatha
Sent forth such a wail of anguish,
Such a fearful lamentation,
That the bison paused to listen,
And the wolves howled from the prairies,
And the thunder in the distance
Starting answered "Baim-wawa!"
    Then his face with black he painted,
With his robe his head he covered,
In his wigwam sat lamenting,
Seven long weeks he sat lamenting,
Uttering still this moan of sorrow: —
    "He is dead, the sweet musician!
He the sweetest of all singers!
He has gone from us forever,
He has moved a little nearer
To the Master of all music,
To the Master of all singing!
O my brother, Chibiabos!"
    And the melancholy fir-trees
Waved their dark green fans above him,
Waved their purple cones above him,
Sighing with him to console him,
Mingling with his lamentation
Their complaining, their lamenting.
    Came the Spring, and all the forest
Looked in vain for Chibiabos;
Sighed the rivulet, Sebowisha,
Sighed the rushes in the meadow.
    From the tree-tops sang the bluebird,
Sang the bluebird, the Owaissa,
"Chibiabos! Chibiabos!
He is dead, the sweet musician!"
    From the wigwam sang the robin,
Sang the robin, the Opechee,
"Chibiabos! Chibiabos!
He is dead, the sweetest singer!"
    And at night through all the forest
Went the whippoorwill complaining,

Wailing went the Wawonaissa,
"Chibiabos! Chibiabos!
He is dead, the sweet musician!
He the sweetest of all singers!"
  Then the Medicine-men, the Medas,
The magicians, the Wabenos,
And the Jossakeeds, the Prophets,
Came to visit Hiawatha;
Built a Sacred Lodge beside him,
To appease him, to console him,
Walked in silent, grave procession,
Bearing each a pouch of healing,
Skin of beaver, lynx, or otter,
Filled with magic roots and simples,
Filled with very potent medicines.
  When he heard their steps approaching,
Hiawatha ceased lamenting,
Called no more on Chibiabos;
Naught he questioned, naught he answered,
But his mournful head uncovered,
From his face the mourning colors
Washed he slowly and in silence,
Slowly and in silence followed
Onward to the Sacred Wigwam.
  There a magic drink they gave him,
Made of Nahma-wusk, the spearmint,
And Wabeno-wusk, the yarrow,
Roots of power, and herbs of healing;
Beat their drums, and shook their rattles;
Chanted singly and in chorus,
Mystic songs like these, they chanted.
  "I myself, myself! behold me!
'T is the great Gray Eagle talking;
Come, ye white crows, come and hear him!
The loud-speaking thunder helps me;
All the unseen spirits help me;
I can hear their voices calling,
All around the sky I hear them!
I can blow you strong, my brother,
I can heal you, Hiawatha!"
  "Hi-au-ha!" replied the chorus,
"Way-ha-way!" the mystic chorus.
  "Friends of mine are all the serpents!

Hear me shake my skin of hen-hawk!
Mahng, the white loon, I can kill him;
I can shoot your heart and kill it!
I can blow you strong, my brother,
I can heal you, Hiawatha!"
  "Hi-au-ha!" replied the chorus,
"Way-ha-way!" the mystic chorus.
  "I myself, myself! the prophet!
When I speak the wigwam trembles,
Shakes the Sacred Lodge with terror,
Hands unseen begin to shake it!
When I walk, the sky I tread on
Bends and makes a noise beneath me!
I can blow you strong, my brother!
Rise and speak, O Hiawatha!"
  "Hi-au-ha!" replied the chorus,
"Way-ha-way!" the mystic chorus.
  Then they shook their medicine-pouches
O'er the head of Hiawatha,
Danced their medicine-dance around him;
And upstarting wild and haggard,
Like a man from dreams awakened,
He was healed of all his madness.
As the clouds are swept from heaven,
Straightway from his brain departed
All his moody melancholy;
As the ice is swept from rivers,
Straightway from his heart departed
All his sorrow and affliction.
  Then they summoned Chibiabos
From his grave beneath the waters,
From the sands of Gitche Gumee
Summoned Hiawatha's brother.
And so mighty was the magic
Of that cry and invocation,
That he heard it as he lay there
Underneath the Big-Sea-Water;
From the sand he rose and listened,
Heard the music and the singing,
Came, obedient to the summons,
To the doorway of the wigwam,
But to enter they forbade him.
  Through a chink a coal they gave him,

Through the door a burning fire-brand;
Ruler in the Land of Spirits,
Ruler o'er the dead, they made him,
Telling him a fire to kindle
For all those that died thereafter,
Camp-fires for their night encampments
On their solitary journey
To the kingdom of Ponemah,
To the land of the Hereafter.
  From the village of his childhood,
From the homes of those who knew him,
Passing silent through the forest,
Like a smoke-wreath wafted sideways,
Slowly vanished Chibiabos!
Where he passed, the branches moved not,
Where he trod, the grasses bent not,
And the fallen leaves of last year
Made no sound beneath his footstep.
  Four whole days he journeyed onward
Down the pathway of the dead men;
On the dead-man's strawberry feasted,
Crossed the melancholy river,
On the swinging log he crossed it,
Came unto the Lake of Silver,
In the Stone Canoe was carried
To the Islands of the Blessed,
To the land of ghosts and shadows.
  On that journey, moving slowly,
Many weary spirits saw he,
Panting under heavy burdens,
Laden with war-clubs, bows and arrows,
Robes of fur, and pots and kettles,
And with food that friends had given
For that solitary journey.
  "Ay! why do the living," said they,
"Lay such heavy burdens on us!
Better were it to go naked,
Better were it to go fasting,
Than to bear such heavy burdens
On our long and weary journey!"
Forth then issued Hiawatha,
Wandered eastward, wandered westward,
Teaching men the use of simples

And the antidotes for poisons,
And the cure of all diseases.
Thus was first made known to mortals
All the mystery of Medamin,
All the sacred art of healing.

XVI

PAU-PUK-KEEWIS

You shall hear how Pau-Puk-Keewis,
He, the handsome Yenadizze,
Whom the people called the Storm-Fool,
Vexed the village with disturbance;
You shall hear of all his mischief,
And his flight from Hiawatha,
And his wondrous transmigrations,
And the end of his adventures.
  On the shores of Gitche Gumee,
On the dunes of Nagow Wudjoo,
By the shining Big-Sea-Water
Stood the lodge of Pau-Puk-Keewis.
It was he who in his frenzy
Whirled these drifting sands together,
On the dunes of Nagow Wudjoo,
When, among the guests assembled,
He so merrily and madly
Danced at Hiawatha's wedding,
Danced the Beggar's Dance to please them.
  Now, in search of new adventures,
From his lodge went Pau-Puk-Keewis,
Came with speed into the village,
Found the young men all assembled
In the lodge of old Iagoo,
Listening to his monstrous stories,
To his wonderful adventures.
  He was telling them the story
Of Ojeeg, the Summer-Maker,
How he made a hole in heaven,
How he climbed up into heaven,
And let out the summer-weather,
The perpetual, pleasant Summer;

How the Otter first essayed it;
How the Beaver, Lynx, and Badger
Tried in turn the great achievement,
From the summit of the mountain
Smote their fists against the heavens,
Smote against the sky their foreheads,
Cracked the sky, but could not break it;
How the Wolverine, uprising,
Made him ready for the encounter,
Bent his knees down, like a squirrel,
Drew his arms back, like a cricket.
    "Once he leaped," said old Iagoo,
"Once he leaped, and lo! above him
Bent the sky, as ice in rivers
When the waters rise beneath it;
Twice he leaped, and lo! above him
Cracked the sky, as ice in rivers
When the freshet is at highest!
Thrice he leaped, and lo! above him
Broke the shattered sky asunder,
And he disappeared within it,
And Ojeeg, the Fisher Weasel,
With a bound went in behind him!"
    "Hark you!" shouted Pau-Puk-Keewis
As he entered at the doorway;
"I am tired of all this talking,
Tired of old Iagoo's stories,
Tired of Hiawatha's wisdom.
Here is something to amuse you,
Better than this endless talking."
    Then from out his pouch of wolf-skin
Forth he drew, with solemn manner,
All the game of Bowl and Counters,
Pugasaing, with thirteen pieces.
White on one side were they painted,
And vermilion on the other;
Two Kenabeeks or great serpents,
Two Ininewug or wedge-men,
One great war-club, Pugamaugun,
And one slender fish, the Keego,
Four round pieces, Ozawabeeks,
And three Sheshebwug or ducklings.
All were made of bone and painted,

All except the Ozawabeeks;
These were brass, on one side burnished,
And were black upon the other.
  In a wooden bowl he placed them,
Shook and jostled them together,
Threw them on the ground before him,
Thus exclaiming and explaining:
"Red side up are all the pieces,
And one great Kenabeek standing
On the bright side of a brass piece,
On a burnished Ozawabeek;
Thirteen tens and eight are counted."
  Then again he shook the pieces,
Shook and jostled them together,
Threw them on the ground before him,
Still exclaiming and explaining:
"White are both the great Kenabeeks,
White the Ininewug, the wedge-men,
Red are all the other pieces;
Five tens and an eight are counted."
  Thus he taught the game of hazard,
Thus displayed it and explained it,
Running through its various chances,
Various changes, various meanings:
Twenty curious eyes stared at him,
Full of eagerness stared at him.
  "Many games," said old Iagoo,
"Many games of skill and hazard
Have I seen in different nations,
Have I played in different countries.
He who plays with old Iagoo
Must have very nimble fingers;
Though you think yourself so skilful,
I can beat you, Pau-Puk-Keewis,
I can even give you lessons
In your game of Bowl and Counters!"
  So they sat and played together,
All the old men and the young men,
Played for dresses, weapons, wampum,
Played till midnight, played till morning,
Played until the Yenadizze,
Till the cunning Pau-Puk-Keewis,
Of their treasures had despoiled them,

Of the best of all their dresses,
Shirts of deer-skin, robes of ermine,
Belts of wampum, crests of feathers,
Warlike weapons, pipes and pouches.
Twenty eyes glared wildly at him,
Like the eyes of wolves glared at him.
  Said the lucky Pau-Puk-Keewis:
"In my wigwam I am lonely,
In my wanderings and adventures
I have need of a companion,
Fain would have a Meshinauwa,
An attendant and pipe-bearer.
I will venture all these winnings,
All these garments heaped about me,
All this wampum, all these feathers,
On a single throw will venture
All against the young man yonder!"
'T was a youth of sixteen summers,
'T was a nephew of Iagoo;
Face-in-a-Mist, the people called him.
  As the fire burns in a pipe-head
Dusky red beneath the ashes,
So beneath his shaggy eyebrows
Glowed the eyes of old Iagoo.
"Ugh!" he answered very fiercely;
"Ugh!" they answered all and each one.
  Seized the wooden bowl the old man,
Closely in his bony fingers
Clutched the fatal bowl, Onagon,
Shook it fiercely and with fury,
Made the pieces ring together
As he threw them down before him.
  Red were both the great Kenabeeks,
Red the Ininewug, the wedge-men,
Red the Sheshebwug, the ducklings,
Black the four brass Ozawabeeks,
White alone the fish, the Keego;
Only five the pieces counted!
  Then the smiling Pau-Puk-Keewis
Shook the bowl and threw the pieces;
Lightly in the air he tossed them,
And they fell about him scattered;
Dark and bright the Ozawabeeks,

Red and white the other pieces,
And upright among the others
One Ininewug was standing,
Even as crafty Pau-Puk-Keewis
Stood alone among the players,
Saying, "Five tens! mine the game is!"
  Twenty eyes glared at him fiercely,
Like the eyes of wolves glared at him,
As he turned and left the wigwam,
Followed by his Meshinauwa,
By the nephew of Iagoo,
By the tall and graceful stripling,
Bearing in his arms the winnings,
Shirts of deer-skin, robes of ermine,
Belts of wampum, pipes and weapons.
  "Carry them," said Pau-Puk-Keewis,
Pointing with his fan of feathers,
"To my wigwam far to eastward,
On the dunes of Nagow Wudjoo!"
  Hot and red with smoke and gambling
Were the eyes of Pau-Puk-Keewis
As he came forth to the freshness
Of the pleasant Summer morning.
All the birds were singing gayly,
All the streamlets flowing swiftly,
And the heart of Pau-Puk-Keewis
Sang with pleasure as the birds sing,
Beat with triumph like the streamlets,
As he wandered through the village,
In the early gray of morning,
With his fan of turkey-feathers,
With his plumes and tufts of swan's down,
Till he reached the farthest wigwam,
Reached the lodge of Hiawatha.
  Silent was it and deserted;
No one met him at the doorway,
No one came to bid him welcome;
But the birds were singing round it,
In and out and round the doorway,
Hopping, singing, fluttering, feeding,
And aloft upon the ridge-pole
Kahgahgee, the King of Ravens,
Sat with fiery eyes, and, screaming,

Flapped his wings at Pau-Puk-Keewis.
"All are gone! the lodge is empty!"
Thus it was spake Pau-Puk-Keewis,
In his heart resolving mischief;—
"Gone is wary Hiawatha,
Gone the silly Laughing Water,
Gone Nokomis, the old woman,
And the lodge is left unguarded!"
  By the neck he seized the raven,
Whirled it round him like a rattle,
Like a medicine-pouch he shook it,
Strangled Kahgahgee, the raven,
From the ridge-pole of the wigwam
Left its lifeless body hanging,
As an insult to its master,
As a taunt to Hiawatha.
  With a stealthy step he entered,
Round the lodge in wild disorder
Threw the household things about him,
Piled together in confusion
Bowls of wood and earthen kettles,
Robes of buffalo and beaver,
Skins of otter, lynx, and ermine,
As an insult to Nokomis,
As a taunt to Minnehaha.
  Then departed Pau-Puk-Keewis,
Whistling, singing through the forest,
Whistling gayly to the squirrels,
Who from hollow boughs above him
Dropped their acorn-shells upon him,
Singing gayly to the wood birds,
Who from out the leafy darkness
Answered with a song as merry.
  Then he climbed the rocky headlands,
Looking o'er the Gitche Gumee,
Perched himself upon their summit,
Waiting full of mirth and mischief
The return of Hiawatha.
  Stretched upon his back he lay there;
Far below him plashed the waters,
Plashed and washed the dreamy waters;
Far above him swam the heavens,
Swam the dizzy, dreamy heavens;

Round him hovered, fluttered, rustled
Hiawatha's mountain chickens,
Flock-wise swept and wheeled about him,
Almost brushed him with their pinions.
  And he killed them as he lay there,
Slaughtered them by tens and twenties,
Threw their bodies down the headland,
Threw them on the beach below him,
Till at length Kayoshk, the sea-gull,
Perched upon a crag above them,
Shouted: "It is Pau-Puk-Keewis!
He is slaying us by hundreds!
Send a message to our brother,
Tidings send to Hiawatha!"

XVII

THE HUNTING OF PAU-PUK-KEEWIS

Full of wrath was Hiawatha
When he came into the village,
Found the people in confusion,
Heard of all the misdemeanors,
All the malice and the mischief,
Of the cunning Pau-Puk-Keewis.
  Hard his breath came through his nostrils,
Through his teeth he buzzed and muttered
Words of anger and resentment,
Hot and humming, like a hornet.
"I will slay this Pau-Puk-Keewis,
Slay this mischief-maker!" said he.
"Not so long and wide the world is,
Not so rude and rough the way is,
That my wrath shall not attain him,
That my vengeance shall not reach him!"
   Then in swift pursuit departed
Hiawatha and the hunters
On the trail of Pau-Puk-Keewis,
Through the forest, where he passed it,
To the headlands where he rested;
But they found not Pau-Puk-Keewis,
Only in the trampled grasses,

In the whortleberry-bushes,
Found the couch where he had rested,
Found the impress of his body.
  From the lowlands far beneath them,
From the Muskoday, the meadow,
Pau-Puk-Keewis, turning backward,
Made a gesture of defiance,
Made a gesture of derision;
And aloud cried Hiawatha,
From the summit of the mountains:
"Not so long and wide the world is,
Not so rude and rough the way is,
But my wrath shall overtake you,
And my vengeance shall attain you!"
  Over rock and over river,
Through bush, and brake, and forest,
Ran the cunning Pau-Puk-Keewis;
Like an antelope he bounded,
Till he came unto a streamlet
In the middle of the forest,
To a streamlet still and tranquil,
That had overflowed its margin,
To a dam made by the beavers,
To a pond of quiet water,
Where knee-deep the trees were standing,
Where the water lilies floated,
Where the rushes waved and whispered.
  On the dam stood Pau-Puk-Keewis,
On the dam of trunks and branches,
Through whose chinks the water spouted,
O'er whose summit flowed the streamlet.
From the bottom rose the beaver,
Looked with two great eyes of wonder,
Eyes that seemed to ask a question,
At the stranger, Pau-Puk-Keewis.
  On the dam stood Pau-Puk-Keewis,
O'er his ankles flowed the streamlet,
Flowed the bright and silvery water,
And he spake unto the beaver,
With a smile he spake in this wise:
  "O my friend Ahmeek, the beaver,
Cool and pleasant is the water;
Let me dive into the water,

Let me rest there in your lodges;
Change me, too, into a beaver!"
  Cautiously replied the beaver,
With reserve he thus made answer:
"Let me first consult the others,
Let me ask the other beavers."
Down he sank into the water,
Heavily sank he, as a stone sinks,
Down among the leaves and branches,
Brown and matted at the bottom.
  On the dam stood Pau-Puk-Keewis,
O'er his ankles flowed the streamlet,
Spouted through the chinks below him,
Dashed upon the stones beneath him,
Spread serene and calm before him,
And the sunshine and the shadows
Fell in flecks and gleams upon him,
Fell in little shining patches,
Through the waving, rustling branches.
  From the bottom rose the beavers,
Silently above the surface
Rose one head and then another,
Till the pond seemed full of beavers,
Full of black and shining faces.
  To the beavers Pau-Puk-Keewis
Spake entreating, said in this wise:
"Very pleasant is your dwelling,
O my friends! and safe from danger;
Can you not, with all your cunning,
All your wisdom and contrivance,
Change me, too, into a beaver?"
  "Yes!" replied Ahmeek, the beaver,
He the King of all the beavers,
"Let yourself slide down among us,
Down into the tranquil water."
  Down into the pond among them
Silently sank Pau-Puk-Keewis;
Black became his shirt of deer-skin,
Black his moccasins and leggings,
In a broad black tail behind him
Spread his fox-tails and his fringes;
He was changed into a beaver.
  "Make me large," said Pau-Puk-Keewis,

"Make me large and make me larger,
Larger than the other beavers."
"Yes," the beaver chief responded,
"When our lodge below you enter,
In our wigwam we will make you
Ten times larger than the others."
  Thus into the clear, brown water
Silently sank Pau-Puk-Keewis:
Found the bottom covered over
With the trunks of trees and branches,
Hoards of food against the winter,
Piles and heaps against the famine;
Found the lodge with arching doorway,
Leading into spacious chambers.
  Here they made him large and larger,
Made him largest of the beavers,
Ten times larger than the others.
"You shall be our ruler," said they;
"Chief and King of all the beavers."
  But not long had Pau-Puk-Keewis
Sat in state among the beavers,
When there came a voice of warning
From the watchman at his station
In the water-flags and lilies,
Saying, "Here Is Hiawatha!
Hiawatha with his hunters!"
  Then they heard a cry above them,
Heard a shouting and a tramping,
Heard a crashing and a rushing,
And the water round and o'er them
Sank and sucked away in eddies,
And they knew their dam was broken.
  On the lodge's roof the hunters
Leaped, and broke it all asunder;
Streamed the sunshine through the crevice,
Sprang the beavers through the doorway,
Hid themselves in deeper water,
In the channel of the streamlet;
But the mighty Pau-Puk-Keewis
Could not pass beneath the doorway;
He was puffed with pride and feeding,
He was swollen like a bladder.
  Through the roof looked Hiawatha,

Cried aloud, "O Pau-Puk-Keewis
Vain are all your craft and cunning,
Vain your manifold disguises!
Well I know you, Pau-Puk-Keewis!"
  With their clubs they beat and bruised him,
Beat to death poor Pau-Puk-Keewis,
Pounded him as maize is pounded,
Till his skull was crushed to pieces.
  Six tall hunters, lithe and limber,
Bore him home on poles and branches,
Bore the body of the beaver;
But the ghost, the Jeebi in him,
Thought and felt as Pau-Puk-Keewis,
Still lived on as Pau-Puk-Keewis.
  And it fluttered, strove, and struggled,
Waving hither, waving thither,
As the curtains of a wigwam
Struggle with their thongs of deer-skin,
When the wintry wind is blowing;
Till it drew itself together,
Till it rose up from the body,
Till it took the form and features
Of the cunning Pau-Puk-Keewis
Vanishing into the forest.
  But the wary Hiawatha
Saw the figure ere it vanished,
Saw the form of Pau-Puk-Keewis
Glide into the soft blue shadow
Of the pine-trees of the forest;
Toward the squares of white beyond it,
Toward an opening in the forest.
Like a wind it rushed and panted,
Bending all the boughs before it,
And behind it, as the rain comes,
Came the steps of Hiawatha.
  To a lake with many islands
Came the breathless Pau-Puk-Keewis,
Where among the water-lilies
Pishnekuh, the brant, were sailing;
Through the tufts of rushes floating,
Steering through the reedy islands.
Now their broad black beaks they lifted,
Now they plunged beneath the water,

Now they darkened in the shadow,
Now they brightened in the sunshine.
  "Pishnekuh!" cried Pau-Puk-Keewis,
"Pishnekuh! my brothers!" said he,
"Change me to a brant with plumage,
With a shining neck and feathers,
Make me large, and make me larger,
Ten times larger than the others."
  Straightway to a brant they changed him,
With two huge and dusky pinions,
With a bosom smooth and rounded,
With a bill like two great paddles,
Made him larger than the others,
Ten times larger than the largest,
Just as, shouting from the forest,
On the shore stood Hiawatha.
  Up they rose with cry and clamor,
With a whir and beat of pinions,
Rose up from the reedy Islands,
From the water-flags and lilies.
And they said to Pau-Puk-Keewis:
"In your flying, look not downward,
Take good heed and look not downward,
Lest some strange mischance should happen,
Lest some great mishap befall you!"
  Fast and far they fled to northward,
Fast and far through mist and sunshine,
Fed among the moors and fen-lands,
Slept among the reeds and rushes.
  On the morrow as they journeyed,
Buoyed and lifted by the South-wind,
Wafted onward by the South-wind,
Blowing fresh and strong behind them,
Rose a sound of human voices,
Rose a clamor from beneath them,
From the lodges of a village,
From the people miles beneath them.
  For the people of the village
Saw the flock of brant with wonder,
Saw the wings of Pau-Puk-Keewis
Flapping far up in the ether,
Broader than two doorway curtains.
  Pau-Puk-Keewis heard the shouting,

Knew the voice of Hiawatha,
Knew the outcry of Iagoo,
And, forgetful of the warning,
Drew his neck in, and looked downward,
And the wind that blew behind him
Caught his mighty fan of feathers,
Sent him wheeling, whirling downward!
  All in vain did Pau-Puk-Keewis
Struggle to regain his balance!
Whirling round and round and downward,
He beheld in turn the village
And in turn the flock above him,
Saw the village coming nearer,
And the flock receding farther,
Heard the voices growing louder,
Heard the shouting and the laughter;
Saw no more the flocks above him,
Only saw the earth beneath him;
Dead out of the empty heaven,
Dead among the shouting people,
With a heavy sound and sullen,
Fell the brant with broken pinions.
  But his soul, his ghost, his shadow,
Still survived as Pau-Puk-Keewis,
Took again the form and features
Of the handsome Yenadizze,
And again went rushing onward,
Followed fast by Hiawatha,
Crying: "Not so wide the world is,
Not so long and rough the way is,
But my wrath shall overtake you,
But my vengeance shall attain you!"
  And so near he came, so near him,
That his hand was stretched to seize him,
His right hand to seize and hold him,
When the cunning Pau-Puk-Keewis
Whirled and spun about in circles,
Fanned the air into a whirlwind,
Danced the dust and leaves about him,
And amid the whirling eddies
Sprang into a hollow oak-tree,
Changed himself into a serpent,
Gliding out through root and rubbish.

With his right hand Hiawatha
Smote amain the hollow oak-tree,
Rent it into shreds and splinters,
Left it lying there in fragments.
But in vain; for Pau-Puk-Keewis,
Once again in human figure,
Full in sight ran on before him,
Sped away in gust and whirlwind,
On the shores of Gitche Gumee,
Westward by the Big-Sea-Water,
Came unto the rocky headlands,
To the Pictured Rocks of sandstone,
Looking over lake and landscape.
    And the Old Man of the Mountain,
He the Manito of Mountains,
Opened wide his rocky doorways,
Opened wide his deep abysses,
Giving Pau-Puk-Keewis shelter
In his caverns dark and dreary,
Bidding Pau-Puk-Keewis welcome
To his gloomy lodge of sandstone.
    There without stood Hiawatha,
Found the doorways closed against him,
With his mittens, Minjekahwun,
Smote great caverns in the sandstone,
Cried aloud in tones of thunder,
"Open! I am Hiawatha!"
But the Old Man of the Mountain
Opened not, and made no answer
From the silent crags of sandstone,
From the gloomy rock abysses.
    Then he raised his hands to heaven,
Called imploring on the tempest,
Called Waywassimo, the lightning,
And the thunder, Annemeekee;
And they came with night and darkness,
Sweeping down the Big-Sea-Water
From the distant Thunder Mountains;
And the trembling Pau-Puk-Keewis
Heard the footsteps of the thunder,
Saw the red eyes of the lightning,
Was afraid, and crouched and trembled.
    Then Waywassimo, the lightning,

Smote the doorways of the caverns,
With his war-club smote the doorways,
Smote the jutting crags of sandstone,
And the thunder, Annemeekee,
Shouted down into the caverns,
Saying, "Where is Pau-Puk-Keewis!"
And the crags fell, and beneath them
Dead among the rocky ruins
Lay the cunning Pau-Puk-Keewis,
Lay the handsome Yenadizze,
Slain in his own human figure.
  Ended were his wild adventures,
Ended were his tricks and gambols,
Ended all his craft and cunning,
Ended all his mischief-making,
All his gambling and his dancing,
All his wooing of the maidens.
  Then the noble Hiawatha
Took his soul, his ghost, his shadow,
Spake and said: "O Pau-Puk-Keewis,
Never more in human figure
Shall you search for new adventures;
Never more with jest and laughter
Dance the dust and leaves in whirlwinds;
But above there in the heavens
You shall soar and sail in circles;
I will change you to an eagle,
To Keneu, the great war-eagle,
Chief of all the fowls with feathers,
Chief of Hiawatha's chickens."
  And the name of Pau-Puk-Keewis
Lingers still among the people,
Lingers still among the singers,
And among the story-tellers;
And in Winter, when the snow-flakes
Whirl in eddies round the lodges,
When the wind in gusty tumult
O'er the smoke-flue pipes and whistles,
"There," they cry, "comes Pau-Puk-Keewis;
He is dancing through the village,
He is gathering in his harvest!"

XVIII

THE DEATH OF KWASIND

Far and wide among the nations
Spread the name and fame of Kwasind;
No man dared to strive with Kwasind,
No man could compete with Kwasind.
But the mischievous Puk-Wudjies,
They the envious Little People,
They the fairies and the pygmies,
Plotted and conspired against him.
 "If this hateful Kwasind," said they,
"If this great, outrageous fellow
Goes on thus a little longer,
Tearing everything he touches,
Rending everything to pieces,
Filling all the world with wonder,
What becomes of the Puk-Wudjies?
Who will care for the Puk-Wudjies?
He will tread us down like mushrooms,
Drive us all into the water,
Give our bodies to be eaten
By the wicked Nee-ba-naw-baigs,
By the Spirits of the water!
 So the angry Little People
All conspired against the Strong Man,
All conspired to murder Kwasind,
Yes, to rid the world of Kwasind,
The audacious, overbearing,
Heartless, haughty, dangerous Kwasind!
 Now this wondrous strength of Kwasind
In his crown alone was seated;
In his crown too was his weakness;
There alone could he be wounded,
Nowhere else could weapon pierce him,
Nowhere else could weapon harm him.
 Even there the only weapon
That could wound him, that could slay him,
Was the seed-cone of the pine-tree,
Was the blue cone of the fir-tree.
This was Kwasind's fatal secret,
Known to no man among mortals;

But the cunning Little People,
The Puk-Wudjies, knew the secret,
Knew the only way to kill him.
  So they gathered cones together,
Gathered seed-cones of the pine-tree,
Gathered blue cones of the fir-tree,
In the woods by Taquamenaw,
Brought them to the river's margin,
Heaped them in great piles together,
Where the red rocks from the margin
Jutting overhang the river.
There they lay in wait for Kwasind,
The malicious Little People.
  'T was an afternoon in Summer;
Very hot and still the air was,
Very smooth the gliding river,
Motionless the sleeping shadows:
Insects glistened in the sunshine,
Insects skated on the water,
Filled the drowsy air with buzzing,
With a far resounding war-cry.
  Down the river came the Strong Man,
In his birch canoe came Kwasind,
Floating slowly down the current
Of the sluggish Taquamenaw,
Very languid with the weather,
Very sleepy with the silence.
  From the overhanging branches,
From the tassels of the birch-trees,
Soft the Spirit of Sleep descended;
By his airy hosts surrounded,
His invisible attendants,
Came the Spirit of Sleep, Nepahwin;
Like a burnished Dush-kwo-ne-she,
Like a dragon-fly, he hovered
O'er the drowsy head of Kwasind.
  To his ear there came a murmur
As of waves upon a sea-shore,
As of far-off tumbling waters,
As of winds among the pine-trees;
And he felt upon his forehead
Blows of little airy war-clubs,
Wielded by the slumbrous legions

Of the Spirit of Sleep, Nepahwin,
As of some one breathing on him.
  At the first blow of their war-clubs,
Fell a drowsiness on Kwasind;
At the second blow they smote him,
Motionless his paddle rested;
At the third, before his vision
Reeled the landscape into darkness,
Very sound asleep was Kwasind.
  So he floated down the river,
Like a blind man seated upright,
Floated down the Taquamenaw,
Underneath the trembling birch-trees,
Underneath the wooded headlands,
Underneath the war encampment
Of the pygmies, the Puk-Wudjies.
  There they stood, all armed and waiting,
Hurled the pine-cones down upon him,
Struck him on his brawny shoulders,
On his crown defenceless struck him.
"Death to Kwasind!" was the sudden
War-cry of the Little People.
  And he sideways swayed and tumbled,
Sideways fell into the river,
Plunged beneath the sluggish water
Headlong, as an otter plunges;
And the birch canoe, abandoned,
Drifted empty down the river,
Bottom upward swerved and drifted:
Nothing more was seen of Kwasind.
  But the memory of the Strong Man
Lingered long among the people,
And whenever through the forest
Raged and roared the wintry tempest,
And the branches, tossed and troubled,
Creaked and groaned and split asunder,
"Kwasind!" cried they; "that is Kwasind!
He is gathering in his fire-wood!"

IX

THE GHOSTS

Never stoops the soaring vulture
On his quarry in the desert,
On the sick or wounded bison,
But another vulture, watching
From his high aerial look-out,
Sees the downward plunge, and follows;
And a third pursues the second,
Coming from the invisible ether,
First a speck, and then a vulture,
Till the air is dark with pinions.
  So disasters come not singly;
But as if they watched and waited,
Scanning one another's motions,
When the first descends, the others
Follow, follow, gathering flock-wise
Round their victim, sick and wounded,
First a shadow, then a sorrow,
Till the air is dark with anguish.
  Now, o'er all the dreary North-land,
Mighty Peboan, the Winter,
Breathing on the lakes and rivers,
Into stone had changed their waters.
From his hair he shook the snow-flakes,
Till the plains were strewn with whiteness,
One uninterrupted level,
As if, stooping, the Creator
With his hand had smoothed them over.
Through the forest, wide and wailing,
Roamed the hunter on his snow-shoes;
In the village worked the women,
Pounded maize, or dressed the deer-skin;
And the young men played together
On the ice the noisy ball-play,
On the plain the dance of snow-shoes.
  One dark evening, after sundown,
In her wigwam Laughing Water
Sat with old Nokomis, waiting
For the steps of Hiawatha
Homeward from the hunt returning.

On their faces gleamed the firelight,
Painting them with streaks of crimson,
In the eyes of old Nokomis
Glimmered like the watery moonlight,
In the eyes of Laughing Water
Glistened like the sun in water;
And behind them crouched their shadows
In the corners of the wigwam,
And the smoke in wreaths above them
Climbed and crowded through the smoke-flue.
   Then the curtain of the doorway
From without was slowly lifted;
Brighter glowed the fire a moment,
And a moment swerved the smoke-wreath,
As two women entered softly,
Passed the doorway uninvited,
Without word of salutation,
Without sign of recognition,
Sat down in the farthest corner,
Crouching low among the shadows.
   From their aspect and their garments,
Strangers seemed they in the village;
Very pale and haggard were they,
As they sat there sad and silent,
Trembling, cowering with the shadows.
   Was it the wind above the smoke-flue,
Muttering down into the wigwam?
Was it the owl, the Koko-koho,
Hooting from the dismal forest?
Sure a voice said in the silence:
"These are corpses clad in garments,
These are ghosts that come to haunt you,
From the kingdom of Ponemah,
From the land of the Hereafter!"
   Homeward now came Hiawatha
From his hunting in the forest,
With the snow upon his tresses,
And the red deer on his shoulders.
At the feet of Laughing Water
Down he threw his lifeless burden;
Nobler, handsomer she thought him,
Than when first he came to woo her,
First threw down the deer before her,

As a token of his wishes,
As a promise of the future.
  Then he turned and saw the strangers,
Cowering, crouching with the shadows;
Said within himself, "Who are they?
What strange guests has Minnehaha?"
But he questioned not the strangers,
Only spake to bid them welcome
To his lodge, his food, his fireside.
  When the evening meal was ready,
And the deer had been divided,
Both the pallid guests, the strangers,
Springing from among the shadows,
Seized upon the choicest portions,
Seized the white fat of the roebuck,
Set apart for Laughing Water,
For the wife of Hiawatha;
Without asking, without thanking,
Eagerly devoured the morsels,
Flitted back among the shadows
In the corner of the wigwam.
  Not a word spake Hiawatha,
Not a motion made Nokomis,
Not a gesture Laughing Water;
Not a change came o'er their features;
Only Minnehaha softly
Whispered, saying, "They are famished;
Let them do what best delights them;
Let them eat, for they are famished."
  Many a daylight dawned and darkened,
Many a night shook off the daylight
As the pine shakes off the snow-flakes
From the midnight of its branches;
Day by day the guests unmoving
Sat there silent in the wigwam;
But by night, in storm or starlight,
Forth they went into the forest,
Bringing fire-wood to the wigwam,
Bringing pine-cones for the burning,
Always sad and always silent.
  And whenever Hiawatha
Came from fishing or from hunting,
When the evening meal was ready,

And the food had been divided,
Gliding from their darksome corner,
Came the pallid guests, the strangers,
Seized upon the choicest portions
Set aside for Laughing Water,
And without rebuke or question
Flitted back among the shadows.
  Never once had Hiawatha
By a word or look reproved them;
Never once had old Nokomis
Made a gesture of impatience;
Never once had Laughing Water
Shown resentment at the outrage.
All had they endured in silence,
That the rights of guest and stranger,
That the virtue of free-giving,
By a look might not be lessened,
By a word might not be broken.
  Once at midnight Hiawatha,
Ever wakeful, ever watchful,
In the wigwam, dimly lighted
By the brands that still were burning,
By the glimmering, flickering firelight
Heard a sighing, oft repeated,
Heard a sobbing, as of sorrow.
  From his couch rose Hiawatha,
From his shaggy hides of bison,
Pushed aside the deer-skin curtain,
Saw the pallid guests, the shadows,
Sitting upright on their couches,
Weeping in the silent midnight.
  And he said: "O guests! why is it
That your hearts are so afflicted,
That you sob so in the midnight?
Has perchance the old Nokomis,
Has my wife, my Minnehaha,
Wronged or grieved you by unkindness,
Failed in hospitable duties?"
  Then the shadows ceased from weeping,
Ceased from sobbing and lamenting,
And they said, with gentle voices:
"We are ghosts of the departed,
Souls of those who once were with you.

From the realms of Chibiabos
Hither have we come to try you,
Hither have we come to warn you.
  "Cries of grief and lamentation
Reach us in the Blessed Islands;
Cries of anguish from the living,
Calling back their friends departed,
Sadden us with useless sorrow.
Therefore have we come to try you;
No one knows us, no one heeds us.
We are but a burden to you,
And we see that the departed
Have no place among the living.
  "Think of this, O Hiawatha!
Speak of it to all the people,
That henceforward and forever
They no more with lamentations
Sadden the souls of the departed
In the Islands of the Blessed.
  "Do not lay such heavy burdens
In the graves of those you bury,
Not such weight of furs and wampum,
Not such weight of pots and kettles,
For the spirits faint beneath them.
Only give them food to carry,
Only give them fire to light them.
  "Four days is the spirit's journey
To the land of ghosts and shadows,
Four its lonely night encampments;
Four times must their fires be lighted.
Therefore, when the dead are buried,
Let a fire, as night approaches,
Four times on the grave be kindled,
That the soul upon its journey
May not lack the cheerful firelight,
May not grope about in darkness.
  "Farewell, noble Hiawatha!
We have put you to the trial,
To the proof have put your patience,
By the insult of our presence,
By the outrage of our actions.
We have found you great and noble.
Fail not in the greater trial,

Faint not in the harder struggle."
  When they ceased, a sudden darkness
Fell and filled the silent wigwam.
Hiawatha heard a rustle
As of garments trailing by him,
Heard the curtain of the doorway
Lifted by a hand he saw not,
Felt the cold breath of the night air,
For a moment saw the starlight;
But he saw the ghosts no longer,
Saw no more the wandering spirits
From the kingdom of Ponemah,
From the land of the Hereafter.

XX

THE FAMINE

Oh the long and dreary Winter!
Oh the cold and cruel Winter!
Ever thicker, thicker, thicker
Froze the ice on lake and river,
Ever deeper, deeper, deeper
Fell the snow o'er all the landscape,
Fell the covering snow, and drifted
Through the forest, round the village.
Hardly from his buried wigwam
Could the hunter force a passage;
With his mittens and his snow-shoes
Vainly walked he through the forest,
Sought for bird or beast and found none,
Saw no track of deer or rabbit,
In the snow beheld no footprints,
In the ghastly, gleaming forest
Fell, and could not rise from weakness,
Perished there from cold and hunger.
  Oh the famine and the fever!
Oh the wasting of the famine!
Oh the blasting of the fever!
Oh the wailing of the children!
Oh the anguish of the women!
  All the earth was sick and famished;

Hungry was the air around them,
Hungry was the sky above them,
And the hungry stars in heaven
Like the eyes of wolves glared at them!
  Into Hiawatha's wigwam
Came two other guests, as silent
As the ghosts were, and as gloomy,
Waited not to be invited
Did not parley at the doorway
Sat there without word of welcome
In the seat of Laughing Water;
Looked with haggard eyes and hollow
At the face of Laughing Water.
  And the foremost said: "Behold me!
I am Famine, Bukadawin!"
And the other said: "Behold me!
I am Fever, Ahkosewin!"
  And the lovely Minnehaha
Shuddered as they looked upon her,
Shuddered at the words they uttered,
Lay down on her bed in silence,
Hid her face, but made no answer;
Lay there trembling, freezing, burning
At the looks they cast upon her,
At the fearful words they uttered.
  Forth into the empty forest
Rushed the maddened Hiawatha;
In his heart was deadly sorrow,
In his face a stony firmness;
On his brow the sweat of anguish
Started, but it froze and fell not.
  Wrapped in furs and armed for hunting,
With his mighty bow of ash-tree,
With his quiver full of arrows,
With his mittens, Minjekahwun,
Into the vast and vacant forest
On his snow-shoes strode he forward.
  "Gitche Manito, the Mighty!"
Cried he with his face uplifted
In that bitter hour of anguish,
"Give your children food, O father!
Give us food, or we must perish!
Give me food for Minnehaha,

For my dying Minnehaha!"
  Through the far-resounding forest,
Through the forest vast and vacant
Rang that cry of desolation,
But there came no other answer
Than the echo of his crying,
Than the echo of the woodlands,
"Minnehaha! Minnehaha!"
  All day long roved Hiawatha
In that melancholy forest,
Through the shadow of whose thickets,
In the pleasant days of Summer,
Of that ne'er forgotten Summer,
He had brought his young wife homeward
From the land of the Dacotahs;
When the birds sang in the thickets,
And the streamlets laughed and glistened,
And the air was full of fragrance,
And the lovely Laughing Water
Said with voice that did not tremble,
"I will follow you, my husband!"
  In the wigwam with Nokomis,
With those gloomy guests that watched her,
With the Famine and the Fever,
She was lying, the Beloved,
She, the dying Minnehaha.
  "Hark!" she said; "I hear a rushing,
Hear a roaring and a rushing,
Hear the Falls of Minnehaha
Calling to me from a distance!"
"No, my child!" said old Nokomis,
"'T is the night-wind in the pine-trees!"
"Look!" she said; "I see my father
Standing lonely at his doorway,
Beckoning to me from his wigwam
In the land of the Dacotahs!"
"No, my child!" said old Nokomis.
"'T is the smoke, that waves and beckons!"
"Ah!" said she, "the eyes of Pauguk
Glare upon me in the darkness,
I can feel his icy fingers
Clasping mine amid the darkness!
Hiawatha! Hiawatha!"

And the desolate Hiawatha,
Far away amid the forest,
Miles away among the mountains,
Heard that sudden cry of anguish,
Heard the voice of Minnehaha
Calling to him in the darkness,
"Hiawatha! Hiawatha!"
  Over snow-fields waste and pathless,
Under snow-encumbered branches,
Homeward hurried Hiawatha,
Empty-handed, heavy-hearted,
Heard Nokomis moaning, wailing:
"Wahonowin! Wahonowin!
Would that I had perished for you,
Would that I were dead as you are!
Wahonowin! Wahonowin!"
  And he rushed into the wigwam,
Saw the old Nokomis slowly
Rocking to and fro and moaning,
Saw his lovely Minnehaha
Lying dead and cold before him,
And his bursting heart within him
Uttered such a cry of anguish,
That the forest moaned and shuddered,
That the very stars in heaven
Shook and trembled with his anguish.
  Then he sat down, still and speechless,
On the bed of Minnehaha,
At the feet of Laughing Water,
At those willing feet, that never
More would lightly run to meet him,
Never more would lightly follow.
  With both hands his face he covered,
Seven long days and nights he sat there,
As if in a swoon he sat there,
Speechless, motionless, unconscious
Of the daylight or the darkness.
  Then they buried Minnehaha;
In the snow a grave they made her
In the forest deep and darksome
Underneath the moaning hemlocks;
Clothed her in her richest garments
Wrapped her in her robes of ermine,

Covered her with snow, like ermine;
Thus they buried Minnehaha.
  And at night a fire was lighted,
On her grave four times was kindled,
For her soul upon its journey
To the Islands of the Blessed.
From his doorway Hiawatha
Saw it burning in the forest,
Lighting up the gloomy hemlocks;
From his sleepless bed uprising,
From the bed of Minnehaha,
Stood and watched it at the doorway,
That it might not be extinguished,
Might not leave her in the darkness.
  "Farewell!" said he, "Minnehaha!
Farewell, O my Laughing Water!
All my heart is buried with you,
All my thoughts go onward with you!
Come not back again to labor,
Come not back again to suffer,
Where the Famine and the Fever
Wear the heart and waste the body.
Soon my task will be completed,
Soon your footsteps I shall follow
To the Islands of the Blessed,
To the Kingdom of Ponemah,
To the Land of the Hereafter!"

XXI

THE WHITE MAN'S FOOT

In his lodge beside a river,
Close beside a frozen river,
Sat an old man, sad and lonely.
White his hair was as a snow-drift;
Dull and low his fire was burning,
And the old man shook and trembled,
Folded in his Waubewyon,
In his tattered white-skin-wrapper,
Hearing nothing but the tempest
As it roared along the forest,

Seeing nothing but the snow-storm,
As it whirled and hissed and drifted.
  All the coals were white with ashes,
And the fire was slowly dying,
As a young man, walking lightly,
At the open doorway entered.
Red with blood of youth his cheeks were,
Soft his eyes, as stars in Spring-time,
Bound his forehead was with grasses;
Bound and plumed with scented grasses,
On his lips a smile of beauty,
Filling all the lodge with sunshine,
In his hand a bunch of blossoms
Filling all the lodge with sweetness.
  "Ah, my son!" exclaimed the old man,
"Happy are my eyes to see you.
Sit here on the mat beside me,
Sit here by the dying embers,
Let us pass the night together,
Tell me of your strange adventures,
Of the lands where you have travelled;
I will tell you of my prowess,
Of my many deeds of wonder."
  From his pouch he drew his peace-pipe,
Very old and strangely fashioned;
Made of red stone was the pipe-head,
And the stem a reed with feathers;
Filled the pipe with bark of willow,
Placed a burning coal upon it,
Gave it to his guest, the stranger,
And began to speak in this wise:
"When I blow my breath about me,
When I breathe upon the landscape,
Motionless are all the rivers,
Hard as stone becomes the water!"
  And the young man answered, smiling:
"When I blow my breath about me,
When I breathe upon the landscape,
Flowers spring up o'er all the meadows,
Singing, onward rush the rivers!"
  "When I shake my hoary tresses,"
Said the old man darkly frowning,
"All the land with snow is covered;

All the leaves from all the branches
Fall and fade and die and wither,
For I breathe, and lo! they are not.
From the waters and the marshes,
Rise the wild goose and the heron,
Fly away to distant regions,
For I speak, and lo! they are not.
And where'er my footsteps wander,
All the wild beasts of the forest
Hide themselves in holes and caverns,
And the earth becomes as flintstone!"
  "When I shake my flowing ringlets,"
Said the young man, softly laughing,
"Showers of rain fall warm and welcome,
Plants lift up their heads rejoicing,
Back into their lakes and marshes
Come the wild goose and the heron,
Homeward shoots the arrowy swallow,
Sing the bluebird and the robin,
And where'er my footsteps wander,
All the meadows wave with blossoms,
All the woodlands ring with music,
All the trees are dark with foliage!"
  While they spake, the night departed:
From the distant realms of Wabun,
From his shining lodge of silver,
Like a warrior robed and painted,
Came the sun, and said, "Behold me
Gheezis, the great sun, behold me!"
  Then the old man's tongue was speechless
And the air grew warm and pleasant,
And upon the wigwam sweetly
Sang the bluebird and the robin,
And the stream began to murmur,
And a scent of growing grasses
Through the lodge was gently wafted.
  And Segwun, the youthful stranger,
More distinctly in the daylight
Saw the icy face before him;
It was Peboan, the Winter!
  From his eyes the tears were flowing,
As from melting lakes the streamlets,
And his body shrunk and dwindled

As the shouting sun ascended,
Till into the air it faded,
Till into the ground it vanished,
And the young man saw before him,
On the hearth-stone of the wigwam,
Where the fire had smoked and smouldered,
Saw the earliest flower of Spring-time,
Saw the Beauty of the Spring-time,
Saw the Miskodeed in blossom.
  Thus it was that in the North-land
After that unheard-of coldness,
That intolerable Winter,
Came the Spring with all its splendor,
All its birds and all its blossoms,
All its flowers and leaves and grasses.
  Sailing on the wind to northward,
Flying in great flocks, like arrows,
Like huge arrows shot through heaven,
Passed the swan, the Mahnahbezee,
Speaking almost as a man speaks;
And in long lines waving, bending
Like a bow-string snapped asunder,
Came the white goose, Waw-be-wawa;
And in pairs, or singly flying,
Mahng the loon, with clangorous pinions,
The blue heron, the Shuh-shuh-gah,
And the grouse, the Mushkodasa.
  In the thickets and the meadows
Piped the bluebird, the Owaissa,
On the summit of the lodges
Sang the robin, the Opechee,
In the covert of the pine-trees
Cooed the pigeon, the Omemee;
And the sorrowing Hiawatha,
Speechless in his infinite sorrow,
Heard their voices calling to him,
Went forth from his gloomy doorway,
Stood and gazed into the heaven,
Gazed upon the earth and waters.
  From his wanderings far to eastward,
From the regions of the morning,
From the shining land of Wabun,
Homeward now returned Iagoo,

The great traveller, the great boaster,
Full of new and strange adventures,
Marvels many and many wonders.
  And the people of the village
Listened to him as he told them
Of his marvellous adventures,
Laughing answered him in this wise:
"Ugh! it is indeed Iagoo!
No one else beholds such wonders!"
  He had seen, he said, a water
Bigger than the Big-Sea-Water,
Broader than the Gitche Gumee,
Bitter so that none could drink it!
At each other looked the warriors,
Looked the women at each other,
Smiled, and said, "It cannot be so!"
Kaw!" they said, it cannot be so!"
  O'er it, said he, o'er this water
Came a great canoe with pinions,
A canoe with wings came flying,
Bigger than a grove of pine-trees,
Taller than the tallest tree-tops!
And the old men and the women
Looked and tittered at each other;
"Kaw!" they said, "we don't believe it!"
  From its mouth, he said, to greet him,
Came Waywassimo, the lightning,
Came the thunder, Annemeekee!
And the warriors and the women
Laughed aloud at poor Iagoo;
"Kaw!" they said, "what tales you tell us!"
  In it, said he, came a people,
In the great canoe with pinions
Came, he said, a hundred warriors;
Painted white were all their faces
And with hair their chins were covered!
And the warriors and the women
Laughed and shouted in derision,
Like the ravens on the tree-tops,
Like the crows upon the hemlocks.
"Kaw!" they said, "what lies you tell us!
Do not think that we believe them!"
  Only Hiawatha laughed not,

But he gravely spake and answered
To their jeering and their jesting:
"True is all Iagoo tells us;
I have seen it in a vision,
Seen the great canoe with pinions,
Seen the people with white faces,
Seen the coming of this bearded
People of the wooden vessel
From the regions of the morning,
From the shining land of Wabun.
  "Gitche Manito, the Mighty,
The Great Spirit, the Creator,
Sends them hither on his errand.
Sends them to us with his message.
Wheresoe'er they move, before them
Swarms the stinging fly, the Ahmo,
Swarms the bee, the honey-maker;
Wheresoe'er they tread, beneath them
Springs a flower unknown among us,
Springs the White-man's Foot in blossom.
  "Let us welcome, then, the strangers,
Hail them as our friends and brothers,
And the heart's right hand of friendship
Give them when they come to see us.
Gitche Manito, the Mighty,
Said this to me in my vision.
  "I beheld, too, in that vision
All the secrets of the future,
Of the distant days that shall be.
I beheld the westward marches
Of the unknown, crowded nations.
All the land was full of people,
Restless, struggling, toiling, striving,
Speaking many tongues, yet feeling
But one heart-beat in their bosoms.
In the woodlands rang their axes,
Smoked their towns in all the valleys,
Over all the lakes and rivers
Rushed their great canoes of thunder.
  "Then a darker, drearier vision
Passed before me, vague and cloud-like;
I beheld our nation scattered,
All forgetful of my counsels,

Weakened, warring with each other;
Saw the remnants of our people
Sweeping westward, wild and woful,
Like the cloud-rack of a tempest,
Like the withered leaves of Autumn!"

XXII

HIAWATHA'S DEPARTURE

By the shore of Gitche Gumee,
By the shining Big-Sea-Water,
At the doorway of his wigwam,
In the pleasant Summer morning,
Hiawatha stood and waited.
All the air was full of freshness,
All the earth was bright and joyous,
And before him, through the sunshine,
Westward toward the neighboring forest
Passed in golden swarms the Ahmo,
Passed the bees, the honey-makers,
Burning, singing in the sunshine.
  Bright above him shone the heavens,
Level spread the lake before him;
From its bosom leaped the sturgeon,
Sparkling, flashing in the sunshine;
On its margin the great forest
Stood reflected in the water,
Every tree-top had its shadow,
Motionless beneath the water.
  From the brow of Hiawatha
Gone was every trace of sorrow,
As the fog from off the water,
As the mist from off the meadow.
With a smile of joy and triumph,
With a look of exultation,
As of one who in a vision
Sees what is to be, but is not,
Stood and waited Hiawatha.
  Toward the sun his hands were lifted,
Both the palms spread out against it,
And between the parted fingers

Fell the sunshine on his features,
Flecked with light his naked shoulders,
As it falls and flecks an oak-tree
Through the rifted leaves and branches.
  O'er the water floating, flying,
Something in the hazy distance,
Something in the mists of morning,
Loomed and lifted from the water,
Now seemed floating, now seemed flying,
Coming nearer, nearer, nearer.
  Was it Shingebis the diver?
Or the pelican, the Shada?
Or the heron, the Shuh-shuh-gah?
Or the white goose, Waw-be-wawa,
With the water dripping, flashing,
From its glossy neck and feathers?
  It was neither goose nor diver,
Neither pelican nor heron,
O'er the water floating, flying,
Through the shining mist of morning,
But a birch canoe with paddles,
Rising, sinking on the water,
Dripping, flashing in the sunshine;
And within it came a people
From the distant land of Wabun,
From the farthest realms of morning
Came the Black-Robe chief, the Prophet,
He the Priest of Prayer, the Pale-face,
With his guides and his companions.
  And the noble Hiawatha,
With his hands aloft extended,
Held aloft in sign of welcome,
Waited, full of exultation,
Till the birch canoe with paddles
Grated on the shining pebbles,
Stranded on the sandy margin,
Till the Black-Robe chief, the Pale-face,
With the cross upon his bosom,
Landed on the sandy margin.
  Then the joyous Hiawatha
Cried aloud and spake in this wise:
"Beautiful is the sun, O strangers,
When you come so far to see us!

All our town in peace awaits you,
All our doors stand open for you;
You shall enter all our wigwams,
For the heart's right hand we give you.
  "Never bloomed the earth so gayly,
Never shone the sun so brightly,
As to-day they shine and blossom
When you come so far to see us!
Never was our lake so tranquil,
Nor so free from rocks, and sand-bars;
For your birch canoe in passing
Has removed both rock and sand-bar.
  "Never before had our tobacco
Such a sweet and pleasant flavor,
Never the broad leaves of our cornfields
Were so beautiful to look on,
As they seem to us this morning,
When you come so far to see us!'
  And the Black-Robe chief made answer,
Stammered in his speech a little,
Speaking words yet unfamiliar:
"Peace be with you, Hiawatha,
Peace be with you and your people,
Peace of prayer, and peace of pardon,
Peace of Christ, and joy of Mary!"
  Then the generous Hiawatha
Led the strangers to his wigwam,
Seated them on skins of bison,
Seated them on skins of ermine,
And the careful old Nokomis
Brought them food in bowls of basswood,
Water brought in birchen dippers,
And the calumet, the peace-pipe,
Filled and lighted for their smoking.
  All the old men of the village,
All the warriors of the nation,
All the Jossakeeds, the Prophets,
The magicians, the Wabenos,
And the Medicine-men, the Medas,
Came to bid the strangers welcome;
"It is well", they said, "O brothers,
That you come so far to see us!"
  In a circle round the doorway,

With their pipes they sat in silence,
Waiting to behold the strangers,
Waiting to receive their message;
Till the Black-Robe chief, the Pale-face,
From the wigwam came to greet them,
Stammering in his speech a little,
Speaking words yet unfamiliar;
"It is well," they said, "O brother,
That you come so far to see us!"
　Then the Black-Robe chief, the Prophet,
Told his message to the people,
Told the purport of his mission,
Told them of the Virgin Mary,
And her blessed Son, the Saviour,
How in distant lands and ages
He had lived on earth as we do;
How he fasted, prayed, and labored;
How the Jews, the tribe accursed,
Mocked him, scourged him, crucified him;
How he rose from where they laid him,
Walked again with his disciples,
And ascended into heaven.
　And the chiefs made answer, saying:
"We have listened to your message,
We have heard your words of wisdom,
We will think on what you tell us.
It is well for us, O brothers,
That you come so far to see us!"
　Then they rose up and departed
Each one homeward to his wigwam,
To the young men and the women
Told the story of the strangers
Whom the Master of Life had sent them
From the shining land of Wabun.
　Heavy with the heat and silence
Grew the afternoon of Summer;
With a drowsy sound the forest
Whispered round the sultry wigwam,
With a sound of sleep the water
Rippled on the beach below it;
From the cornfields shrill and ceaseless
Sang the grasshopper, Pah-puk-keena;
And the guests of Hiawatha,

378

Weary with the heat of Summer,
Slumbered in the sultry wigwam.
  Slowly o'er the simmering landscape
Fell the evening's dusk and coolness,
And the long and level sunbeams
Shot their spears into the forest,
Breaking through its shields of shadow,
Rushed into each secret ambush,
Searched each thicket, dingle, hollow;
Still the guests of Hiawatha
Slumbered in the silent wigwam.
  From his place rose Hiawatha,
Bade farewell to old Nokomis,
Spake in whispers, spake in this wise,
Did not wake the guests, that slumbered.
  "I am going, O Nokomis,
On a long and distant journey,
To the portals of the Sunset.
To the regions of the home-wind,
Of the Northwest-Wind, Keewaydin.
But these guests I leave behind me,
In your watch and ward I leave them;
See that never harm comes near them,
See that never fear molests them,
Never danger nor suspicion,
Never want of food or shelter,
In the lodge of Hiawatha!"
  Forth into the village went he,
Bade farewell to all the warriors,
Bade farewell to all the young men,
Spake persuading, spake in this wise:
  "I am going, O my people,
On a long and distant journey;
Many moons and many winters
Will have come, and will have vanished,
Ere I come again to see you.
But my guests I leave behind me;
Listen to their words of wisdom,
Listen to the truth they tell you,
For the Master of Life has sent them
From the land of light and morning!"
  On the shore stood Hiawatha,
Turned and waved his hand at parting;

On the clear and luminous water
Launched his birch canoe for sailing,
From the pebbles of the margin
Shoved it forth into the water;
Whispered to it, "Westward! westward!"
And with speed it darted forward.
  And the evening sun descending
Set the clouds on fire with redness,
Burned the broad sky, like a prairie,
Left upon the level water
One long track and trail of splendor,
Down whose stream, as down a river,
Westward, westward Hiawatha
Sailed into the fiery sunset,
Sailed into the purple vapors,
Sailed into the dusk of evening:
  And the people from the margin
Watched him floating, rising, sinking,
Till the birch canoe seemed lifted
High into that sea of splendor,
Till it sank into the vapors
Like the new moon slowly, slowly
Sinking in the purple distance.
  And they said, "Farewell forever!"
Said, "Farewell, O Hiawatha!"
And the forests, dark and lonely,
Moved through all their depths of darkness,
Sighed, "Farewell, O Hiawatha!"
And the waves upon the margin
Rising, rippling on the pebbles,
Sobbed, "Farewell, O Hiawatha!"
And the heron, the Shuh-shuh-gah,
From her haunts among the fen-lands,
Screamed, "Farewell, O Hiawatha!"
  Thus departed Hiawatha,
Hiawatha the Beloved,
In the glory of the sunset,.
In the purple mists of evening,
To the regions of the home-wind,
Of the Northwest-Wind, Keewaydin,
To the Islands of the Blessed,
To the Kingdom of Ponemah,
To the Land of the Hereafter!

NOTES
THE SONG OF HIAWATHA.

This Indian Edda—if I may so call it—is founded on a tradition prevalent among the North American Indians, of a personage of miraculous birth, who was sent among them to clear their rivers, forests, and fishing-grounds, and to teach them the arts of peace.

He was known among different tribes by the several names of Michabou, Chiabo, Manabozo, Tarenyawagon, and Hiawatha. Mr. Schoolcraft gives an account of him in his Algic Researches, Vol. I. p. 134; and in his History, Condition, and Prospects of the Indian Tribes of the United States, Part III. p. 314, may be found the Iroquois form of the tradition, derived from the verbal narrations of an Onondaga chief.

Into this old tradition I have woven other curious Indian legends, drawn chiefly from the various and valuable writings of Mr. Schoolcraft, to whom the literary world is greatly indebted for his indefatigable zeal in rescuing from oblivion so much of the legendary lore of the Indians.

The scene of the poem is among the Ojibways on the southern shore of Lake Superior, in the region between the Pictured Rocks and the Grand Sable.

VOCABULARY

Adjidau'mo, the red squirrel.
Ahdeek', the reindeer.
Ahkose'win, fever.
Ahmeek', the beaver.
Algon'quin, Ojibway.
Annemee'kee, the thunder.
Apuk'wa. a bulrush.
Baim-wa'wa, the sound of the thunder.
Bemah'gut, the grapevine.
Be'na, the pheasant.
Big-Sea-Water, Lake Superior.
Bukada'win, famine.
Chemaun', a birch canoe.
Chetowaik', the plover.

Chibia'bos, a musician; friend of Hiawatha; ruler in the Land of Spirits.

Dahin'da, the bull frog.

Dush-kwo-ne'she or Kwo-ne'she, the dragon fly.

Esa, shame upon you.

Ewa-yea', lullaby.

Ghee'zis, the sun.

Gitche Gu'mee, The Big-Sea-Water, Lake Superior.

Gitche Man'ito, the Great Spirit, the Master of Life.

Gushkewau', the darkness.

Hiawa'tha, the Wise Man, the Teacher, son of Mudjekeewis, the WestWind and Wenonah, daughter of Nokomis.

Ia'goo, a great boaster and story-teller.

Inin'ewug, men, or pawns in the Game of the Bowl.

Ishkoodah', fire, a comet.

Jee'bi, a ghost, a spirit.

Joss'akeed, a prophet.

Kabibonok'ka, the North-Wind.

Kagh, the hedge-hog.

Ka'go, do not.

Kahgahgee', the raven.

Kaw, no.

Kaween', no indeed.

Kayoshk', the sea-gull.

Kee'go, a fish.

Keeway'din, the Northwest wind, the Home-wind.

Kena'beek, a serpent.

Keneu', the great war-eagle.

Keno'zha, the pickerel.

Ko'ko-ko'ho, the owl.

Kuntasoo', the Game of Plum-stones.

Kwa'sind, the Strong Man.

Kwo-ne'she, or Dush-kwo-ne'she, the dragon-fly.

Mahnahbe'zee, the swan.

Mahng, the loon.

Mahn-go-tay'see, loon-hearted, brave.

Mahnomo'nee, wild rice.

Ma'ma, the woodpecker.

Maskeno'zha, the pike.

Me'da, a medicine-man.

Meenah'ga, the blueberry.

Megissog'won, the great Pearl-Feather, a magician, and the Manito of Wealth.

Meshinau'wa, a pipe-bearer.

Minjekah'wun, Hiawatha's mittens.

Minneha'ha, Laughing Water; wife of Hiawatha; a water-fall in a
stream running into the Mississippi between Fort Snelling and the
   Falls of St. Anthony.

Minne-wa'wa, a pleasant sound, as of the wind in the trees.

Mishe-Mo'kwa, the Great Bear.

Mishe-Nah'ma, the Great Sturgeon.

Miskodeed', the Spring-Beauty, the Claytonia Virginica.

Monda'min, Indian corn.

Moon of Bright Nights, April.

Moon of Leaves, May.

Moon of Strawberries, June.

Moon of the Falling Leaves, September.

Moon of Snow-shoes, November.

Mudjekee'wis, the West-Wind; father of Hiawatha.

Mudway-aush'ka, sound of waves on a shore.

Mushkoda'sa, the grouse.

Nah'ma, the sturgeon.

Nah'ma-wusk, spearmint.

Na'gow Wudj'oo, the Sand Dunes of Lake Superior.

Nee-ba-naw'-baigs, water-spirits.

Nenemoo'sha, sweetheart.

Nepah'win, sleep.

Noko'mis, a grandmother, mother of Wenonah.

No'sa, my father.

Nush'ka, look! look!

Odah'min, the strawberry.

Okahah'wis, the fresh-water herring.

Ome'me, the pigeon.

Ona'gon, a bowl.

Onaway', awake.

Ope'chee, the robin.

Osse'o, Son of the Evening Star.

Owais'sa, the bluebird.

Oweenee', wife of Osseo.

Ozawa'beek, a round piece of brass or copper in the Game of the
   Bowl.

Pah-puk-kee'na, the grasshopper.

Pau'guk, death.

Pau-Puk-Kee'wis, the handsome Yenadizze, the son of Storm Fool.

Pauwa'ting, Saut Sainte Marie.

Pe'boan, Winter.

Pem'ican, meat of the deer or buffalo dried and pounded.
Pezhekee', the bison.
Pishnekuh', the brant.
Pone'mah, hereafter.
Pugasaing', Game of the Bowl.
Puggawau'gun, a war-club.
Puk-Wudj'ies, little wild men of the woods; pygmies.
Sah-sah-je'wun, rapids.
Sah'wa, the perch.
Segwun', Spring.
Sha'da, the pelican.
Shahbo'min, the gooseberry.
Shah-shah, long ago.
Shaugoda'ya, a coward.
Shawgashee', the craw-fish.
Shawonda'see, the South-Wind.
Shaw-shaw, the swallow.
Shesh'ebwug, ducks; pieces in the Game of the Bowl.
Shin'gebis, the diver, or grebe.
Showain' neme'shin, pity me.
Shuh-shuh'gah, the blue heron.
Soan-ge-ta'ha, strong-hearted.
Subbeka'she, the spider.
Sugge'me, the mosquito.
To'tem, family coat-of-arms.
Ugh, yes.
Ugudwash', the sun-fish.
Unktahee', the God of Water.
Wabas'so, the rabbit, the North.
Wabe'no, a magician, a juggler.
Wabe'no-wusk, yarrow.
Wa'bun, the East-Wind.
Wa'bun An'nung, the Star of the East, the Morning Star.
Wahono'win, a cry of lamentation.
Wah-wah-tay'see, the fire-fly.
Wam'pum, beads of shell.
Waubewy'on, a white skin wrapper.
Wa'wa, the wild goose.
Waw'beek, a rock.
Waw-be-wa'wa, the white goose.
Wawonais'sa, the whippoorwill.
Way-muk-kwa'na, the caterpillar.
Wen'digoes, giants.

Weno'nah, Hiawatha's mother, daughter of Nokomis.
Yenadiz'ze, an idler and gambler; an Indian dandy.

In the Vale of Tawasentha.

This valley, now called Norman's Kill; is in Albany County, New York.

On the Mountains of the Prairie.

Mr. Catlin, in his Letters and Notes on the Manners, Customs, and

Condition of the North American Indians, Vol. II p. 160, gives an interesting account of the Coteau des Prairies, and the Red Pipestone Quarry. He says: —

"Here (according to their traditions) happened the mysterious birth of the red pipe, which has blown its fumes of peace and war to the remotest corners of the continent; which has visited every warrior, and passed through its reddened stem the irrevocable oath of war and desolation. And here, also, the peace-breathing calumet was born, and fringed with the eagle's quills, which has shed its thrilling fumes over the land, and soothed the fury of the relentless savage.

"The Great Spirit at an ancient period here called the Indian nations together, and, standing on the precipice of the red pipe- stone rock, broke from its wall a piece, and made a huge pipe by turning it in his hand, which he smoked over them, and to the North, the South, the East, and the West, and told them that this stone was red, —that it was their flesh, —that they must use it for their pipes of peace, —that it belonged to them all, and that the war-club and scalping-knife must not be raised on its ground. At the last whiff of his pipe his head went into a great cloud, and the whole surface of the rock for several miles was melted and glazed; two great ovens were opened beneath, and two women (guardian spirits of the place) entered them in a blaze of fire; and they are heard there yet (Tso-mec-cos-tee aud Tso-me-cos-te-won-dee), answering to the invocations of the high-priests or medicine-men, who consult them when they are visitors to this sacred place. "

Hark you, Bear! you are a coward.

This anecdote is from Heckewelder. In his account of the Indian Nations, he describes an Indian hunter as addressing a bear in nearly these words. "I was present, " he says, "at the delivery of this curious invective; when the hunter had despatched the bear, I asked him how he thought that poor animal could understand what he said to it. 'O, ' said he in answer, 'the bear understood me very well; did you not observe how ashamed he looked while I was upbraiding him? '" —Transactions of the American Philosophical Society, Vol. I. p. 240.

Hush! the Naked Bear will hear thee!

Heckewelder, in a letter published in the Transactions of the American Philosophical Society, Vol. IV. p. 260, speaks of this tradition as prevalent among the Mohicans and Delawares.

"Their reports, " he says, "run thus: that among all animals that had been formerly in this country, this was the most ferocious; that it was much larger than the largest of the common bears, and remarkably long-bodied; all over (except a spot of hair on its back of a white color) naked. . . . .

"The history of this animal used to be a subject of conversation among the Indians, especially when in the woods a hunting. I have also heard them say to their children when crying: 'Hush! the naked bear will hear you, be upon you, and devour you, '"

Where the Falls of Minnehaha, etc.

"The scenery about Fort Snelling is rich in beauty. The Falls of St. Anthony are familiar to travellers, and to readers of Indian sketches. Between the fort and these falls are the 'Little Falls, ' forty feet in height, on a stream that empties into the Mississippi. The Indians called them Mine-hah-hah, or 'laughing waters. '" — MRS. EASTMAN'S Dacotah, or Legends of the Sioux, Introd., p. ii.

Sand Hills of the Nagow Wudjoo.

A description of the Grand Sable, or great sand-dunes of Lake Superior, is given in Foster and Whitney's Report on the Geology of the Lake Superior Land District, Part II. p. 131.

"The Grand Sable possesses a scenic interest little inferior to that of the Pictured Rocks. The explorer passes abruptly from a coast of consolidated sand to one of loose materials; and although in the one case the cliffs are less precipitous, yet in the other they attain a higher altitude. He sees before him a long reach of coast, resembling a vast sand-bank, more than three hundred and fifty feet in height, without a trace of vegetation. Ascending to the top, rounded hillocks of blown sand are observed, with occasional clumps of trees standing out like oases in the desert. "

Onaway! Awake, beloved!

The original of this song may be found in Littell's Living Age, Vol. XXV. p. 45.

On the Red Swan floating, flying.

The fanciful tradition of the Red Swan may be found in Schoolcraft's Algic Researches, Vol. II. p. 9. Three brothers were hunting on a wager to see who would bring home the first game.

"They were to shoot no other animal, " so the legend says, "but such as each was in the habit of killing. They set out different ways: Odjibwa, the youngest, had not gone far before he saw a bear, an animal he was not to kill, by the agreement. He followed him close, and drove an arrow through him, which brought him to the ground. Although contrary to the bet, he immediately commenced skinning him, when suddenly something red tinged all the air around him. He rubbed his eyes, thinking he was perhaps deceived; but without effect, for the red hue continued. At length he heard a strange noise at a distance. It first appeared like a human voice, but after following the sound for some distance, he reached the shores of a lake, and soon saw the object he was looking for. At a distance out in the lake sat a most beautiful Red Swan, whose plumage glittered in the sun, and who would now and then make the same noise he had heard. He was within long bow-shot, and, pulling the arrow from the bowstring up to his ear, took deliberate aim and shot. The arrow took no effect; and he shot and shot again till his quiver was empty. Still the swan remained, moving round and round, stretching its long neck and dipping its bill into the water, as if heedless of the arrows shot at it. Odjibwa ran home, and got all his own and his brother's arrows and shot them all away. He then stood and gazed at the beautiful bird. While standing, he remembered his brother's saying that in their deceased father's medicine-sack were three magic arrows. Off he started, his anxiety to kill the swan overcoming all scruples. At any other time, he would have deemed it sacrilege to open his father's medicine-sack; but now he hastily seized the three arrows and ran back, leaving the other contents of the sack scattered over the lodge. The swan was still there. He shot the first arrow with great precision, and came very near to it. The second came still closer; as he took the last arrow, he felt his arm firmer, and, drawing it up with vigor, saw it pass through the neck of the swan a little above the breast. Still it did not prevent the bird from flying off, which it did, however, at first slowly, flapping its wings and rising gradually into the airs and teen flying off toward the sinking of the sun. " — pp. 10-12.

When I think of my beloved.

The original of this song may be found in Oneota, p. 15.

Sing the mysteries of Mondamin. The Indians hold the maize, or Indian corn, in great veneration.

"They esteem it so important and divine a grain, " says Schoolcraft, "that their story-tellers invented various tales, in which this idea is symbolized under the form of a special gift from the Great Spirit. The Odjibwa-Algonquins, who call it Mon-da-min, that is, the Spirit's grain or berry, have a pretty story of this kind, in which the stalk in full tassel is represented as descending from the sky, under the guise of a handsome youth, in answer to the prayers of a young man at his fast of virility, or coming to manhood.

"It is well known that corn-planting and corn-gathering, at least among all the still uncolonized tribes, are left entirely to the females and children, and a few superannuated old men. It is not generally known, perhaps, that this labor is not compulsory, and that it is assumed by the females as a just equivalent, in their view, for the onerous and continuous labor of the other sex, in providing meats, and skins for clothing, by the chase, and in defending their villages against their enemies, and keeping intruders off their territories. A good Indian housewife deems this a part of her prerogative, and prides herself to have a store of corn to exercise her hospitality, or duly honor her husband's hospitality, in the entertainment of the lodge guests. " — Oneota, p. 82.

Thus the fields shall be more fruitful.

"A singular proof of this belief, in both sexes, of the mysterious influence of the steps of a woman on the vegetable and in sect creation, is found in an ancient custom, which was related to me, respecting corn-planting. It was the practice of the hunter's wife, when the field of corn had been planted, to choose the first dark or overclouded evening to perform a secret circuit, sans habillement, around the field. For this purpose she slipped out of the lodge in the evening, unobserved, to some obscure nook, where she completely disrobed. Then, taking her matchecota, or principal garment, in one hand, she dragged it around the field. This was thought to insure a prolific crop, and to prevent the assaults of insects and worms upon the grain. It was supposed they could not creep over the charmed line. " — Oneota, p. 83.

With his prisoner-string he bound him.

"These cords, " says Mr. Tanner "are made of the bark of the elm-tree, by boiling and then immersing it in cold water. . ... The leader of a war party commonly carries several fastened about his waist, and if, in the course of the fight, any one of his young men take a prisoner, it is his duty to bring him immediately to the chief, to be tied, and the latter is responsible for his safe keeping. " — Narrative of Captivity and Adventures, p. 412.

Wagemin, the thief of cornfields, Paimosaid, who steals the maize-ear.

"If one of the young female huskers finds a red ear of corn, it is typical of a brave admirer, and is regarded as a fitting present to some young warrior. But if the ear be crooked, and tapering to a point, no matter what color, the whole circle is set in a roar, and wa-ge-min is the word shouted aloud. It is the symbol of a thief in the cornfield. It is considered as the image of an old man stooping as he enters the lot. Had the chisel of Praxiteles been employed to produce this image, it could not more vividly bring to the minds of the merry group the idea of a pilferer of their favorite mondamin. . . . .

"The literal meaning of the term is, a mass, or crooked ear of grain; but the ear of corn so called is a conventional type of a little old man pilfering ears of corn in a cornfield. It is in this manner that a single word or term, in these curious languages, becomes the fruitful parent of many ideas. And we can thus perceive why it is that the word wagemin is alone competent to excite merriment in the husking circle.

"This term is taken as the basis of the cereal chorus, or corn song, as sung by the Northern Algonquin tribes. It is coupled with the phrase Paimosaid, —a permutative form of the Indian substantive, made from the verb pim-o-sa, to walk. Its literal meaning is, he who walks, or the walker; but the ideas conveyed by it are, he who walks by night to pilfer corn. It offers, therefore, a kind of parallelism in expression to the preceding term. " — Oneota, p. 254.

Pugasaing, with thirteen pieces.

This Game of the Bowl is the principal game of hazard among the Northern tribes of Indians. Mr. Schoolcraft gives a particular account of it in Oneota, p. 85. "This game, " he says, "is very fascinating to some portions of the Indians. They stake at it their ornaments, weapons, clothing, canoes, horses, everything in fact they possess; and have been known, it is said, to set up their wives and children and even to forfeit their own liberty. Of such desperate stakes I have seen no examples, nor do I think the game itself in common use. It is rather confined to certain persons, who hold the relative rank of gamblers in Indian society, —men who are not noted as hunters or warriors, or steady providers for their families. Among these are persons who bear the term of Iena-dizze- wug, that is, wanderers about the country, braggadocios, or fops. It can hardly be classed with the popular games of amusement, by which skill and dexterity are acquired. I have generally found the chiefs and graver men of the tribes, who encouraged the young men to play ball, and are sure to be present at the customary sports, to witness, and sanction, and applaud them, speak lightly and disparagingly of this game of hazard. Yet it cannot be denied that some of the chiefs, distinguished in war and the chase, at the West, can be referred to as lending their example to its fascinating power. "

See also his history, Condition, and Prospects of the Indian Tribes, Part II, p. 72.

To the Pictured Rocks of sandstone.

The reader will find a long description of the Pictured Rocks in Foster and Whitney's Report on the Geology of the Lake Superior

Land District, Part II. p. 124. From this I make the following extract: —

"The Pictured Rocks may be described, in general terms, as a series of sandstone bluffs extending along the shore of Lake Superior for about five miles, and rising, in most places, vertically from the water, without any beach at the base, to a height varying from fifty to nearly two hundred feet. Were they simply a line of cliffs, they might not, so far as relates to height or extent, be worthy of a rank among great natural curiosities, although such an assemblage of rocky strata, washed by the waves of the great lake, would not, under any circumstances, be destitute of grandeur. To the voyager, coasting along their base in his frail canoe, they would, at all times, be an object of dread; the recoil of the surf, the rock-bound coast, affording, for miles, no place of refuge, —the lowering sky, the rising wind, — all these would excite his apprehension, and induce him to ply a vigorous oar until the dreaded wall was passed. But in the Pictured Rocks there are two features which communicate to the scenery a wonderful and almost unique character. These are, first, the curious manner in which the cliffs have been excavated and worn away by the action of the lake, which, for centuries, has dashed an ocean-like surf against their base; and, second, the equally curious manner in which large portions of the surface have been colored by bands of brilliant hues.

"It is from the latter circumstance that the name, by which these cliffs are known to the American traveller, is derived; while that applied to them by the French voyageurs ('Les Portails') is derived from the former, and by far the most striking peculiarity.

"The term Pictured Rocks has been in use for a great length of time; but when it was first applied, we have been unable to discover. It would seem that the first travellers were more impressed with the novel and striking distribution of colors on the surface than with the astonishing variety of form into which the cliffs themselves have been worn. . . .

"Our voyageurs had many legends to relate of the pranks of the Menni-bojou in these caverns, and, in answer to our inquiries, seemed disposed to fabricate stories, without end, of the achievements of this Indian deity. "

Toward the Sun his hands were lifted.

In this manner, and with such salutations, was Father Marquette received by the Illinois. See his Voyages et Decouvertes, Section V.

END HIAWATHA NOTES

THE COURTSHIP OF MILES STANDISH

I

MILES STANDISH

In the Old Colony days, in Plymouth the land of the Pilgrims,
To and fro in a room of his simple and primitive dwelling,
Clad in doublet and hose, and boots of Cordovan leather,
Strode, with a martial air, Miles Standish the Puritan Captain.
Buried in thought he seemed, with his hands behind him, and pausing
Ever and anon to behold his glittering weapons of warfare,
Hanging in shining array along the walls of the chamber, —
Cutlass and corselet of steel, and his trusty sword of Damascus,
Curved at the point and inscribed with its mystical Arabic sentence,
While underneath, in a corner, were fowling-piece, musket, and matchlock.
Short of stature he was, but strongly built and athletic,
Broad in the shoulders, deep-chested, with muscles and sinews of iron;
Brown as a nut was his face, but his russet beard was already
Flaked with patches of snow, as hedges sometimes in November.
Near him was seated John Alden, his friend, and household companion,
Writing with diligent speed at a table of pine by the window;
Fair-haired, azure-eyed, with delicate Saxon complexion,
Having the dew of his youth, and the beauty thereof, as the captives
Whom Saint Gregory saw, and exclaimed, "Not Angles, but Angels."
Youngest of all was he of the men who came in the Mayflower.

  Suddenly breaking the silence, the diligent scribe interrupting,
Spake, in the pride of his heart, Miles Standish the Captain of Plymouth.
"Look at these arms," he said, "the warlike weapons that hang here
Burnished and bright and clean, as if for parade or inspection!
This is the sword of Damascus I fought with in Flanders; this breastplate,
Well I remember the day! once saved my life in a skirmish;
Here in front you can see the very dint of the bullet
Fired point-blank at my heart by a Spanish arcabucero.
Had it not been of sheer steel, the forgotten bones of Miles Standish
Would at this moment be mould, in their grave in the Flemish morasses."
Thereupon answered John Alden, but looked not up from his writing:
"Truly the breath of the Lord hath slackened the speed of the bullet;
He in his mercy preserved you, to be our shield and our weapon!"
Still the Captain continued, unheeding the words of the stripling:
"See, how bright they are burnished, as if in an arsenal hanging;

That is because I have done it myself, and not left it to others.
Serve yourself, would you be well served, is an excellent adage;
So I take care of my arms, as you of your pens and your inkhorn.
Then, too, there are my soldiers, my great, invincible army,
Twelve men, all equipped, having each his rest and his matchlock,
Eighteen shillings a month, together with diet and pillage,
And, like Caesar, I know the name of each of my soldiers!"
This he said with a smile, that danced in his eyes, as the sunbeams
Dance on the waves of the sea, and vanish again in a moment.
Alden laughed as he wrote, and still the Captain continued:
"Look! you can see from this window my brazen howitzer planted
High on the roof of the church, a preacher who speaks to the purpose,
Steady, straight-forward, and strong, with irresistible logic,
Orthodox, flashing conviction right into the hearts of the heathen.
Now we are ready, I think, for any assault of the Indians;
Let them come, if they like, and the sooner they try it the better,—
Let them come if they like, be it sagamore, sachem, or pow-wow,
Aspinet, Samoset, Corbitant, Squanto, or Tokamahamon!"

Long at the window he stood, and wistfully gazed on the landscape,
Washed with a cold gray mist, the vapory breath of the east-wind,
Forest and meadow and hill, and the steel-blue rim of the ocean,
Lying silent and sad, in the afternoon shadows and sunshine.
Over his countenance flitted a shadow like those on the landscape,
Gloom intermingled with light; and his voice was subdued with emotion,
Tenderness, pity, regret, as after a pause he proceeded:
"Yonder there, on the hill by the sea, lies buried Rose Standish;
Beautiful rose of love, that bloomed for me by the wayside!
She was the first to die of all who came in the Mayflower!
Green above her is growing the field of wheat we have sown there,
Better to hide from the Indian scouts the graves of our people,
Lest they should count them and see how many already have perished!"
Sadly his face he averted, and strode up and down, and was thoughtful.

Fixed to the opposite wall was a shelf of books, and among them
Prominent three, distinguished alike for bulk and for binding;
Bariffe's Artillery Guide, and the Commentaries of Caesar,
Out of the Latin translated by Arthur Goldinge of London,
And, as if guarded by these, between them was standing the Bible.
Musing a moment before them, Miles Standish paused, as if doubtful
Which of the three he should choose for his consolation and comfort,
Whether the wars of the Hebrews, the famous campaigns of the
      Romans,

Or the Artillery practice, designed for belligerent Christians.
Finally down from its shelf he dragged the ponderous Roman,
Seated himself at the window, and opened the book, and in silence
Turned o'er the well-worn leaves, where thumb-marks thick on the margin,
Like the trample of feet, proclaimed the battle was hottest.
Nothing was heard in the room but the hurrying pen of the stripling,
Busily writing epistles important, to go by the Mayflower,
Ready to sail on the morrow, or next day at latest, God willing!
Homeward bound with the tidings of all that terrible winter,
Letters written by Alden, and full of the name of Priscilla,
Full of the name and the fame of the Puritan maiden Priscilla!

II

LOVE AND FRIENDSHIP

Nothing was heard in the room but the hurrying pen of the stripling,
Or an occasional sigh from the laboring heart of the Captain,
Reading the marvellous words and achievements of Julius Caesar.
After a while he exclaimed, as he smote with his hand, palm downwards,
Heavily on the page: "A wonderful man was this Caesar!
You are a writer, and I am a fighter, but here is a fellow
Who could both write and fight, and in both was equally skilful!"
Straightway answered and spake John Alden, the comely, the youthful:
"Yes, he was equally skilled, as you say, with his pen and his weapons.
Somewhere have I read, but where I forget, he could dictate
Seven letters at once, at the same time writing his memoirs."
"Truly," continued the Captain, not heeding or hearing the other,
"Truly a wonderful man was Caius Julius Caesar!
Better be first, he said, in a little Iberian village,
Than be second in Rome, and I think he was right when he said it.
Twice was he married before he was twenty, and many times after;
Battles five hundred he fought, and a thousand cities he conquered;
He, too, fought in Flanders, as he himself has recorded;
Finally he was stabbed by his friend, the orator Brutus!
Now, do you know what he did on a certain occasion in Flanders,
When the rear-guard of his army retreated, the front giving way too,
And the immortal Twelfth Legion was crowded so closely together
There was no room for their swords? Why, he seized a shield from a soldier,
Put himself straight at the head of his troops, and commanded the captains,
Calling on each by his name, to order forward the ensigns;
Then to widen the ranks, and give more room for their weapons;

So he won the day, the battle of something-or-other.
That's what I always say; if you wish a thing to be well done,
You must do it yourself, you must not leave it to others!"

   All was silent again; the Captain continued his reading.
Nothing was heard in the room but the hurrying pen of the stripling
Writing epistles important to go next day by the Mayflower,
Filled with the name and the fame of the Puritan maiden Priscilla;
Every sentence began or closed with the name of Priscilla,
Till the treacherous pen, to which he confided the secret,
Strove to betray it by singing and shouting the name of Priscilla!
Finally closing his book, with a bang of the ponderous cover,
Sudden and loud as the sound of a soldier grounding his musket,
Thus to the young man spake Miles Standish the Captain of Plymouth:
"When you have finished your work, I have something important to tell you.
Be not however in haste; I can wait; I shall not be impatient!"
Straightway Alden replied, as he folded the last of his letters,
Pushing his papers aside, and giving respectful attention:
"Speak; for whenever you speak, I am always ready to listen,
Always ready to hear whatever pertains to Miles Standish."
Thereupon answered the Captain, embarrassed, and culling his phrases:
"'T is not good for a man to be alone, say the Scriptures.
This I have said before, and again and again I repeat it;
Every hour in the day, I think it, and feel it, and say it.
Since Rose Standish died, my life has been weary and dreary;
Sick at heart have I been, beyond the healing of friendship.
Oft in my lonely hours have I thought of the maiden Priscilla.
She is alone in the world; her father and mother and brother
Died in the winter together; I saw her going and coming,
Now to the grave of the dead, and now to the bed of the dying,
Patient, courageous, and strong, and said to myself, that if ever
There were angels on earth, as there are angels in heaven,
Two have I seen and known; and the angel whose name is Priscilla
Holds in my desolate life the place which the other abandoned.
Long have I cherished the thought, but never have dared to reveal it,
Being a coward in this, though valiant enough for the most part.
Go to the damsel Priscilla, the loveliest maiden of Plymouth,
Say that a blunt old Captain, a man not of words but of actions,
Offers his hand and his heart, the hand and heart of a soldier.
Not in these words, you know, but this in short is my meaning;
I am a maker of war, and not a maker of phrases.
You, who are bred as a scholar, can say it in elegant language,
Such as you read in your books of the pleadings and wooings of lovers,

Such as you think best adapted to win the heart of a maiden."

When he had spoken, John Alden, the fair-haired, taciturn stripling,
All aghast at his words, surprised, embarrassed, bewildered,
Trying to mask his dismay by treating the subject with lightness,
Trying to smile, and yet feeling his heart stand still in his bosom,
Just as a timepiece stops in a house that is stricken by lightning,
Thus made answer and spake, or rather stammered than answered:
"Such a message as that, I am sure I should mangle and mar it;
If you would have it well done,—I am only repeating your maxim,—
You must do it yourself, you must not leave it to others!"
But with the air of a man whom nothing can turn from his purpose,
Gravely shaking his head, made answer the Captain of Plymouth:
"Truly the maxim is good, and I do not mean to gainsay it;
But we must use it discreetly, and not waste powder for nothing.
Now, as I said before, I was never a maker of phrases.
I can march up to a fortress and summon the place to surrender,
But march up to a woman with such a proposal, I dare not.
I'm not afraid of bullets, nor shot from the mouth of a cannon,
But of a thundering "No!" point-blank from the mouth of a woman,
That I confess I'm afraid of, nor am I ashamed to confess it!
So you must grant my request, for you are an elegant scholar,
Having the graces of speech, and skill in the turning of phrases."
Taking the hand of his friend, who still was reluctant and doubtful,
Holding it long in his own, and pressing it kindly, he added:
"Though I have spoken thus lightly, yet deep is the feeling that
prompts me;
Surely you cannot refuse what I ask in the name of our friendship!"
Then made answer John Alden: "The name of friendship is sacred;
What you demand in that name, I have not the power to deny you!"
So the strong will prevailed, subduing and moulding the gentler,
Friendship prevailed over love, and Alden went on his errand.

        III

THE LOVER'S ERRAND

So the strong will prevailed, and Alden went on his errand,
Out of the street of the village, and into the paths of the forest,
Into the tranquil woods, where blue-birds and robins were building
Towns in the populous trees, with hanging gardens of verdure,
Peaceful, aerial cities of joy and affection and freedom.

All around him was calm, but within him commotion and conflict,
Love contending with friendship, and self with each generous impulse.
To and fro in his breast his thoughts were heaving and dashing,
As in a foundering ship, with every roll of the vessel,
Washes the bitter sea, the merciless surge of the ocean!
"Must I relinquish it all," he cried with a wild lamentation,
"Must I relinquish it all, the joy, the hope, the illusion?
Was it for this I have loved, and waited, and worshipped in silence?
Was it for this I have followed the flying feet and the shadow
Over the wintry sea, to the desolate shores of New England?
Truly the heart is deceitful, and out of its depths of corruption
Rise, like an exhalation, the misty phantoms of passion;
Angels of light they seem, but are only delusions of Satan.
All is clear to me now; I feel it, I see it distinctly!
This is the hand of the Lord; it is laid upon me in anger,
For I have followed too much the heart's desires and devices,
Worshipping Astaroth blindly, and impious idols of Baal.
This is the cross I must bear; the sin and the swift retribution."

  So through the Plymouth woods John Alden went on his errand;
Crossing the brook at the ford, where it brawled over pebble and shallow,
Gathering still, as he went, the May-flowers blooming around him,
Fragrant, filling the air with a strange and wonderful sweetness,
Children lost in the woods, and covered with leaves in their slumber.
"Puritan flowers," he said, "and the type of Puritan maidens,
Modest and simple and sweet, the very type of Priscilla!
So I will take them to her; to Priscilla the May-flower of Plymouth,
Modest and simple and sweet, as a parting gift will I take them;
Breathing their silent farewells, as they fade and wither and perish,
Soon to be thrown away as is the heart of the giver."
So through the Plymouth woods John Alden went on his errand;
Came to an open space, and saw the disk of the ocean,
Sailless, sombre and cold with the comfortless breath of the east-wind;
Saw the new-built house and people at work in a meadow;
Heard, as he drew near the door, the musical voice of Priscilla
Singing the hundredth Psalm, the grand old Puritan anthem,
Music that Luther sang to the sacred words of the Psalmist,
Full of the breath of the Lord, consoling and comforting many.
Then, as he opened the door, he beheld the form of the maiden
Seated beside her wheel, and the carded wool like a snow-drift
Piled at her knee, her white hands feeding the ravenous spindle,
While with her foot on the treadle she guided the wheel in its motion.
Open wide on her lap lay the well-worn psalm-book of Ainsworth,

Printed in Amsterdam, the words and the music together,
Rough-hewn, angular notes, like stones in the wall of a churchyard,
Darkened and overhung by the running vine of the verses.
Such was the book from whose pages she sang the old Puritan anthem,
She, the Puritan girl, in the solitude of the forest,
Making the humble house and the modest apparel of home-spun
Beautiful with her beauty, and rich with the wealth of her being!
Over him rushed, like a wind that is keen and cold and relentless,
Thoughts of what might have been, and the weight and woe of his errand;
All the dreams that had faded, and all the hopes that had vanished,
All his life henceforth a dreary and tenantless mansion,
Haunted by vain regrets, and pallid, sorrowful faces.
Still he said to himself, and almost fiercely he said it,
"Let not him that putteth his hand to the plough look backwards;
Though the ploughshare cut through the flowers of life to its fountains,
Though it pass o'er the graves of the dead and the hearths of the living,
It is the will of the Lord; and his mercy endureth for ever!"

So he entered the house: and the hum of the wheel and the singing
Suddenly ceased; for Priscilla, aroused by his step on the threshold,
Rose as he entered, and gave him her hand, in signal of welcome,
Saying, "I knew it was you, when I heard your step in the passage;
For I was thinking of you, as I sat there singing and spinning."
Awkward and dumb with delight, that a thought of him had been mingled
Thus in the sacred psalm, that came from the heart of the maiden,
Silent before her he stood, and gave her the flowers for an answer,
Finding no words for his thought. He remembered that day in the winter,
After the first great snow, when he broke a path from the village,
Reeling and plunging along through the drifts that encumbered the doorway,
Stamping the snow from his feet as he entered the house, and Priscilla
Laughed at his snowy locks, and gave him a seat by the fireside,
Grateful and pleased to know he had thought of her in the snow-storm.
Had he but spoken then! perhaps not in vain had he spoken;
Now it was all too late; the golden moment had vanished!
So he stood there abashed, and gave her the flowers for an answer.

Then they sat down and talked of the birds and the beautiful Spring-time,
Talked of their friends at home, and the Mayflower that sailed on the morrow.
"I have been thinking all day," said gently the Puritan maiden,
"Dreaming all night, and thinking all day, of the hedge-rows of England, —
They are in blossom now, and the country is all like a garden;
Thinking of lanes and fields, and the song of the lark and the linnet,
Seeing the village street, and familiar faces of neighbors

Going about as of old, and stopping to gossip together,
And, at the end of the street, the village church, with the ivy
Climbing the old gray tower, and the quiet graves in the churchyard.
Kind are the people I live with, and dear to me my religion;
Still my heart is so sad, that I wish myself back in Old England.
You will say it is wrong, but I cannot help it: I almost
Wish myself back in Old England, I feel so lonely and wretched."

Thereupon answered the youth: — "Indeed I do not condemn you;
Stouter hearts than a woman's have quailed in this terrible winter.
Yours is tender and trusting, and needs a stronger to lean on;
So I have come to you now, with an offer and proffer of marriage
Made by a good man and true, Miles Standish the Captain of
        Plymouth!"

Thus he delivered his message, the dexterous writer of letters, —
Did not embellish the theme, nor array it in beautiful phrases,
But came straight to the point, and blurted it out like a schoolboy;
Even the Captain himself could hardly have said it more bluntly.
Mute with amazement and sorrow, Priscilla the Puritan maiden
Looked into Alden's face, her eyes dilated with wonder,
Feeling his words like a blow, that stunned her and rendered her speechless;
Till at length she exclaimed, interrupting the ominous silence:
"If the great Captain of Plymouth is so very eager to wed me,
Why does he not come himself, and take the trouble to woo me?
If I am not worth the wooing, I surely am not worth the winning!"
Then John Alden began explaining and smoothing the matter,
Making it worse as he went, by saying the Captain was busy, —
Had no time for such things; — such things! the words grating harshly
Fell on the ear of Priscilla; and swift as a flash she made answer:
"Has he no time for such things, as you call it, before he is married,
Would he be likely to find it, or make it, after the wedding?
That is the way with you men; you don't understand us, you cannot.
When you have made up your minds, after thinking of this one and that one,
Choosing, selecting, rejecting, comparing one with another,
Then you make known your desire, with abrupt and sudden avowal,
And are offended and hurt, and indignant perhaps, that a woman
Does not respond at once to a love that she never suspected,
Does not attain at a bound the height to which you have been climbing.
This is not right nor just: for surely a woman's affection
Is not a thing to be asked for, and had for only the asking.
When one is truly in love, one not only says it, but shows it.
Had he but waited awhile, had he only showed that he loved me,

Even this Captain of yours—who knows?—at last might have won me,
Old and rough as he is; but now it never can happen."

  Still John Alden went on, unheeding the words of Priscilla,
Urging the suit of his friend, explaining, persuading, expanding;
Spoke of his courage and skill, and of all his battles in Flanders,
How with the people of God he had chosen to suffer affliction,
How, in return for his zeal, they had made him Captain of Plymouth;
He was a gentleman born, could trace his pedigree plainly
Back to Hugh Standish of Duxbury Hall, in Lancashire, England,
Who was the son of Ralph, and the grandson of Thurston de Standish;
Heir unto vast estates, of which he was basely defrauded,
Still bore the family arms, and had for his crest a cock argent
Combed and wattled gules, and all the rest of the blazon.
He was a man of honor, of noble and generous nature;
Though he was rough, he was kindly; she knew how during the winter
He had attended the sick, with a hand as gentle as woman's;
Somewhat hasty and hot, he could not deny it, and headstrong,
Stern as a soldier might be, but hearty, and placable always,
Not to be laughed at and scorned, because he was little of stature;
For he was great of heart, magnanimous, courtly, courageous;
Any woman in Plymouth, nay, any woman in England,
Might be happy and proud to be called the wife of Miles Standish!

  But as he warmed and glowed, in his simple and eloquent language,
Quite forgetful of self, and full of the praise of his rival,
Archly the maiden smiled, and, with eyes over-running with laughter,
Said, in a tremulous voice, "Why don't you speak for yourself, John?"

        IV

JOHN ALDEN

Into the open air John Alden, perplexed and bewildered,
Rushed like a man insane, and wandered alone by the sea-side;
Paced up and down the sands, and bared his head to the east-wind,
Cooling his heated brow, and the fire and fever within him.
Slowly as out of the heavens, with apocalyptical splendors,
Sank the City of God, in the vision of John the Apostle,
So, with its cloudy walls of chrysolite, jasper, and sapphire,
Sank the broad red sun, and over its turrets uplifted
Glimmered the golden reed of the angel who measured the city.

"Welcome, O wind of the East!" he exclaimed in his wild exultation,
"Welcome, O wind of the East, from the caves of the misty Atlantic!
Blowing o'er fields of dulse, and measureless meadows of sea-grass,
Blowing o'er rocky wastes, and the grottos and gardens of ocean!
Lay thy cold, moist hand on my burning forehead, and wrap me
Close in thy garments of mist, to allay the fever within me!"

Like an awakened conscience, the sea was moaning and tossing,
Beating remorseful and loud the mutable sands of the sea-shore.
Fierce in his soul was the struggle and tumult of passions contending;
Love triumphant and crowned, and friendship wounded and bleeding,
Passionate cries of desire, and importunate pleadings of duty!
"Is it my fault," he said, "that the maiden has chosen between us?
Is it my fault that he failed, — my fault that I am the victor?"
Then within him there thundered a voice, like the voice of the Prophet:
"It hath displeased the Lord!" — and he thought of David's
        transgression,
Bathsheba's beautiful face, and his friend in the front of the battle!
Shame and confusion of guilt, and abasement and self-condemnation,
Overwhelmed him at once; and he cried in the deepest contrition:
"It hath displeased the Lord! It is the temptation of Satan!"

Then, uplifting his head, he looked at the sea, and beheld there
Dimly the shadowy form of the Mayflower riding at anchor,
Rocked on the rising tide, and ready to sail on the morrow;
Heard the voices of men through the mist, the rattle of cordage
Thrown on the deck, the shouts of the mate, and the sailors' "Ay, ay, Sir!"
Clear and distinct, but not loud, in the dripping air of the twilight.
Still for a moment he stood, and listened, and stared at the vessel,
Then went hurriedly on, as one who, seeing a phantom,
Stops, then quickens his pace, and follows the beckoning shadow.
"Yes, it is plain to me now," he murmured; "the hand of the Lord is
Leading me out of the land of darkness, the bondage of error,
Through the sea, that shall lift the walls of its waters around me,
Hiding me, cutting me off, from the cruel thoughts that pursue me.
Back will I go o'er the ocean, this dreary land will abandon,
Her whom I may not love, and him whom my heart has offended.
Better to be in my grave in the green old churchyard in England,
Close by my mother's side, and among the dust of my kindred;
Better be dead and forgotten, than living in shame and dishonor!
Sacred and safe and unseen, in the dark of the narrow chamber
With me my secret shall lie, like a buried jewel that glimmers
Bright on the hand that is dust, in the chambers of silence and darkness, —

Yes, as the marriage ring of the great espousal hereafter!"

  Thus as he spake, he turned, in the strength of his strong resolution,
Leaving behind him the shore, and hurried along in the twilight,
Through the congenial gloom of the forest silent and sombre,
Till he beheld the lights in the seven houses of Plymouth,
Shining like seven stars in the dusk and mist of the evening.
Soon he entered his door, and found the redoubtable Captain
Sitting alone, and absorbed in the martial pages of Caesar,
Fighting some great campaign in Hainault or Brabant or Flanders.
"Long have you been on your errand," he said with a cheery demeanor,
Even as one who is waiting an answer, and fears not the issue.
"Not far off is the house, although the woods are between us;
But you have lingered so long, that while you were going and coming
I have fought ten battles and sacked and demolished a city.
Come, sit down, and in order relate to me all that has happened."

  Then John Alden spake, and related the wondrous adventure,
From beginning to end, minutely, just as it happened;
How he had seen Priscilla, and how he had sped in his courtship,
Only smoothing a little, and softening down her refusal.
But when he came at length to the words Priscilla had spoken,
Words so tender and cruel: "Why don't you speak for yourself, John?"
Up leaped the Captain of Plymouth, and stamped on the floor, till
          his armor
Clanged on the wall, where it hung, with a sound of sinister omen.
All his pent-up wrath burst forth in a sudden explosion,
Even as a hand-grenade, that scatters destruction around it.
Wildly he shouted, and loud: "John Alden! you have betrayed me!
Me, Miles Standish, your friend! have supplanted, defrauded,
          betrayed me!
One of my ancestors ran his sword through the heart of Wat Tyler;
Who shall prevent me from running my own through the heart of a traitor?
Yours is the greater treason, for yours is a treason to friendship!
You, who lived under my roof, whom I cherished and loved as a brother;
You, who have fed at my board, and drunk at my cup, to whose keeping
I have intrusted my honor, my thoughts the most sacred and secret, —
You too, Brutus! ah woe to the name of friendship hereafter!
Brutus was Caesar's friend, and you were mine, but henceforward
Let there be nothing between us save war, and implacable hatred!"

  So spake the Captain of Plymouth, and strode about in the chamber,
Chafing and choking with rage; like cords were the veins on his temples.

But in the midst of his anger a man appeared at the doorway,
Bringing in uttermost haste a message of urgent importance,
Rumors of danger and war and hostile incursions of Indians!
Straightway the Captain paused, and, without further question or parley,
Took from the nail on the wall his sword with its scabbard of iron,
Buckled the belt round his waist, and, frowning fiercely, departed.
Alden was left alone. He heard the clank of the scabbard
Growing fainter and fainter, and dying away in the distance.
Then he arose from his seat, and looked forth into the darkness,
Felt the cool air blow on his cheek, that was hot with the insult,
Lifted his eyes to the heavens, and, folding his hands as in childhood,
Prayed in the silence of night to the Father who seeth in secret.

Meanwhile the choleric Captain strode wrathful away to the council,
Found it already assembled, impatiently waiting his coming;
Men in the middle of life, austere and grave in deportment,
Only one of them old, the hill that was nearest to heaven,
Covered with snow, but erect, the excellent Elder of Plymouth.
God had sifted three kingdoms to find the wheat for this planting,
Then had sifted the wheat, as the living seed of a nation;
So say the chronicles old, and such is the faith of the people!
Near them was standing an Indian, in attitude stern and defiant,
Naked down to the waist, and grim and ferocious in aspect;
While on the table before them was lying unopened a Bible,
Ponderous, bound in leather, brass-studded, printed in Holland,
And beside it outstretched the skin of a rattle-snake glittered,
Filled, like a quiver, with arrows; a signal and challenge of warfare,
Brought by the Indian, and speaking with arrowy tongues of defiance.
This Miles Standish beheld, as he entered, and heard them debating
What were an answer befitting the hostile message and menace,
Talking of this and of that, contriving, suggesting, objecting;
One voice only for peace, and that the voice of the Elder,
Judging it wise and well that some at least were converted,
Rather than any were slain, for this was but Christian behavior!
Then out spake Miles Standish, the stalwart Captain of Plymouth,
Muttering deep in his throat, for his voice was husky with anger,
"What! do you mean to make war with milk and the water of roses?
Is it to shoot red squirrels you have your howitzer planted
There on the roof of the church, or is it to shoot red devils?
Truly the only tongue that is understood by a savage
Must be the tongue of fire that speaks from the mouth of the cannon!"
Thereupon answered and said the excellent Elder of Plymouth,
Somewhat amazed and alarmed at this irreverent language:

"Not so thought Saint Paul, nor yet the other Apostles;
Not from the cannon's mouth were the tongues of fire they spake with!"
But unheeded fell this mild rebuke on the Captain,
Who had advanced to the table, and thus continued discoursing:
"Leave this matter to me, for to me by right it pertaineth.
War is a terrible trade; but in the cause that is righteous,
Sweet is the smell of powder; and thus I answer the challenge!"

   Then from the rattlesnake's skin, with a sudden, contemptuous gesture,
Jerking the Indian arrows, he filled it with powder and bullets
Full to the very jaws, and handed it back to the savage,
Saying, in thundering tones: "Here, take it! this is your answer!"
Silently out of the room then glided the glistening savage,
Bearing the serpent's skin, and seeming himself like a serpent,
Winding his sinuous way in the dark to the depths of the forest.

   V

THE SAILING OF THE MAYFLOWER

Just in the gray of the dawn, as the mists uprose from the meadows,
There was a stir and a sound in the slumbering village of Plymouth;
Clanging and clicking of arms, and the order imperative, "Forward!"
Given in tone suppressed, a tramp of feet, and then silence.
Figures ten, in the mist, marched slowly out of the village.
Standish the stalwart it was, with eight of his valorous army,
Led by their Indian guide, by Hobomok, friend of the white men,
Northward marching to quell the sudden revolt of the savage.
Giants they seemed in the mist, or the mighty men of King David;
Giants in heart they were, who believed in God and the Bible, —
Ay, who believed in the smiting of Midianites and Philistines.
Over them gleamed far off the crimson banners of morning;
Under them loud on the sands, the serried billows, advancing,
Fired along the line, and in regular order retreated.

   Many a mile had they marched, when at length the village of Plymouth
Woke from its sleep, and arose, intent on its manifold labors.
Sweet was the air and soft; and slowly the smoke from the chimneys
Rose over roofs of thatch, and pointed steadily eastward;
Men came forth from the doors, and paused and talked of the weather,
Said that the wind had changed, and was blowing fair for the
      Mayflower;

Talked of their Captain's departure, and all the dangers that menaced,
He being gone, the town, and what should be done in his absence.
Merrily sang the birds, and the tender voices of women
Consecrated with hymns the common cares of the household.
Out of the sea rose the sun, and the billows rejoiced at his coming;
Beautiful were his feet on the purple tops of the mountains;
Beautiful on the sails of the Mayflower riding at anchor,
Battered and blackened and worn by all the storms of the winter.
Loosely against her masts was hanging and flapping her canvas,
Rent by so many gales, and patched by the hands of the sailors.
Suddenly from her side, as the sun rose over the ocean,
Darted a puff of smoke, and floated seaward; anon rang
Loud over field and forest the cannon's roar, and the echoes
Heard and repeated the sound, the signal-gun of departure!
Ah! but with louder echoes replied the hearts of the people!
Meekly, in voices subdued, the chapter was read from the Bible,
Meekly the prayer was begun, but ended in fervent entreaty!
Then from their houses in haste came forth the Pilgrims of Plymouth,
Men and women and children, all hurrying down to the sea-shore,
Eager, with tearful eyes, to say farewell to the Mayflower,
Homeward bound o'er the sea, and leaving them here in the desert.

  Foremost among them was Alden. All night he had lain without slumber,
Turning and tossing about in the heat and unrest of his fever.
He had beheld Miles Standish, who came back late from the council,
Stalking into the room, and heard him mutter and murmur,
Sometimes it seemed a prayer, and sometimes it sounded like swearing.
Once he had come to the bed, and stood there a moment in silence;
Then he had turned away, and said: "I will not awake him;
Let him sleep on, it is best; for what is the use of more talking!"
Then he extinguished the light, and threw himself down on his pallet,
Dressed as he was, and ready to start at the break of the morning, —
Covered himself with the cloak he had worn in his campaigns in Flanders, —
Slept as a soldier sleeps in his bivouac, ready for action.
But with the dawn he arose; in the twilight Alden beheld him
Put on his corselet of steel, and all the rest of his armor,
Buckle about his waist his trusty blade of Damascus,
Take from the corner his musket, and so stride out of the chamber.
Often the heart of the youth had burned and yearned to embrace him,
Often his lips had essayed to speak, imploring for pardon;
All the old friendship came back, with its tender and grateful emotions;
But his pride overmastered the nobler nature within him, —
Pride, and the sense of his wrong, and the burning fire of the insult.

So he beheld his friend departing in anger, but spake not,
Saw him go forth to danger, perhaps to death, and he spake not!
Then he arose from his bed, and heard what the people were saying,
Joined in the talk at the door, with Stephen and Richard and Gilbert,
Joined in the morning prayer, and in the reading of Scripture,
And, with the others, in haste went hurrying down to the sea-shore,
Down to the Plymouth Rock, that had been to their feet as a door-step
Into a world unknown,—the corner-stone of a nation!

There with his boat was the Master, already a little impatient
Lest he should lose the tide, or the wind might shift to the eastward,
Square-built, hearty, and strong, with an odor of ocean about him,
Speaking with this one and that, and cramming letters and parcels
Into his pockets capacious, and messages mingled together
Into his narrow brain, till at last he was wholly bewildered.
Nearer the boat stood Alden, with one foot placed on the gunwale,
One still firm on the rock, and talking at times with the sailors,
Seated erect on the thwarts, all ready and eager for starting.
He too was eager to go, and thus put an end to his anguish,
Thinking to fly from despair, that swifter than keel is or canvas,
Thinking to drown in the sea the ghost that would rise and pursue him.
But as he gazed on the crowd, he beheld the form of Priscilla
Standing dejected among them, unconscious of all that was passing.
Fixed were her eyes upon his, as if she divined his intention,
Fixed with a look so sad, so reproachful, imploring, and patient,
That with a sudden revulsion his heart recoiled from its purpose,
As from the verge of a crag, where one step more is destruction.
Strange is the heart of man, with its quick, mysterious instincts!
Strange is the life of man, and fatal or fated are moments,
Whereupon turn, as on hinges, the gates of the wall adamantine!
"Here I remain!" he exclaimed, as he looked at the heavens above him,
Thanking the Lord whose breath had scattered the mist and the madness,
Wherein, blind and lost, to death he was staggering headlong.
"Yonder snow-white cloud, that floats in the ether above me,
Seems like a hand that is pointing and beckoning over the ocean.
There is another hand, that is not so spectral and ghost-like,
Holding me, drawing me back, and clasping mine for protection.
Float, O hand of cloud, and vanish away in the ether!
Roll thyself up like a fist, to threaten and daunt me; I heed not
Either your warning or menace, or any omen of evil!
There is no land so sacred, no air so pure and so wholesome,
As is the air she breathes, and the soil that is pressed by her footsteps.
Here for her sake will I stay, and like an invisible presence

Hover around her for ever, protecting, supporting her weakness;
Yes! as my foot was the first that stepped on this rock at the landing,
So, with the blessing of God, shall it be the last at the leaving!"

  Meanwhile the Master alert, but with dignified air and important,
Scanning with watchful eye the tide and the wind and the weather,
Walked about on the sands; and the people crowded around him
Saying a few last words, and enforcing his careful remembrance.
Then, taking each by the hand, as if he were grasping a tiller,
Into the boat he sprang, and in haste shoved off to his vessel,
Glad in his heart to get rid of all this worry and flurry,
Glad to be gone from a land of sand and sickness and sorrow,
Short allowance of victual, and plenty of nothing but Gospel!
Lost in the sound of the oars was the last farewell of the Pilgrims.
O strong hearts and true! not one went back in the Mayflower!
No, not one looked back, who had set his hand to this ploughing!

  Soon were heard on board the shouts and songs of the sailors
Heaving the windlass round, and hoisting the ponderous anchor.
Then the yards were braced, and all sails set to the west-wind,
Blowing steady and strong; and the Mayflower sailed from the harbor,
Rounded the point of the Gurnet, and leaving far to the southward
Island and cape of sand, and the Field of the First Encounter,
Took the wind on her quarter, and stood for the open Atlantic,
Borne on the send of the sea, and the swelling hearts of the Pilgrims.

  Long in silence they watched the receding sail of the vessel,
Much endeared to them all, as something living and human;
Then, as if filled with the spirit, and wrapt in a vision prophetic,
Baring his hoary head, the excellent Elder of Plymouth
Said, "Let us pray!" and they prayed, and thanked the Lord and took courage.
Mournfully sobbed the waves at the base of the rock, and above them
Bowed and whispered the wheat on the hill of death, and their kindred
Seemed to awake in their graves, and to join in the prayer that they uttered.
Sun-illumined and white, on the eastern verge of the ocean
Gleamed the departing sail, like a marble slab in a graveyard;
Buried beneath it lay for ever all hope of escaping.
Lo! as they turned to depart, they saw the form of an Indian,
Watching them from the hill; but while they spake with each other,
Pointing with outstretched hands, and saying, "Look!" he had vanished.
So they returned to their homes; but Alden lingered a little,
Musing alone on the shore, and watching the wash of the billows
Round the base of the rock, and the sparkle and flash of the sunshine,

Like the spirit of God, moving visibly over the waters.

VI

PRISCILLA

Thus for a while he stood, and mused by the shore of the ocean,
Thinking of many things, and most of all of Priscilla;
And as if thought had the power to draw to itself, like the loadstone,
Whatsoever it touches, by subtile laws of its nature,
Lo! as he turned to depart, Priscilla was standing beside him.

"Are you so much offended, you will not speak to me?" said she.
"Am I so much to blame, that yesterday, when you were pleading
Warmly the cause of another, my heart, impulsive and wayward,
Pleaded your own, and spake out, forgetful perhaps of decorum?
Certainly you can forgive me for speaking so frankly, for saying
What I ought not to have said, yet now I can never unsay it;
For there are moments in life, when the heart is so full of emotion,
That if by chance it be shaken, or into its depths like a pebble
Drops some careless word, it overflows, and its secret,
Spilt on the ground like water, can never be gathered together.
Yesterday I was shocked, when I heard you speak of Miles Standish,
Praising his virtues, transforming his very defects into virtues,
Praising his courage and strength, and even his fighting in Flanders,
As if by fighting alone you could win the heart of a woman,
Quite overlooking yourself and the rest, in exalting your hero.
Therefore I spake as I did, by an irresistible impulse.
You will forgive me, I hope, for the sake of the friendship between us,
Which is too true and too sacred to be so easily broken!"
Thereupon answered John Alden, the scholar, the friend of Miles Standish:
"I was not angry with you, with myself alone I was angry,
Seeing how badly I managed the matter I had in my keeping."
"No!" interrupted the maiden, with answer prompt and decisive;
"No; you were angry with me, for speaking so frankly and freely.
It was wrong, I acknowledge; for it is the fate of a woman
Long to be patient and silent, to wait like a ghost that is speechless,
Till some questioning voice dissolves the spell of its silence.
Hence is the inner life of so many suffering women
Sunless and silent and deep, like subterranean rivers
Running through caverns of darkness, unheard, unseen, and unfruitful,
Chafing their channels of stone, with endless and profitless murmurs."

Thereupon answered John Alden, the young man, the lover of women:
"Heaven forbid it, Priscilla; and truly they seem to me always
More like the beautiful rivers that watered the garden of Eden,
More like the river Euphrates, through deserts of Havilah flowing,
Filling the land with delight, and memories sweet of the garden!"
"Ah, by these words, I can see," again interrupted the maiden,
"How very little you prize me, or care for what I am saying.
When from the depths of my heart, in pain and with secret misgiving,
Frankly I speak to you, asking for sympathy only and kindness,
Straightway you take up my words, that are plain and direct and in earnest,
Turn them away from their meaning, and answer with flattering phrases.
This is not right, is not just, is not true to the best that is in you;
For I know and esteem you, and feel that your nature is noble,
Lifting mine up to a higher, a more ethereal level.
Therefore I value your friendship, and feel it perhaps the more keenly
If you say aught that implies I am only as one among many,
If you make use of those common and complimentary phrases
Most men think so fine, in dealing and speaking with women,
But which women reject as insipid, if not as insulting."

  Mute and amazed was Alden; and listened and looked at Priscilla,
Thinking he never had seen her more fair, more divine in her beauty.
He who but yesterday pleaded so glibly the cause of another,
Stood there embarrassed and silent, and seeking in vain for an answer.
So the maiden went on, and little divined or imagined
What was at work in his heart, that made him so awkward and speechless.
"Let us, then, be what we are, and speak what we think, and in all things
Keep ourselves loyal to truth, and the sacred professions of
          friendship.
It is no secret I tell you, nor am I ashamed to declare it:
I have liked to be with you, to see you, to speak with you always.
So I was hurt at your words, and a little affronted to hear you
Urge me to marry your friend, though he were the Captain Miles Standish.
For I must tell you the truth: much more to me is your friendship
Than all the love he could give, were he twice the hero you think him."
Then she extended her hand, and Alden, who eagerly grasped it,
Felt all the wounds in his heart, that were aching and bleeding so sorely,
Healed by the touch of that hand, and he said, with a voice full of feeling:
"Yes, we must ever be friends; and of all who offer you friendship
Let me be ever the first, the truest, the nearest and dearest!"

  Casting a farewell look at the glimmering sail of the Mayflower,
Distant, but still in sight, and sinking below the horizon,

Homeward together they walked, with a strange, indefinite feeling,
That all the rest had departed and left them alone in the desert.
But, as they went through the fields in the blessing and smile of the sunshine,
Lighter grew their hearts, and Priscilla said very archly:
"Now that our terrible Captain has gone in pursuit of the Indians,
Where he is happier far than he would be commanding a household,
You may speak boldly, and tell me of all that happened between you,
When you returned last night, and said how ungrateful you found me."
Thereupon answered John Alden, and told her the whole of the story, —
Told her his own despair, and the direful wrath of Miles Standish.
Whereat the maiden smiled, and said between laughing and earnest,
"He is a little chimney, and heated hot in a moment!"
But as he gently rebuked her, and told her how much he had suffered, —
How he had even determined to sail that day in the Mayflower,
And had remained for her sake, on hearing the dangers that threatened, —
All her manner was changed, and she said with a faltering accent,
"Truly I thank you for this: how good you have been to me always!"

    Thus, as a pilgrim devout, who toward Jerusalem journeys,
Taking three steps in advance, and one reluctantly backward,
Urged by importunate zeal, and withheld by pangs of contrition;
Slowly but steadily onward, receding yet ever advancing,
Journeyed this Puritan youth to the Holy Land of his longings,
Urged by the fervor of love, and withheld by remorseful misgivings.

        VII

THE MARCH OF MILES STANDISH

Meanwhile the stalwart Miles Standish was marching steadily
        northward,
Winding through forest and swamp, and along the trend of the sea-shore,
All day long, with hardly a halt, the fire of his anger
Burning and crackling within, and the sulphurous odor of powder
Seeming more sweet to his nostrils than all the scents of the forest.
Silent and moody he went, and much he revolved his discomfort;
He who was used to success, and to easy victories always,
Thus to be flouted, rejected, and laughed to scorn by a maiden,
Thus to be mocked and betrayed by the friend whom most he had trusted!
Ah! 't was too much to be borne, and he fretted and chafed in his armor!

    "I alone am to blame," he muttered, "for mine was the folly.

What has a rough old soldier, grown grim and gray in the harness,
Used to the camp and its ways, to do with the wooing of maidens?
'T was but a dream, — let it pass, — let it vanish like so many others!
What I thought was a flower, is only a weed, and is worthless;
Out of my heart will I pluck it, and throw it away, and henceforward
Be but a fighter of battles, a lover and wooer of dangers!"
Thus he revolved in his mind his sorry defeat and discomfort,
While he was marching by day or lying at night in the forest,
Looking up at the trees, and the constellations beyond them.

   After a three days' march he came to an Indian encampment
Pitched on the edge of a meadow, between the sea and the forest;
Women at work by the tents, and the warriors, horrid with war-paint,
Seated about a fire, and smoking and talking together;
Who, when they saw from afar the sudden approach of the white men,
Saw the flash of the sun on breastplate and sabre and musket,
Straightway leaped to their feet, and two, from among them advancing,
Came to parley with Standish, and offer him furs as a present;
Friendship was in their looks, but in their hearts there was hatred.
Braves of the tribe were these, and brothers gigantic in stature,
Huge as Goliath of Gath, or the terrible Og, king of Bashan;
One was Pecksuot named, and the other was called Wattawamat.
Round their necks were suspended their knives in scabbards of wampum,
Two-edged, trenchant knives, with points as sharp as a needle.
Other arms had they none, for they were cunning and crafty.
"Welcome, English!" they said, — these words they had learned from the traders
Touching at times on the coast, to barter and chaffer for peltries.
Then in their native tongue they began to parley with Standish,
Through his guide and interpreter Hobomok, friend of the white man,
Begging for blankets and knives, but mostly for muskets and powder,
Kept by the white man, they said, concealed, with the plague, in his cellars,
Ready to be let loose, and destroy his brother the red man!
But when Standish refused, and said he would give them the Bible,

Suddenly changing their tone, they began to boast and to bluster.
Then Wattawamat advanced with a stride in front of the other,
And, with a lofty demeanor, thus vauntingly spake to the Captain:
"Now Wattawamat can see, by the fiery eyes of the Captain,
Angry is he in his heart; but the heart of the brave Wattawamat
Is not afraid at the sight. He was not born of a woman,
But on a mountain, at night, from an oak-tree riven by lightning,
Forth he sprang at a bound, with all his weapons about him,
Shouting, 'Who is there here to fight with the brave Wattawamat?'"

Then he unsheathed his knife, and, whetting the blade on his left hand,
Held it aloft and displayed a woman's face on the handle,
Saying, with bitter expression and look of sinister meaning:
"I have another at home, with the face of a man on the handle;
By and by they shall marry; and there will be plenty of children!"

  Then stood Pecksuot forth, self-vaunting, insulting Miles Standish:
While with his fingers he petted the knife that hung at his bosom,
Drawing it half from its sheath, and plunging it back, as he muttered,
"By and by it shall see; it shall eat; ah, ha! but shall speak not!
This is the mighty Captain the white men have sent to destroy us!
He is a little man; let him go and work with the women!"

  Meanwhile Standish had noted the faces and figures of Indians
Peeping and creeping about from bush to tree in the forest,
Feigning to look for game, with arrows set on their bow-strings,
Drawing about him still closer and closer the net of their ambush.
But undaunted he stood, and dissembled and treated them smoothly;
So the old chronicles say, that were writ in the days of the fathers.
But when he heard their defiance, the boast, the taunt, and the insult,
All the hot blood of his race, of Sir Hugh and of Thurston de Standish,
Boiled and beat in his heart, and swelled in the veins of his temples.
Headlong he leaped on the boaster, and, snatching his knife from its scabbard,
Plunged it into his heart, and, reeling backward, the savage
Fell with his face to the sky, and a fiendlike fierceness upon it.
Straight there arose from the forest the awful sound of the war-whoop,
And, like a flurry of snow on the whistling wind of December,
Swift and sudden and keen came a flight of feathery arrows,
Then came a cloud of smoke, and out of the cloud came the
        lightning,
Out of the lightning thunder, and death unseen ran before it.
Frightened the savages fled for shelter in swamp and in thicket,
Hotly pursued and beset; but their sachem, the brave Wattawamat,
Fled not; he was dead. Unswerving and swift had a bullet
Passed through his brain, and he fell with both hands clutching the
        greensward,
Seeming in death to hold back from his foe the land of his fathers.

  There on the flowers of the meadow the warriors lay, and above them,
Silent, with folded arms, stood Hobomok, friend of the white man.
Smiling at length he exclaimed to the stalwart Captain of Plymouth:
"Pecksuot bragged very loud, of his courage, his strength, and his stature,—
Mocked the great Captain, and called him a little man; but I see now

Big enough have you been to lay him speechless before you!"

  Thus the first battle was fought and won by the stalwart Miles Standish.
When the tidings thereof were brought to the village of Plymouth,
And as a trophy of war the head of the brave Wattawamat
Scowled from the roof of the fort, which at once was a church and a fortress,
All who beheld it rejoiced, and praised the Lord, and took courage.
Only Priscilla averted her face from this spectre of terror,
Thanking God in her heart that she had not married Miles Standish;
Shrinking, fearing almost, lest, coming home from his battles,
He should lay claim to her hand, as the prize and reward of his valor.

    VIII

THE SPINNING-WHEEL

Month after month passed away, and in Autumn the ships of the merchants
Came with kindred and friends, with cattle and corn for the
        Pilgrims.
All in the village was peace; the men were intent on their labors,
Busy with hewing and building, with garden-plot and with
        merestead,
Busy with breaking the glebe, and mowing the grass in the
meadows,
Searching the sea for its fish, and hunting the deer in the forest.
All in the village was peace; but at times the rumor of warfare
Filled the air with alarm, and the apprehension of danger.
Bravely the stalwart Miles Standish was scouring the land with his forces,
Waxing valiant in fight and defeating the alien armies,
Till his name had become a sound of fear to the nations.
Anger was still in his heart, but at times the remorse and contrition
Which in all noble natures succeed the passionate outbreak,
Came like a rising tide, that encounters the rush of a river,
Staying its current awhile, but making it bitter and brackish.

  Meanwhile Alden at home had built him a new habitation,
Solid, substantial, of timber rough-hewn from the firs of the forest.
Wooden-barred was the door, and the roof was covered with rushes;
Latticed the windows were, and the window-panes were of paper,
Oiled to admit the light, while wind and rain were excluded.
There too he dug a well, and around it planted an orchard:
Still may be seen to this day some trace of the well and the orchard.

Close to the house was the stall, where, safe and secure from annoyance,
Raghorn, the snow-white steer, that had fallen to Alden's allotment
In the division of cattle, might ruminate in the night-time
Over the pastures he cropped, made fragrant by sweet pennyroyal.

Oft when his labor was finished, with eager feet would the dreamer
Follow the pathway that ran through the woods to the house of Priscilla,
Led by illusions romantic and subtile deceptions of fancy,
Pleasure disguised as duty, and love in the semblance of friendship.
Ever of her he thought, when he fashioned the walls of his dwelling;
Ever of her he thought, when he delved in the soil of his garden;
Ever of her he thought, when he read in his Bible on Sunday
Praise of the virtuous woman, as she is described in the Proverbs, —
How the heart of her husband doth safely trust in her always,
How all the days of her life she will do him good, and not evil,
How she seeketh the wool and the flax and worketh with gladness,
How she layeth her hand to the spindle and holdeth the distaff,
How she is not afraid of the snow for herself or her household,
Knowing her household are clothed with the scarlet cloth of her weaving!

So as she sat at her wheel one afternoon in the Autumn,
Alden, who opposite sat, and was watching her dexterous fingers,
As if the thread she was spinning were that of his life and his fortune,
After a pause in their talk, thus spake to the sound of the spindle.
"Truly, Priscilla," he said, "when I see you spinning and spinning,
Never idle a moment, but thrifty and thoughtful of others,
Suddenly you are transformed, are visibly changed in a moment;
You are no longer Priscilla, but Bertha the Beautiful Spinner."
Here the light foot on the treadle grew swifter and swifter; the spindle
Uttered an angry snarl, and the thread snapped short in her fingers;
While the impetuous speaker, not heeding the mischief, continued:
"You are the beautiful Bertha, the spinner, the queen of Helvetia;
She whose story I read at a stall in the streets of Southampton,
Who, as she rode on her palfrey, o'er valley and meadow and mountain,
Ever was spinning her thread from a distaff fixed to her saddle.
She was so thrifty and good, that her name passed into a proverb.
So shall it be with your own, when the spinning-wheel shall no longer
Hum in the house of the farmer, and fill its chambers with music.
Then shall the mothers, reproving, relate how it was in their
        childhood,
Praising the good old times, and the days of Priscilla the spinner!"
Straight uprose from her wheel the beautiful Puritan maiden,
Pleased with the praise of her thrift from him whose praise was the sweetest,

Drew from the reel on the table a snowy skein of her spinning,
Thus making answer, meanwhile, to the flattering phrases of Alden:
"Come, you must not be idle; if I am a pattern for housewives,
Show yourself equally worthy of being the model of husbands.
Hold this skein on your hands, while I wind it, ready for knitting;
Then who knows but hereafter, when fashions have changed and the manners,
Fathers may talk to their sons of the good old times of John Alden!"
Thus, with a jest and a laugh, the skein on his hands she adjusted,
He sitting awkwardly there, with his arms extended before him,
She standing graceful, erect, and winding the thread from his fingers,
Sometimes chiding a little his clumsy manner of holding,
Sometimes touching his hands, as she disentangled expertly
Twist or knot in the yarn, unawares—for how could she help it?—
Sending electrical thrills through every nerve in his body.

　Lo! in the midst of this scene, a breathless messenger entered,
Bringing in hurry and heat the terrible news from the village.
Yes; Miles Standish was dead!—an Indian had brought them the tidings,—
Slain by a poisoned arrow, shot down in the front of the battle,
Into an ambush beguiled, cut off with the whole of his forces;
All the town would be burned, and all the people be murdered!
Such were the tidings of evil that burst on the hearts of the hearers.
Silent and statue-like stood Priscilla, her face looking backward
Still at the face of the speaker, her arms uplifted in horror;
But John Alden, upstarting, as if the barb of the arrow
Piercing the heart of his friend had struck his own, and had sundered
Once and for ever the bonds that held him bound as a captive,
Wild with excess of sensation, the awful delight of his freedom,
Mingled with pain and regret, unconscious of what he was doing,
Clasped, almost with a groan, the motionless form of Priscilla,
Pressing her close to his heart, as for ever his own, and exclaiming:
"Those whom the Lord hath united, let no man put them asunder!"

　Even as rivulets twain, from distant and separate sources,
Seeing each other afar, as they leap from the rocks, and pursuing
Each one its devious path, but drawing nearer and nearer,
Rush together at last, at their trysting-place in the forest;
So these lives that had run thus far in separate channels,
Coming in sight of each other, then swerving and flowing asunder,
Parted by barriers strong, but drawing nearer and nearer,
Rushed together at last, and one was lost in the other.

IX

THE WEDDING-DAY

Forth from the curtain of clouds, from the tent of purple and scarlet,
Issued the sun, the great High-Priest, in his garments resplendent,
Holiness unto the Lord, in letters of light, on his forehead,
Round the hem of his robe the golden bells and pomegranates.
Blessing the world he came, and the bars of vapor beneath him
Gleamed like a grate of brass, and the sea at his feet was a laver!

This was the wedding morn of Priscilla the Puritan maiden.
Friends were assembled together; the Elder and Magistrate also
Graced the scene with their presence, and stood like the Law and the
        Gospel,
One with the sanction of earth and one with the blessing of heaven.
Simple and brief was the wedding, as that of Ruth and of Boaz.
Softly the youth and the maiden repeated the words of betrothal,
Taking each other for husband and wife in the Magistrate's presence,
After the Puritan way, and the laudable custom of Holland.
Fervently then, and devoutly, the excellent Elder of Plymouth
Prayed for the hearth and the home, that were founded that day in
        affection,
Speaking of life and of death, and imploring divine benedictions.

Lo! when the service was ended, a form appeared on the threshold,
Clad in armor of steel, a sombre and sorrowful figure!
Why does the bridegroom start and stare at the strange apparition?
Why does the bride turn pale, and hide her face on his shoulder?
Is it a phantom of air, —a bodiless, spectral illusion?
Is it a ghost from the grave, that has come to forbid the betrothal?
Long had it stood there unseen, a guest uninvited, unwelcomed;
Over its clouded eyes there had passed at times an expression
Softening the gloom and revealing the warm heart hidden beneath them,
As when across the sky the driving rack of the rain-cloud
Grows for a moment thin, and betrays the sun by its brightness.
Once it had lifted its hand, and moved its lips, but was silent,
As if an iron will had mastered the fleeting intention.
But when were ended the troth and the prayer and the last
        benediction,
Into the room it strode, and the people beheld with amazement
Bodily there in his armor Miles Standish, the Captain of Plymouth!
Grasping the bridegroom's hand, he said with emotion, "Forgive me!

I have been angry and hurt, — too long have I cherished the feeling;
I have been cruel and hard, but now, thank God! it is ended.
Mine is the same hot blood that leaped in the veins of Hugh Standish,
Sensitive, swift to resent, but as swift in atoning for error.
Never so much as now was Miles Standish the friend of John Alden."
Thereupon answered the bridegroom: "Let all be forgotten between us, —
All save the dear, old friendship, and that shall grow older and dearer!"
Then the Captain advanced, and, bowing, saluted Priscilla,
Gravely, and after the manner of old-fashioned gentry in England,
Something of camp and of court, of town and of country,
       commingled,
Wishing her joy of her wedding, and loudly lauding her husband.
Then he said with a smile: "I should have remembered the adage, —
If you would be well served, you must serve yourself; and moreover,
No man can gather cherries in Kent at the season of Christmas!"

  Great was the people's amazement, and greater yet their rejoicing,
Thus to behold once more the sun-burnt face of their Captain,
Whom they had mourned as dead; and they gathered and crowded
      about him,
Eager to see him and hear him, forgetful of bride and of bridegroom,
Questioning, answering, laughing, and each interrupting the other,
Till the good Captain declared, being quite overpowered and bewildered,
He had rather by far break into an Indian encampment,
Than come again to a wedding to which he had not been invited.

  Meanwhile the bridegroom went forth and stood with the bride at
      the doorway,
Breathing the perfumed air of that warm and beautiful morning.
Touched with autumnal tints, but lonely and sad in the sunshine,
Lay extended before them the land of toil and privation;
There were the graves of the dead, and the barren waste of the sea-shore,
There the familiar fields, the groves of pine, and the meadows;
But to their eyes transfigured, it seemed as the Garden of Eden,
Filled with the presence of God, whose voice was the sound of the ocean.

  Soon was their vision disturbed by the noise and stir of departure,
Friends coming forth from the house, and impatient of longer delaying,
Each with his plan for the day, and the work that was left uncompleted.
Then from a stall near at hand, amid exclamations of wonder,
Alden the thoughtful, the careful, so happy, so proud of Priscilla,
Brought out his snow-white steer, obeying the hand of its master,
Led by a cord that was tied to an iron ring in its nostrils,

Covered with crimson cloth, and a cushion placed for a saddle.
She should not walk, he said, through the dust and heat of the noonday;
Nay, she should ride like a queen, not plod along like a peasant.
Somewhat alarmed at first, but reassured by the others,
Placing her hand on the cushion, her foot in the hand of her husband,
Gayly, with joyous laugh, Priscilla mounted her palfrey.
"Nothing is wanting now," he said with a smile, "but the distaff;
Then you would be in truth my queen, my beautiful Bertha!"

  Onward the bridal procession now moved to their new habitation,
Happy husband and wife, and friends conversing together.
Pleasantly murmured the brook, as they crossed the ford in the forest,
Pleased with the image that passed, like a dream of love through its bosom,
Tremulous, floating in air, o'er the depths of the azure abysses.
Down through the golden leaves the sun was pouring his splendors,
Gleaming on purple grapes, that, from branches above them
      suspended,
Mingled their odorous breath with the balm of the pine and the fir-tree,
Wild and sweet as the clusters that grew in the valley of Eshcol.
Like a picture it seemed of the primitive, pastoral ages,
Fresh with the youth of the world, and recalling Rebecca and Isaac,
Old and yet ever new, and simple and beautiful always,
Love immortal and young in the endless succession of lovers,
So through the Plymouth woods passed onward the bridal
      procession.

BIRDS OF PASSAGE.

FLIGHT THE FIRST

. . come i gru van cantando lor lai,
Facendo in aer di se lunga riga. — DANTE

BIRDS OF PASSAGE

Black shadows fall
From the lindens tall,
That lift aloft their massive wall
  Against the southern sky;

And from the realms
Of the shadowy elms
A tide-like darkness overwhelms
  The fields that round us lie.

But the night is fair,
And everywhere
A warm, soft vapor fills the air,
  And distant sounds seem near,

And above, in the light
Of the star-lit night,
Swift birds of passage wing their flight
  Through the dewy atmosphere.

I hear the beat
Of their pinions fleet,
As from the land of snow and sleet
  They seek a southern lea.

I hear the cry
Of their voices high
Falling dreamily through the sky,
  But their forms I cannot see.

O, say not so!
Those sounds that flow

In murmurs of delight and woe
  Come not from wings of birds.

They are the throngs
Of the poet's songs,
Murmurs of pleasures, and pains, and wrongs,
  The sound of winged words.

This is the cry
Of souls, that high
On toiling, beating pinions, fly,
  Seeking a warmer clime,

From their distant flight
Through realms of light
It falls into our world of night,
  With the murmuring sound of rhyme.

PROMETHEUS

OR THE POET'S FORETHOUGHT

Of Prometheus, how undaunted
  On Olympus' shining bastions
His audacious foot he planted,
Myths are told and songs are chanted,
  Full of promptings and suggestions.

Beautiful is the tradition
  Of that flight through heavenly portals,
The old classic superstition
Of the theft and the transmission
  Of the fire of the Immortals!

First the deed of noble daring,
  Born of heavenward aspiration,
Then the fire with mortals sharing,
Then the vulture, — the despairing
  Cry of pain on crags Caucasian.

All is but a symbol painted
  Of the Poet, Prophet, Seer;
Only those are crowned and sainted
Who with grief have been acquainted,
  Making nations nobler, freer.

In their feverish exultations,
  In their triumph and their yearning,
In their passionate pulsations,
In their words among the nations,
  The Promethean fire is burning.

Shall it, then, be unavailing,
  All this toil for human culture?
Through the cloud-rack, dark and trailing,
Must they see above them sailing
  O'er life's barren crags the vulture?

Such a fate as this was Dante's,
  By defeat and exile maddened;

Thus were Milton and Cervantes,
Nature's priests and Corybantes,
  By affliction touched and saddened.

But the glories so transcendent
  That around their memories cluster,
And, on all their steps attendant,
Make their darkened lives resplendent
  With such gleams of inward lustre!

All the melodies mysterious,
  Through the dreary darkness chanted;
Thoughts in attitudes imperious,
Voices soft, and deep, and serious,
  Words that whispered, songs that haunted!

All the soul in rapt suspension,
  All the quivering, palpitating
Chords of life in utmost tension,
With the fervor of invention,
  With the rapture of creating!

Ah, Prometheus! heaven-scaling!
  In such hours of exultation
Even the faintest heart, unquailing,
Might behold the vulture sailing
  Round the cloudy crags Caucasian!

Though to all there is not given
  Strength for such sublime endeavor,
Thus to scale the walls of heaven,
And to leaven with fiery leaven
  All the hearts of men for ever;

Yet all bards, whose hearts unblighted
  Honor and believe the presage,
Hold aloft their torches lighted,
Gleaming through the realms benighted,
  As they onward bear the message!

EPIMETHEUS

OR THE POET'S AFTERTHOUGHT

Have I dreamed? or was it real,
  What I saw as in a vision,
When to marches hymeneal
In the land of the Ideal
  Moved my thought o'er Fields Elysian?

What! are these the guests whose glances
  Seemed like sunshine gleaming round me?
These the wild, bewildering fancies,
That with dithyrambic dances
  As with magic circles bound me?

Ah! how cold are their caresses!
  Pallid cheeks, and haggard bosoms!
Spectral gleam their snow-white dresses,
And from loose dishevelled tresses
  Fall the hyacinthine blossoms!

O my songs! whose winsome measures
  Filled my heart with secret rapture!
Children of my golden leisures!
Must even your delights and pleasures
  Fade and perish with the capture?

Fair they seemed, those songs sonorous,
  When they came to me unbidden;
Voices single, and in chorus,
Like the wild birds singing o'er us
  In the dark of branches hidden.

Disenchantment! Disillusion!
  Must each noble aspiration
Come at last to this conclusion,
Jarring discord, wild confusion,
  Lassitude, renunciation?

Not with steeper fall nor faster,

From the sun's serene dominions,
Not through brighter realms nor vaster,
In swift ruin and disaster,
  Icarus fell with shattered pinions!

Sweet Pandora! dear Pandora!
  Why did mighty Jove create thee
Coy as Thetis, fair as Flora,
Beautiful as young Aurora,
  If to win thee is to hate thee?

No, not hate thee! for this feeling
  Of unrest and long resistance
Is but passionate appealing,
A prophetic whisper stealing
  O'er the chords of our existence.

Him whom thou dost once enamour,
  Thou, beloved, never leavest;
In life's discord, strife, and clamor,
Still he feels thy spell of glamour;
  Him of Hope thou ne'er bereavest.

Weary hearts by thee are lifted,
  Struggling souls by thee are strengthened,
Clouds of fear asunder rifted,
Truth from falsehood cleansed and sifted,
  Lives, like days in summer, lengthened!

Therefore art thou ever clearer,
  O my Sibyl, my deceiver!
For thou makest each mystery clearer,
And the unattained seems nearer,
  When thou fillest my heart with fever!

Muse of all the Gifts and Graces!
  Though the fields around us wither,
There are ampler realms and spaces,
Where no foot has left its traces:
  Let us turn and wander thither!

THE LADDER OF ST. AUGUSTINE

Saint Augustine! well hast thou said,
  That of our vices we can frame
A ladder, if we will but tread
  Beneath our feet each deed of shame!

All common things, each day's events,
  That with the hour begin and end,
Our pleasures and our discontents,
  Are rounds by which we may ascend.

The low desire, the base design,
  That makes another's virtues less;
The revel of the ruddy wine,
  And all occasions of excess;

The longing for ignoble things;
  The strife for triumph more than truth;
The hardening of the heart, that brings
  Irreverence for the dreams of youth;

All thoughts of ill; all evil deeds,
  That have their root in thoughts of ill;
Whatever hinders or impedes
  The action of the nobler will;—

All these must first be trampled down
  Beneath our feet, if we would gain
In the bright fields of fair renown
  The right of eminent domain.

We have not wings, we cannot soar;
  But we have feet to scale and climb
By slow degrees, by more and more,
  The cloudy summits of our time.

The mighty pyramids of stone
  That wedge-like cleave the desert airs,
When nearer seen, and better known,
  Are but gigantic flights of stairs.

The distant mountains, that uprear
  Their solid bastions to the skies,
Are crossed by pathways, that appear
  As we to higher levels rise.

The heights by great men reached and kept
  Were not attained by sudden flight,
But they, while their companions slept,
  Were toiling upward in the night.

Standing on what too long we bore
  With shoulders bent and downcast eyes,
We may discern—unseen before—
  A path to higher destinies.

Nor deem the irrevocable Past,
  As wholly wasted, wholly vain,
If, rising on its wrecks, at last
  To something nobler we attain.

THE PHANTOM SHIP

In Mather's Magnalia Christi,
  Of the old colonial time,
May be found in prose the legend
  That is here set down in rhyme.

A ship sailed from New Haven,
  And the keen and frosty airs,
That filled her sails at parting,
  Were heavy with good men's prayers.

"O Lord! if it be thy pleasure" —
  Thus prayed the old divine —
"To bury our friends in the ocean,
  Take them, for they are thine!"

But Master Lamberton muttered,
  And under his breath said he,
"This ship is so crank and walty
  I fear our grave she will be!"

And the ships that came from England,
  When the winter months were gone,
Brought no tidings of this vessel
  Nor of Master Lamberton.

This put the people to praying
  That the Lord would let them hear
What in his greater wisdom
He had done with friends so dear.

And at last their prayers were answered: —
  It was in the month of June,
An hour before the sunset
  Of a windy afternoon,

When, steadily steering landward,
  A ship was seen below,
And they knew it was Lamberton, Master,
  Who sailed so long ago.

On she came, with a cloud of canvas,
  Right against the wind that blew,
Until the eye could distinguish
  The faces of the crew.

Then fell her straining topmasts,
  Hanging tangled in the shrouds,
And her sails were loosened and lifted,
  And blown away like clouds.

And the masts, with all their rigging,
  Fell slowly, one by one,
And the hulk dilated and vanished,
  As a sea-mist in the sun!

And the people who saw this marvel
  Each said unto his friend,
That this was the mould of their vessel,
  And thus her tragic end.

And the pastor of the village
  Gave thanks to God in prayer,
That, to quiet their troubled spirits,
  He had sent this Ship of Air.

THE WARDEN OF THE CINQUE PORTS

A mist was driving down the British Channel,
    The day was just begun,
And through the window-panes, on floor and panel,
    Streamed the red autumn sun.

It glanced on flowing flag and rippling pennon,
    And the white sails of ships;
And, from the frowning rampart, the black cannon
    Hailed it with feverish lips.

Sandwich and Romney, Hastings, Hithe, and Dover
    Were all alert that day,
To see the French war-steamers speeding over,
    When the fog cleared away.

Sullen and silent, and like couchant lions,
    Their cannon, through the night,
Holding their breath, had watched, in grim defiance,
    The sea-coast opposite.

And now they roared at drum-beat from their stations
    On every citadel;
Each answering each, with morning salutations,
    That all was well.

And down the coast, all taking up the burden,
    Replied the distant forts,
As if to summon from his sleep the Warden
    And Lord of the Cinque Ports.

Him shall no sunshine from the fields of azure,
    No drum-beat from the wall,
No morning gun from the black fort's embrasure,
    Awaken with its call!

No more, surveying with an eye impartial
    The long line of the coast,
Shall the gaunt figure of the old Field Marshal
    Be seen upon his post!

For in the night, unseen, a single warrior,
    In sombre harness mailed,
Dreaded of man, and surnamed the Destroyer,
    The rampart wall has scaled.

He passed into the chamber of the sleeper,
    The dark and silent room,
And as he entered, darker grew, and deeper,
    The silence and the gloom.

He did not pause to parley or dissemble,
    But smote the Warden hoar;
Ah! what a blow! that made all England tremble
    And groan from shore to shore.

Meanwhile, without, the surly cannon waited,
    The sun rose bright o'erhead;
Nothing in Nature's aspect intimated
    That a great man was dead.

HAUNTED HOUSES

All houses wherein men have lived and died
  Are haunted houses. Through the open doors
The harmless phantoms on their errands glide,
  With feet that make no sound upon the floors.

We meet them at the door-way, on the stair,
  Along the passages they come and go,
Impalpable impressions on the air,
  A sense of something moving to and fro.

There are more guests at table, than the hosts
  Invited; the illuminated hall
Is thronged with quiet, inoffensive ghosts,
  As silent as the pictures on the wall.

The stranger at my fireside cannot see
  The forms I see, nor hear the sounds I hear;
He but perceives what is; while unto me
  All that has been is visible and clear.

We have no title-deeds to house or lands;
  Owners and occupants of earlier dates
From graves forgotten stretch their dusty hands,
  And hold in mortmain still their old estates.

The spirit-world around this world of sense
  Floats like an atmosphere, and everywhere
Wafts through these earthly mists and vapors dense
  A vital breath of more ethereal air.

Our little lives are kept in equipoise
  By opposite attractions and desires;
The struggle of the instinct that enjoys,
  And the more noble instinct that aspires.

These perturbations, this perpetual jar
  Of earthly wants and aspirations high,
Come from the influence of an unseen star,
  An undiscovered planet in our sky.

432

And as the moon from some dark gate of cloud
  Throws o'er the sea a floating bridge of light,
Across whose trembling planks our fancies crowd
  Into the realm of mystery and night, —

So from the world of spirits there descends
  A bridge of light, connecting it with this,
O'er whose unsteady floor, that sways and bends,
  Wander our thoughts above the dark abyss.

IN THE CHURCHYARD AT CAMBRIDGE

In the village churchyard she lies,
Dust is in her beautiful eyes,
  No more she breathes, nor feels, nor stirs;
At her feet and at her head
Lies a slave to attend the dead,
  But their dust is white as hers.

Was she a lady of high degree,
So much in love with the vanity
  And foolish pomp of this world of ours?
Or was it Christian charity,
And lowliness and humility,
  The richest and rarest of all dowers?

Who shall tell us? No one speaks;
No color shoots into those cheeks,
  Either of anger or of pride,
At the rude question we have asked;
Nor will the mystery be unmasked
  By those who are sleeping at her side.

Hereafter?—And do you think to look
On the terrible pages of that Book
  To find her failings, faults, and errors?
Ah, you will then have other cares,
In your own short-comings and despairs,
  In your own secret sins and terrors!

THE EMPEROR'S BIRD'S-NEST

Once the Emperor Charles of Spain,
  With his swarthy, grave commanders,
I forget in what campaign,
Long besieged, in mud and rain,
  Some old frontier town of Flanders.

Up and down the dreary camp,
  In great boots of Spanish leather,
Striding with a measured tramp,
These Hidalgos, dull and damp,
  Cursed the Frenchmen, cursed the weather.

Thus as to and fro they went,
  Over upland and through hollow,
Giving their impatience vent,
Perched upon the Emperor's tent,
  In her nest, they spied a swallow.

Yes, it was a swallow's nest,
  Built of clay and hair of horses,
Mane, or tail, or dragoon's crest,
Found on hedge-rows east and west,
  After skirmish of the forces.

Then an old Hidalgo said,
  As he twirled his gray mustachio,
"Sure this swallow overhead
Thinks the Emperor's tent a shed,
  And the Emperor but a Macho!"

Hearing his imperial name
  Coupled with those words of malice,
Half in anger, half in shame,
Forth the great campaigner came
  Slowly from his canvas palace.

"Let no hand the bird molest,"
  Said he solemnly, "nor hurt her!"
Adding then, by way of jest,
"Golondrina is my guest,

'Tis the wife of some deserter!"

Swift as bowstring speeds a shaft,
  Through the camp was spread the rumor,
And the soldiers, as they quaffed
Flemish beer at dinner, laughed
  At the Emperor's pleasant humor.

So unharmed and unafraid
  Sat the swallow still and brooded,
Till the constant cannonade
Through the walls a breach had made,
  And the siege was thus concluded.

Then the army, elsewhere bent,
  Struck its tents as if disbanding,
Only not the Emperor's tent,
For he ordered, ere he went,
  Very curtly, "Leave it standing!"

So it stood there all alone,
  Loosely flapping, torn and tattered,
Till the brood was fledged and flown,
Singing o'er those walls of stone
  Which the cannon-shot had shattered.

THE TWO ANGELS

Two angels, one of Life and one of Death,
  Passed o'er our village as the morning broke;
The dawn was on their faces, and beneath,
  The sombre houses hearsed with plumes of smoke.

Their attitude and aspect were the same,
  Alike their features and their robes of white;
But one was crowned with amaranth, as with flame,
  And one with asphodels, like flakes of light.

I saw them pause on their celestial way;
  Then said I, with deep fear and doubt oppressed,
"Beat not so loud, my heart, lest thou betray
  The place where thy beloved are at rest!"

And he who wore the crown of asphodels,
  Descending, at my door began to knock,
And my soul sank within me, as in wells
  The waters sink before an earthquake's shock.

I recognized the nameless agony,
  The terror and the tremor and the pain,
That oft before had filled or haunted me,
  And now returned with threefold strength again.

The door I opened to my heavenly guest,
  And listened, for I thought I heard God's voice;
And, knowing whatsoe'er he sent was best,
  Dared neither to lament nor to rejoice.

Then with a smile, that filled the house with light,
  "My errand is not Death, but Life," he said;
And ere I answered, passing out of sight,
  On his celestial embassy he sped.

'T was at thy door, O friend! and not at mine,
  The angel with the amaranthine wreath,
Pausing, descended, and with voice divine,
  Whispered a word that had a sound like Death.

Then fell upon the house a sudden gloom,
  A shadow on those features fair and thin;
And softly, from that hushed and darkened room,
  Two angels issued, where but one went in.

All is of God! If he but wave his hand,
  The mists collect, the rain falls thick and loud,
Till, with a smile of light on sea and land,
  Lo! he looks back from the departing cloud.

Angels of Life and Death alike are his;
  Without his leave they pass no threshold o'er;
Who, then, would wish or dare, believing this,
  Against his messengers to shut the door?

DAYLIGHT AND MOONLIGHT

In broad daylight, and at noon,
Yesterday I saw the moon
Sailing high, but faint and white,
As a school-boy's paper kite.

In broad daylight, yesterday,
I read a Poet's mystic lay;
And it seemed to me at most
As a phantom, or a ghost.

But at length the feverish day
Like a passion died away,
And the night, serene and still,
Fell on village, vale, and hill.

Then the moon, in all her pride,
Like a spirit glorified,
Filled and overflowed the night
With revelations of her light.

And the Poet's song again
Passed like music through my brain;
Night interpreted to me
All its grace and mystery.

THE JEWISH CEMETERY AT NEWPORT

How strange it seems! These Hebrews in their graves,
  Close by the street of this fair seaport town,
Silent beside the never-silent waves,
  At rest in all this moving up and down!

The trees are white with dust, that o'er their sleep
  Wave their broad curtains in the south-wind's breath,
While underneath such leafy tents they keep
  The long, mysterious Exodus of Death.

And these sepulchral stones, so old and brown,
  That pave with level flags their burial-place,
Seem like the tablets of the Law, thrown down
  And broken by Moses at the mountain's base.

The very names recorded here are strange,
  Of foreign accent, and of different climes;
Alvares and Rivera interchange
  With Abraham and Jacob of old times.

"Blessed be God! for he created Death!"
  The mourners said, "and Death is rest and peace";
Then added, in the certainty of faith,
  "And giveth Life that never more shall cease."

Closed are the portals of their Synagogue,
  No Psalms of David now the silence break,
No Rabbi reads the ancient Decalogue
  In the grand dialect the Prophets spake.

Gone are the living, but the dead remain,
  And not neglected; for a hand unseen,
Scattering its bounty, like a summer rain,
  Still keeps their graves and their remembrance green.

How came they here? What burst of Christian hate,
  What persecution, merciless and blind,
Drove o'er the sea—that desert desolate—
  These Ishmaels and Hagars of mankind?

They lived in narrow streets and lanes obscure,
  Ghetto and Judenstrass, in mirk and mire;
Taught in the school of patience to endure
  The life of anguish and the death of fire.

All their lives long, with the unleavened bread
  And bitter herbs of exile and its fears,
The wasting famine of the heart they fed,
  And slaked its thirst with marah of their tears.

Anathema maranatha! was the cry
  That rang from town to town, from street to street;
At every gate the accursed Mordecai
  Was mocked and jeered, and spurned by Christian feet.

Pride and humiliation hand in hand
  Walked with them through the world where'er they went;
Trampled and beaten were they as the sand,
  And yet unshaken as the continent.

For in the background figures vague and vast
  Of patriarchs and of prophets rose sublime,
And all the great traditions of the Past
  They saw reflected in the coming time.

And thus for ever with reverted look
  The mystic volume of the world they read,
Spelling it backward, like a Hebrew book,
  Till life became a Legend of the Dead.

But ah! what once has been shall be no more!
  The groaning earth in travail and in pain
Brings forth its races, but does not restore,
  And the dead nations never rise again.

OLIVER BASSELIN

In the Valley of the Vire
  Still is seen an ancient mill,
With its gables quaint and queer,
  And beneath the window-sill,
    On the stone,
    These words alone:
"Oliver Basselin lived here."

Far above it, on the steep,
  Ruined stands the old Chateau;
Nothing but the donjon-keep
  Left for shelter or for show.
    Its vacant eyes
    Stare at the skies,
Stare at the valley green and deep.

Once a convent, old and brown,
  Looked, but ah! it looks no more,
From the neighboring hillside down
  On the rushing and the roar
    Of the stream
    Whose sunny gleam
Cheers the little Norman town.

In that darksome mill of stone,
  To the water's dash and din,
Careless, humble, and unknown,
  Sang the poet Basselin
    Songs that fill
    That ancient mill
With a splendor of its own.

Never feeling of unrest
  Broke the pleasant dream he dreamed;
Only made to be his nest,
  All the lovely valley seemed;
    No desire
    Of soaring higher
Stirred or fluttered in his breast.

True, his songs were not divine;
  Were not songs of that high art,
Which, as winds do in the pine,
  Find an answer in each heart;
    But the mirth
    Of this green earth
Laughed and revelled in his line.

From the alehouse and the inn,
  Opening on the narrow street,
Came the loud, convivial din,
  Singing and applause of feet,
    The laughing lays
    That in those days
Sang the poet Basselin.

In the castle, cased in steel,
  Knights, who fought at Agincourt,
Watched and waited, spur on heel;
  But the poet sang for sport
    Songs that rang
    Another clang,
Songs that lowlier hearts could feel.

In the convent, clad in gray,
  Sat the monks in lonely cells,
Paced the cloisters, knelt to pray,
  And the poet heard their bells;
    But his rhymes
    Found other chimes,
Nearer to the earth than they.

Gone are all the barons bold,
  Gone are all the knights and squires,
Gone the abbot stern and cold,
  And the brotherhood of friars;
    Not a name
    Remains to fame,
From those mouldering days of old!

But the poet's memory here
  Of the landscape makes a part;
Like the river, swift and clear,

Flows his song through many a heart;
  Haunting still
  That ancient mill,
In the Valley of the Vire.

VICTOR GALBRAITH

Under the walls of Monterey
At daybreak the bugles began to play,
    Victor Galbraith!
In the mist of the morning damp and gray,
These were the words they seemed to say:
    "Come forth to thy death,
    Victor Galbraith!"

Forth he came, with a martial tread;
Firm was his step, erect his head;
    Victor Galbraith,
He who so well the bugle played,
Could not mistake the words it said:
    "Come forth to thy death,
    Victor Galbraith!"

He looked at the earth, he looked at the sky,
He looked at the files of musketry,
    Victor Galbraith!
And he said, with a steady voice and eye,
"Take good aim; I am ready to die!"
    Thus challenges death
    Victor Galbraith.

Twelve fiery tongues flashed straight and red,
Six leaden balls on their errand sped;
    Victor Galbraith
Falls to the ground, but he is not dead;
His name was not stamped on those balls of lead,
    And they only scath
    Victor Galbraith.

Three balls are in his breast and brain,
But he rises out of the dust again,
    Victor Galbraith!
The water he drinks has a bloody stain;
"O kill me, and put me out of my pain!"
    In his agony prayeth
    Victor Galbraith.

Forth dart once more those tongues of flame,
And the bugler has died a death of shame,
    Victor Galbraith!
His soul has gone back to whence it came,
And no one answers to the name,
    When the Sergeant saith,
    "Victor Galbraith!"

Under the walls of Monterey
By night a bugle is heard to play,
    Victor Galbraith!
Through the mist of the valley damp and gray
The sentinels hear the sound, and say,
    "That is the wraith
    Of Victor Galbraith!"

MY LOST YOUTH

Often I think of the beautiful town
  That is seated by the sea;
Often in thought go up and down
The pleasant streets of that dear old town,
  And my youth comes back to me.
    And a verse of a Lapland song
    Is haunting my memory still:
  "A boy's will is the wind's will,
And the thoughts of youth are long, long thoughts."

I can see the shadowy lines of its trees,
  And catch, in sudden gleams,
The sheen of the far-surrounding seas,
And islands that were the Hersperides
  Of all my boyish dreams.
    And the burden of that old song,
    It murmurs and whispers still:
  "A boy's will is the wind's will,
And the thoughts of youth are long, long thoughts."

I remember the black wharves and the slips,
  And the sea-tides tossing free;
And Spanish sailors with bearded lips,
And the beauty and mystery of the ships,
  And the magic of the sea.
    And the voice of that wayward song
    Is singing and saying still:
  "A boy's will is the wind's will,
And the thoughts of youth are long, long thoughts."

I remember the bulwarks by the shore,
  And the fort upon the hill;
The sunrise gun, with its hollow roar,
The drum-beat repeated o'er and o'er,
  And the bugle wild and shrill.
    And the music of that old song
    Throbs in my memory still:
  "A boy's will is the wind's will,
And the thoughts of youth are long, long thoughts."

I remember the sea-fight far away,
  How it thundered o'er the tide!
And the dead captains, as they lay
In their graves, o'erlooking the tranquil bay,
  Where they in battle died.
    And the sound of that mournful song
    Goes through me with a thrill:
  "A boy's will is the wind's will,
And the thoughts of youth are long, long thoughts."

I can see the breezy dome of groves,
  The shadows of Deering's Woods;
And the friendships old and the early loves
Come back with a sabbath sound, as of doves
  In quiet neighborhoods.
    And the verse of that sweet old song,
    It flutters and murmurs still:
  "A boy's will is the wind's will,
And the thoughts of youth are long, long thoughts."

I remember the gleams and glooms that dart
  Across the schoolboy's brain;
The song and the silence in the heart,
That in part are prophecies, and in part
  Are longings wild and vain.
    And the voice of that fitful song
    Sings on, and is never still:
  "A boy's will is the wind's will,
And the thoughts of youth are long, long thoughts."

There are things of which I may not speak;
  There are dreams that cannot die;
There are thoughts that make the strong heart weak,
And bring a pallor into the cheek,
  And a mist before the eye.
    And the words of that fatal song
    Come over me like a chill:
  "A boy's will is the wind's will,
And the thoughts of youth are long, long thoughts."

Strange to me now are the forms I meet
  When I visit the dear old town;
But the native air is pure and sweet,

And the trees that o'ershadow each well-known street,
  As they balance up and down,
    Are singing the beautiful song,
    Are sighing and whispering still:
   "A boy's will is the wind's will,
And the thoughts of youth are long, long thoughts."

And Deering's Woods are fresh and fair,
  And with joy that is almost pain
My heart goes back to wander there,
And among the dreams of the days that were,
  I find my lost youth again.
    And the strange and beautiful song,
    The groves are repeating it still:
   "A boy's will is the wind's will,
And the thoughts of youth are long, long thoughts."

THE ROPEWALK

In that building, long and low,
With its windows all a-row,
  Like the port-holes of a hulk,
Human spiders spin and spin,
Backward down their threads so thin
  Dropping, each a hempen bulk.

At the end, an open door;
Squares of sunshine on the floor
  Light the long and dusky lane;
And the whirring of a wheel,
Dull and drowsy, makes me feel
  All its spokes are in my brain.

As the spinners to the end
Downward go and reascend,
  Gleam the long threads in the sun;
While within this brain of mine
Cobwebs brighter and more fine
  By the busy wheel are spun.

Two fair maidens in a swing,
Like white doves upon the wing,
  First before my vision pass;
Laughing, as their gentle hands
Closely clasp the twisted strands,
  At their shadow on the grass.

Then a booth of mountebanks,
With its smell of tan and planks,
  And a girl poised high in air
On a cord, in spangled dress,
With a faded loveliness,
  And a weary look of care.

Then a homestead among farms,
And a woman with bare arms
  Drawing water from a well;
As the bucket mounts apace,
With it mounts her own fair face,

As at some magician's spell.

Then an old man in a tower,
Ringing loud the noontide hour,
   While the rope coils round and round
Like a serpent at his feet,
And again, in swift retreat,
   Nearly lifts him from the ground.

Then within a prison-yard,
Faces fixed, and stern, and hard,
   Laughter and indecent mirth;
Ah! it is the gallows-tree!
Breath of Christian charity,
   Blow, and sweep it from the earth!

Then a school-boy, with his kite
Gleaming in a sky of light,
   And an eager, upward look;
Steeds pursued through lane and field;
Fowlers with their snares concealed;
   And an angler by a brook.

Ships rejoicing in the breeze,
Wrecks that float o'er unknown seas,
   Anchors dragged through faithless sand;
Sea-fog drifting overhead,
And, with lessening line and lead,
   Sailors feeling for the land.

All these scenes do I behold,
These, and many left untold,
   In that building long and low;
While the wheel goes round and round,
With a drowsy, dreamy sound,
   And the spinners backward go.

THE GOLDEN MILE-STONE

Leafless are the trees; their purple branches
Spread themselves abroad, like reefs of coral,
    Rising silent
In the Red Sea of the Winter sunset.

From the hundred chimneys of the village,
Like the Afreet in the Arabian story,
    Smoky columns
Tower aloft into the air of amber.

At the window winks the flickering fire-light;
Here and there the lamps of evening glimmer,
    Social watch-fires
Answering one another through the darkness.

On the hearth the lighted logs are glowing,
And like Ariel in the cloven pine-tree
    For its freedom
Groans and sighs the air imprisoned in them.

By the fireside there are old men seated,
Seeing ruined cities in the ashes,
    Asking sadly
Of the Past what it can ne'er restore them.

By the fireside there are youthful dreamers,
Building castles fair, with stately stairways,
    Asking blindly
Of the Future what it cannot give them.

By the fireside tragedies are acted
In whose scenes appear two actors only,
    Wife and husband,
And above them God the sole spectator.

By the fireside there are peace and comfort,
Wives and children, with fair, thoughtful faces,
    Waiting, watching
For a well-known footstep in the passage.

Each man's chimney is his Golden Mile-stone;
Is the central point, from which he measures
    Every distance
Through the gateways of the world around him.

In his farthest wanderings still he sees it;
Hears the talking flame, the answering night-wind,
    As he heard them
When he sat with those who were, but are not.

Happy he whom neither wealth nor fashion,
Nor the march of the encroaching city,
    Drives an exile
From the hearth of his ancestral homestead.

We may build more splendid habitations,
Fill our rooms with paintings and with sculptures,
    But we cannot
Buy with gold the old associations!

CATAWBA WINE

This song of mine
Is a Song of the Vine,
To be sung by the glowing embers
Of wayside inns,
When the rain begins
To darken the drear Novembers.

It is not a song
Of the Scuppernong,
From warm Carolinian valleys,
Nor the Isabel
And the Muscadel
That bask in our garden alleys.

Nor the red Mustang,
Whose clusters hang
O'er the waves of the Colorado,
And the fiery flood
Of whose purple blood
Has a dash of Spanish bravado.

For richest and best
Is the wine of the West,
That grows by the Beautiful River;
Whose sweet perfume
Fills all the room
With a benison on the giver.

And as hollow trees
Are the haunts of bees,
For ever going and coming;
So this crystal hive
Is all alive
With a swarming and buzzing and humming.

Very good in its way
Is the Verzenay,
Or the Sillery soft and creamy;
But Catawba wine
Has a taste more divine,

More dulcet, delicious, and dreamy.

There grows no vine
By the haunted Rhine,
By Danube or Guadalquivir,
Nor on island or cape,
That bears such a grape
As grows by the Beautiful River.

Drugged is their juice
For foreign use,
When shipped o'er the reeling Atlantic,
To rack our brains
With the fever pains,
That have driven the Old World frantic.

To the sewers and sinks
With all such drinks,
And after them tumble the mixer;
For a poison malign
Is such Borgia wine,
Or at best but a Devil's Elixir.

While pure as a spring
Is the wine I sing,
And to praise it, one needs but name it;
For Catawba wine
Has need of no sign,
No tavern-bush to proclaim it.

And this Song of the Vine,
This greeting of mine,
The winds and the birds shall deliver
To the Queen of the West,
In her garlands dressed,
On the banks of the Beautiful River.

SANTA FILOMENA

Whene'er a noble deed is wrought,
Whene'er is spoken a noble thought,
  Our hearts, in glad surprise,
  To higher levels rise.

The tidal wave of deeper souls
Into our inmost being rolls,
  And lifts us unawares
  Out of all meaner cares.

Honor to those whose words or deeds
Thus help us in our daily needs,
  And by their overflow
  Raise us from what is low!

Thus thought I, as by night I read
Of the great army of the dead,
  The trenches cold and damp,
  The starved and frozen camp,—

The wounded from the battle-plain,
In dreary hospitals of pain,
  The cheerless corridors,
  The cold and stony floors.

Lo! in that house of misery
A lady with a lamp I see
  Pass through the glimmering gloom,
  And flit from room to room.

And slow, as in a dream of bliss,
The speechless sufferer turns to kiss
  Her shadow, as it falls
  Upon the darkening walls.

As if a door in heaven should be
Opened and then closed suddenly,
  The vision came and went,
  The light shone and was spent.

On England's annals, through the long
Hereafter of her speech and song,
   That light its rays shall cast
   From portals of the past.

A Lady with a Lamp shall stand
In the great history of the land,
   A noble type of good,
   Heroic womanhood.

Nor even shall be wanting here
The palm, the lily, and the spear,
   The symbols that of yore
   Saint Filomena bore.

THE DISCOVERER OF THE NORTH CAPE

A LEAF FROM KING ALFRED'S OROSIUS

Othere, the old sea-captain,
  Who dwelt in Helgoland,
To King Alfred, the Lover of Truth,
Brought a snow-white walrus-tooth,
  Which he held in his brown right hand.

His figure was tall and stately,
  Like a boy's his eye appeared;
His hair was yellow as hay,
But threads of a silvery gray
  Gleamed in his tawny beard.

Hearty and hale was Othere,
  His cheek had the color of oak;
With a kind of laugh in his speech,
Like the sea-tide on a beach,
  As unto the King he spoke.

And Alfred, King of the Saxons,
  Had a book upon his knees,
And wrote down the wondrous tale
Of him who was first to sail
  Into the Arctic seas.

"So far I live to the northward,
  No man lives north of me;
To the east are wild mountain-chains;
And beyond them meres and plains;
  To the westward all is sea.

"So far I live to the northward,
  From the harbor of Skeringes-hale,
If you only sailed by day,
With a fair wind all the way,
  More than a month would you sail.

"I own six hundred reindeer,
  With sheep and swine beside;

458

I have tribute from the Finns,
Whalebone and reindeer-skins,
  And ropes of walrus-hide.

"I ploughed the land with horses,
  But my heart was ill at ease,
For the old seafaring men
Came to me now and then,
  With their sagas of the seas;—

"Of Iceland and of Greenland,
  And the stormy Hebrides,
And the undiscovered deep;—
I could not eat nor sleep
  For thinking of those seas.

"To the northward stretched the desert,
  How far I fain would know;
So at last I sallied forth,
And three days sailed due north,
  As far as the whale-ships go.

"To the west of me was the ocean,
  To the right the desolate shore,
But I did not slacken sail
For the walrus or the whale,
  Till after three days more.

"The days grew longer and longer,
  Till they became as one,
And southward through the haze
I saw the sullen blaze
  Of the red midnight sun.

"And then uprose before me,
  Upon the water's edge,
The huge and haggard shape
Of that unknown North Cape,
  Whose form is like a wedge.

"The sea was rough and stormy,
  The tempest howled and wailed,
And the sea-fog, like a ghost,

Haunted that dreary coast,
  But onward still I sailed.

"Four days I steered to eastward,
  Four days without a night:
Round in a fiery ring
Went the great sun, O King,
  With red and lurid light."

Here Alfred, King of the Saxons,
  Ceased writing for a while;
And raised his eyes from his book,
With a strange and puzzled look,
  And an incredulous smile.

But Othere, the old sea-captain,
  He neither paused nor stirred,
Till the King listened, and then
Once more took up his pen,
  And wrote down every word.

"And now the land," said Othere,
  "Bent southward suddenly,
And I followed the curving shore
And ever southward bore
  Into a nameless sea.

"And there we hunted the walrus,
  The narwhale, and the seal;
Ha! 't was a noble game!
And like the lightning's flame
  Flew our harpoons of steel.

"There were six of us all together,
  Norsemen of Helgoland;
In two days and no more
We killed of them threescore,
  And dragged them to the strand!"

Here Alfred the Truth-Teller
  Suddenly closed his book,
And lifted his blue eyes,
With doubt and strange surmise

Depicted in their look.

And Othere the old sea-captain
  Stared at him wild and weird,
Then smiled, till his shining teeth
Gleamed white from underneath
  His tawny, quivering beard.

And to the King of the Saxons,
  In witness of the truth,
Raising his noble head,
He stretched his brown hand, and said,
  "Behold this walrus-tooth!"

DAYBREAK

A wind came up out of the sea,
And said, "O mists, make room for me."

It hailed the ships, and cried, "Sail on,
Ye mariners, the night is gone."

And hurried landward far away,
Crying, "Awake! it is the day."

It said unto the forest, "Shout!
Hang all your leafy banners out!"

It touched the wood-bird's folded wing,
And said, "O bird, awake and sing."

And o'er the farms, "O chanticleer,
Your clarion blow; the day is near."

It whispered to the fields of corn,
"Bow down, and hail the coming morn."

It shouted through the belfry-tower,
"Awake, O bell! proclaim the hour."

It crossed the churchyard with a sigh,
And said, "Not yet! in quiet lie."

THE FIFTIETH BIRTHDAY OF AGASSIZ

MAY 28, 1857

It was fifty years ago
  In the pleasant month of May,
In the beautiful Pays de Vaud,
  A child in its cradle lay.

And Nature, the old nurse, took
  The child upon her knee,
Saying: "Here is a story-book
  Thy Father has written for thee."

"Come, wander with me," she said,
  "Into regions yet untrod;
And read what is still unread
  In the manuscripts of God."

And he wandered away and away
  With Nature, the dear old nurse,
Who sang to him night and day
  The rhymes of the universe.

And whenever the way seemed long,
  Or his heart began to fail,
She would sing a more wonderful song,
  Or tell a more marvellous tale.

So she keeps him still a child,
  And will not let him go,
Though at times his heart beats wild
  For the beautiful Pays de Vaud;

Though at times he hears in his dreams
  The Ranz des Vaches of old,
And the rush of mountain streams
  From glaciers clear and cold;

And the mother at home says, "Hark!
  For his voice I listen and yearn;
It is growing late and dark,
  And my boy does not return!"

CHILDREN

Come to me, O ye children!
  For I hear you at your play,
And the questions that perplexed me
  Have vanished quite away.

Ye open the eastern windows,
  That look towards the sun,
Where thoughts are singing swallows
  And the brooks of morning run.

In your hearts are the birds and the sunshine,
  In your thoughts the brooklet's flow,
But in mine is the wind of Autumn
  And the first fall of the snow.

Ah! what would the world be to us
  If the children were no more?
We should dread the desert behind us
  Worse than the dark before.

What the leaves are to the forest,
  With light and air for food,
Ere their sweet and tender juices
  Have been hardened into wood, —

That to the world are children;
  Through them it feels the glow
Of a brighter and sunnier climate
  Than reaches the trunks below.

Come to me, O ye children!
  And whisper in my ear
What the birds and the winds are singing
  In your sunny atmosphere.

For what are all our contrivings,
  And the wisdom of our books,
When compared with your caresses,
  And the gladness of your looks?

Ye are better than all the ballads
  That ever were sung or said;
For ye are living poems,
  And all the rest are dead.

SANDALPHON

Have you read in the Talmud of old,
In the Legends the Rabbins have told
  Of the limitless realms of the air, —
Have you read it, — the marvellous story
Of Sandalphon, the Angel of Glory,
  Sandalphon, the Angel of Prayer?

How, erect, at the outermost gates
Of the City Celestial he waits,
  With his feet on the ladder of light,
That, crowded with angels unnumbered,
By Jacob was seen, as he slumbered
  Alone in the desert at night?

The Angels of Wind and of Fire
Chant only one hymn, and expire
  With the song's irresistible stress;
Expire in their rapture and wonder,
As harp-strings are broken asunder
  By music they throb to express.

But serene in the rapturous throng,
Unmoved by the rush of the song,
  With eyes unimpassioned and slow,
Among the dead angels, the deathless
Sandalphon stands listening breathless
  To sounds that ascend from below; —

From the spirits on earth that adore,
From the souls that entreat and implore
  In the fervor and passion of prayer;
From the hearts that are broken with losses,
And weary with dragging the crosses
  Too heavy for mortals to bear.

And he gathers the prayers as he stands,
And they change into flowers in his hands,
  Into garlands of purple and red;
And beneath the great arch of the portal,
Through the streets of the City Immortal

467

Is wafted the fragrance they shed.

It is but a legend, I know, —
A fable, a phantom, a show,
  Of the ancient Rabbinical lore;
Yet the old mediaeval tradition,
The beautiful, strange superstition,
  But haunts me and holds me the more.

When I look from my window at night,
And the welkin above is all white,
  All throbbing and panting with stars,
Among them majestic is standing
Sandalphon the angel, expanding
  His pinions in nebulous bars.

And the legend, I feel, is a part
Of the hunger and thirst of the heart,
  The frenzy and fire of the brain,
That grasps at the fruitage forbidden,
The golden pomegranates of Eden,
  To quiet its fever and pain.

FLIGHT THE SECOND

THE CHILDREN'S HOUR

Between the dark and the daylight,
  When the night is beginning to lower,
Comes a pause in the day's occupations,
  That is known as the Children's Hour.

I hear in the chamber above me
  The patter of little feet,
The sound of a door that is opened,
  And voices soft and sweet.

From my study I see in the lamplight,
  Descending the broad hall stair,
Grave Alice, and laughing Allegra,
  And Edith with golden hair.

A whisper, and then a silence:
  Yet I know by their merry eyes
They are plotting and planning together
  To take me by surprise.

A sudden rush from the stairway,
  A sudden raid from the hall!
By three doors left unguarded
  They enter my castle wall!

They climb up into my turret
  O'er the arms and back of my chair;
If I try to escape, they surround me;
  They seem to be everywhere.

They almost devour me with kisses,
  Their arms about me entwine,
Till I think of the Bishop of Bingen
  In his Mouse-Tower on the Rhine!

Do you think, o blue-eyed banditti,
  Because you have scaled the wall,
Such an old mustache as I am

Is not a match for you all!

I have you fast in my fortress,
 And will not let you depart,
But put you down into the dungeon
 In the round-tower of my heart.

And there will I keep you forever,
 Yes, forever and a day,
Till the walls shall crumble to ruin,
 And moulder in dust away!

ENCELADUS

Under Mount Etna he lies,
  It is slumber, it is not death;
For he struggles at times to arise,
And above him the lurid skies
  Are hot with his fiery breath.

The crags are piled on his breast,
  The earth is heaped on his head;
But the groans of his wild unrest,
Though smothered and half suppressed,
  Are heard, and he is not dead.

And the nations far away
  Are watching with eager eyes;
They talk together and say,
"To-morrow, perhaps to-day,
  Euceladus will arise!"

And the old gods, the austere
  Oppressors in their strength,
Stand aghast and white with fear
At the ominous sounds they hear,
  And tremble, and mutter, "At length!"

Ah me! for the land that is sown
  With the harvest of despair!
Where the burning cinders, blown
From the lips of the overthrown
  Enceladus, fill the air.

Where ashes are heaped in drifts
  Over vineyard and field and town,
Whenever he starts and lifts
His head through the blackened rifts
  Of the crags that keep him down.

See, see! the red light shines!
  'T is the glare of his awful eyes!
And the storm-wind shouts through the pines
Of Alps and of Apennines,
  "Enceladus, arise!"

THE CUMBERLAND

At anchor in Hampton Roads we lay,
  On board of the cumberland, sloop-of-war;
And at times from the fortress across the bay
    The alarum of drums swept past,
    Or a bugle blast
  From the camp on the shore.

Then far away to the south uprose
  A little feather of snow-white smoke,
And we knew that the iron ship of our foes
    Was steadily steering its course
    To try the force
  Of our ribs of oak.

Down upon us heavily runs,
  Silent and sullen, the floating fort;
Then comes a puff of smoke from her guns,
    And leaps the terrible death,
    With fiery breath,
  From each open port.

We are not idle, but send her straight
  Defiance back in a full broadside!
As hail rebounds from a roof of slate,
    Rebounds our heavier hail
    From each iron scale
  Of the monster's hide.

"Strike your flag!" the rebel cries,
  In his arrogant old plantation strain.
"Never!" our gallant Morris replies;
    "It is better to sink than to yield!"
    And the whole air pealed
  With the cheers of our men.

Then, like a kraken huge and black,
  She crushed our ribs in her iron grasp!
Down went the Cumberland all a wrack,
    With a sudden shudder of death,
    And the cannon's breath

For her dying gasp.

Next morn, as the sun rose over the bay,
  Still floated our flag at the mainmast head.
Lord, how beautiful was Thy day!
    Every waft of the air
    Was a whisper of prayer,
  Or a dirge for the dead.

Ho! brave hearts that went down in the seas
  Ye are at peace in the troubled stream;
Ho! brave land! with hearts like these,
    Thy flag, that is rent in twain,
    Shall be one again,
  And without a seam!

SNOW-FLAKES

Out of the bosom of the Air,
  Out of the cloud-folds of her garments shaken,
Over the woodlands brown and bare,
  Over the harvest-fields forsaken,
    Silent, and soft, and slow
    Descends the snow.

Even as our cloudy fancies take
  Suddenly shape in some divine expression,
Even as the troubled heart doth make
  In the white countenance confession,
    The troubled sky reveals
    The grief it feels.

This is the poem of the air,
  Slowly in silent syllables recorded;
This is the secret of despair,
  Long in its cloudy bosom hoarded,
    Now whispered and revealed
    To wood and field.

A DAY OF SUNSHINE

O gift of God! O perfect day:
Whereon shall no man work, but play;
Whereon it is enough for me,
Not to be doing, but to be!

Through every fibre of my brain,
Through every nerve, through every vein,
I feel the electric thrill, the touch
Of life, that seems almost too much.

I hear the wind among the trees
Playing celestial symphonies;
I see the branches downward bent,
Like keys of some great instrument.

And over me unrolls on high
The splendid scenery of the sky,
Where though a sapphire sea the sun
Sails like a golden galleon,

Towards yonder cloud-land in the West,
Towards yonder Islands of the Blest,
Whose steep sierra far uplifts
Its craggy summits white with drifts.

Blow, winds! and waft through all the rooms
The snow-flakes of the cherry-blooms!
Blow, winds! and bend within my reach
The fiery blossoms of the peach!

O Life and Love! O happy throng
Of thoughts, whose only speech is song!
O heart of man! canst thou not be
Blithe as the air is, and as free?

SOMETHING LEFT UNDONE

Labor with what zeal we will,
  Something still remains undone,
Something uncompleted still
  Waits the rising of the sun.

By the bedside, on the stair,
  At the threshold, near the gates,
With its menace or its prayer,
  Like a mendicant it waits;

Waits, and will not go away;
  Waits, and will not be gainsaid;
By the cares of yesterday
  Each to-day is heavier made;

Till at length the burden seems
  Greater than our strength can bear,
Heavy as the weight of dreams,
  Pressing on us everywhere.

And we stand from day to day,
  Like the dwarfs of times gone by,
Who, as Northern legends say,
  On their shoulders held the sky.

WEARINESS

O little feet! that such long years
Must wander on through hopes and fears,
  Must ache and bleed beneath your load;
I, nearer to the wayside inn
Where toil shall cease and rest begin,
  Am weary, thinking of your road!

O little hands! that, weak or strong,
Have still to serve or rule so long,
  Have still so long to give or ask;
I, who so much with book and pen
Have toiled among my fellow-men,
  Am weary, thinking of your task.

O little hearts! that throb and beat
With such impatient, feverish heat,
  Such limitless and strong desires;
Mine that so long has glowed and burned,
With passions into ashes turned
  Now covers and conceals its fires.

O little souls! as pure and white
And crystalline as rays of light
  Direct from heaven, their source divine;
Refracted through the mist of years,
How red my setting sun appears,
  How lurid looks this soul of mine!